Graph Data Modeling in Python

A practical guide to curating, analyzing, and modeling data with graphs

Gary Hutson

Matt Jackson

<packt>

BIRMINGHAM—MUMBAI

Graph Data Modeling in Python

Group Product Manager: Reshma Raman
Publishing Product Manager: Arindam Majumder
Senior Editor: Nathanya Dias
Technical Editor: Rahul Limbachiya
Copy Editor: Safis Editing
Project Coordinator: Farheen Fathima
Proofreader: Safis Editing
Indexer: Subalakshmi Govindhan
Production Designer: Joshua Misquitta
Marketing Coordinator: Nivedita Singh

First published: July 2023
Production reference: 1210623

Published by Packt Publishing Ltd.
Livery Place
35 Livery Street
Birmingham
B3 2PB, UK.

ISBN 978-1-80461-803-5

www.packtpub.com

To my son, Charlie, my wife, Kerry, and my supportive parents, Carol and Eric, plus my parents-in-law, Patricia and John. Thanks for all your love, support, and always being there to offer sage advice.

– Gary Hutson

To Lori, for her patience and support.

– Matt Jackson

Contributors

About the authors

Gary Hutson is an experienced Python and graph database developer. He has experience in Python, R, C, SQL, and many other programming languages, and has been working with databases of some form for 20+ years. Professionally, he works as the Head of Graph Data Science and Machine Learning for a company that uses **machine learning** (**ML**) and graph data science techniques to detect risks on social media and other platforms. He is experienced in many graph and ML techniques, specializing in natural language processing, computer vision, deep learning, and ML. His passion is using open sourced technologies to create useful toolsets and practical applied solutions, as this was the focus of his master's degree.

Matt Jackson is a lead data scientist specializing in graph theory and network analytics. His interest in graphs was sparked during his PhD in systems biology, where network analysis was used to uncover novel features of cell organization. Since then, he has worked in diverse industries - from academia to intelligence, highlighting patterns and risk in complex data by harnessing the latest in graph algorithms and machine learning.

About the reviewer

Atul Kadlag, a seasoned professional in the business intelligence, data, and analytics industry, possesses diverse experience across different technologies and a proven track record of success. A self-motivated learner, he has excelled at working at various multinational companies for more than 15 years, leading transformative initiatives in business intelligence, data warehouses, and data analytics. Atul has immense experience in handling end-to-end projects in business intelligence and data warehouse technologies, and is dedicated to driving positive change and inspiring others through continuous learning, making a lasting impact in the data industry. His expertise involves SQL, Python, and business intelligence and data warehousing technologies.

Table of Contents

Part 2: Making the Graph Transition

3

Data Model Transformation – Relational to Graph Databases   41

4

Building a Knowledge Graph   63

Part 3: Storing and Productionizing Graphs

5

6

7

Part 4: Graphing Like a Pro

8

Perfect Projections — 163

9

Common Errors and Debugging — 185

Preface

Organizations across the globe are starting to use graph approaches and visualization techniques to make sense of complex networks. These networks are present in many industries, ranging from social network analysis (analyzing the connections of people interacting on social networks) to fraud detection (looking at transactions in a network to spot outliers), modeling the stability of systems such as rail and energy grids, and as critical components of recommendation engines that are used in many of your favorite online streaming services, for example, Netflix, Prime, and so on.

This book provides you with the tools to get up and running with these methods while working with a familiar language, such as Python. We start by looking at how you can create graphs in igraph NetworkX and how these can be used to carry out sophisticated graph analytics. We will then delve into the world of Neo4j and graph databases, as well as equipping you with the knowledge to query graph databases with the Cypher query language.

Who this book is for

The primary aim of this book is to assist existing Python developers of an intermediate level who may have the ambition of getting into graph data modeling. Or, if you are a database developer or IT professional, then the graph database section may give you insights into how graph databases are different from traditional databases.

In essence, this book is targeted at anyone who loves coding in Python and wants to learn more about how to build graph data pipelines, how to ingest and clean data, various ways to store graph data relationships, how to conduct analytical techniques such as community detection and recommendation engine creation, and how to use Cypher to store these relationships and then query the *in-memory* graph with Cypher.

What this book covers

Chapter 1, Introducing Graphs in the Real World, takes you through why you should consider graphs. What are the fundamental attributes of graph data structures, such as nodes and edges? It also covers how graphs are used in various industries and provides a gentle introduction to igraph and NetworkX.

Chapter 2, Working with Graph Data Models, deals with how to work with graphs. From there, you will implement a model in Python to recommend the most popular television show.

Chapter 3, Data Model Transformation – Relational to Graph Databases, gets hands-on with MySQL, considers how data gets ingested into MySQL from your graph databases, and then looks at building a recommendation engine to recommend similar games to a user, based on their gaming history on the popular platform Steam.

Chapter 4, Building a Knowledge Graph, puts your skills to work on building a knowledge graph to analyze medical abstracts, clean the data, and then proceed to perform graph analysis and community detection on the knowledge graph.

Chapter 5, Working with Graph Databases, looks into working with Neo4j and storing data in a graph database using Cypher commands. Python will then be used to interact with our graph database by connecting Neo4j to Python.

Chapter 6, Pipeline Development, includes all you need to know to design a schema and allow it to work with your graph pipeline to finally make product recommendations across Neo4j, igraph, and Python.

Chapter 7, Refactoring and Evolving Schemas, deals with why you would need to refactor, how to evolve effectively, and how to apply these changes to your development life cycle.

Chapter 8, Perfect Projections, deals with understanding, creating, analyzing, and using projections in Neo4j and igraph.

Chapter 9, Common Errors and Debugging, explains how to debug graph issues and how to deal with some of the most common issues in Neo4j and igraph.

To get the most out of this book

You will need to create a virtual environment for these tutorials for Python 3.8, as all code has been tested on Python 3.8, however, they should work on future versions of Python. Furthermore, when working with Neo4j, refer to *Chapter 5, Working with Graph Databases*, as it has comprehensive installation instructions.

Software/hardware covered in the book	Operating system requirements
Python 3.7/3.8/3.9	Windows, macOS, or Linux
Neo4j Community Edition v1.5.7	Windows, macOS, or Linux
MySQL 5.7.39	Windows, macOS, or Linux

Each repository for each chapter has a `requirements.txt` file that you will need to `pip install` in your working Python environment.

If you are using the digital version of this book, we advise you to type the code yourself or access the code from the book's GitHub repository (a link is available in the next section). Doing so will help you avoid any potential errors related to the copying and pasting of code.

Download the example code files

You can download the example code files for this book from GitHub at https://github.com/ PacktPublishing/Graph-Data-Modeling-in-Python. If there's an update to the code, it will be updated in the GitHub repository.

We also have other code bundles from our rich catalog of books and videos available at https:// github.com/PacktPublishing/. Check them out!

Conventions used

There are a number of text conventions used throughout this book.

Code in text: Indicates code words in text, database table names, folder names, filenames, file extensions, pathnames, dummy URLs, user input, and Twitter handles. Here is an example: "Mount the downloaded WebStorm-10*.dmg disk image file as another disk in your system."

A block of code is set as follows:

```
data = [line for line in reader]
print(data[:10])
print(len(data))
```

When we wish to draw your attention to a particular part of a code block, the relevant lines or items are set in bold:

```
[default]
exten => s,1,Dial(Zap/1|30)
exten => s,2,Voicemail(u100)
exten => s,102,Voicemail(b100)
exten => i,1,Voicemail(s0)
```

Any command-line input or output is written as follows:

```
pip install matplotlib
```

Bold: Indicates a new term, an important word, or words that you see onscreen. For instance, words in menus or dialog boxes appear in **bold**. Here is an example: "Select **System info** from the **Administration** panel."

> **Tips or important notes**
> Appear like this.

Get in touch

Feedback from our readers is always welcome.

General feedback: If you have questions about any aspect of this book, email us at `customercare@packtpub.com` and mention the book title in the subject of your message.

Errata: Although we have taken every care to ensure the accuracy of our content, mistakes do happen. If you have found a mistake in this book, we would be grateful if you would report this to us. Please visit www.packtpub.com/support/errata and fill in the form.

Piracy: If you come across any illegal copies of our works in any form on the internet, we would be grateful if you would provide us with the location address or website name. Please contact us at `copyright@packt.com` with a link to the material.

If you are interested in becoming an author: If there is a topic that you have expertise in and you are interested in either writing or contributing to a book, please visit authors.packtpub.com.

Share your thoughts

Once you've read *Graph Data Modeling in Python*, we'd love to hear your thoughts! Scan the QR code below to go straight to the Amazon review page for this book and share your feedback.

https://packt.link/r/1-804-61803-9

Your review is important to us and the tech community and will help us make sure we're delivering excellent quality content.

Download a free PDF copy of this book

Thanks for purchasing this book!

Do you like to read on the go but are unable to carry your print books everywhere?

Is your eBook purchase not compatible with the device of your choice?

Don't worry, now with every Packt book you get a DRM-free PDF version of that book at no cost.

Read anywhere, any place, on any device. Search, copy, and paste code from your favorite technical books directly into your application.

The perks don't stop there, you can get exclusive access to discounts, newsletters, and great free content in your inbox daily

Follow these simple steps to get the benefits:

1. Scan the QR code or visit the link below

https://packt.link/free-ebook/9781804618035

2. Submit your proof of purchase
3. That's it! We'll send your free PDF and other benefits to your email directly

Part 1:
Getting Started
with Graph Data Modeling

This will be our first delve into graph data modelling in Python. This part covers what you need to know with regard to graph data modelling, such as why and when you need to use graphs; analyzing the fundamentals of graphs and how they are used in industry; and introducing the core packages you will be working with in these chapters, igraph and NetworkX.

Moving on from the fundamentals, we will then look at how to work with graph data models and work through a television recommendation use case as a Python pipeline.

This will serve as the entry-level part of this book and it has the following chapters:

- *Chapter 1, Introducing Graphs in the Real World*
- *Chapter 2, Working with Graph Data Models*

1

Introducing Graphs in the Real World

Social network analysis, fraud detection, modeling the stability of systems (for example, rail and energy grids), and recommendation systems all rely on graphs as the lynchpin underpinning these types of networks. In each of these examples, the relationships between individual people, bank accounts, or other single units are fundamental to describe and model the data. As opposed to traditional data models, a graph is a perfect way to represent groups of interacting elements.

This chapter will serve as an introduction to why graphs are important and introduce you to the fundamentals of what makes up a graph network. Moreover, we will look at how to transition from traditional data storage strategies, such as **relational databases** (**RDBs**), to how you can use this knowledge to work with **graph databases** (**GDBs**). Throughout this book, we will be working with a popular graph database, namely Neo4j. This will be followed by an explanation of how graphs are utilized in the *real world* and then a gentle introduction to working with the main package workhorses, known as igraph and NetworkX, which are the best and most stable graph packages for graph data analysis and modeling.

In this chapter, we're going to cover the following topics:

- Why should you use graphs?
- The fundamentals of nodes and edges and the properties of a graph
- Comparing RDBs and GDBs
- The use of graphs across various industries
- Introduction to NetworkX and igraph

Technical requirements

We will be using the Jupyter Notebook to run our coding exercises. For this, you will require `python>=3.8.0`, along with the following packages, which will need to be installed in your environment with the `pip install` command:

- `networkx==2.8.8`
- `igraph==0.9.8`

All notebooks, along with the coding exercises, are available at the following GitHub link: `https://github.com/PacktPublishing/Graph-Data-Modeling-in-Python/tree/main/CH01`.

Why should you use graphs?

In modern, data-driven solutions and enterprises, graph data structures are becoming more and more common. This is because, in our modern, data-driven world, relationships between things are becoming as, if not more important, than the things themselves. In modern industries and enterprises, graphs are starting to become more common and powerful in understanding the relationships between entities. I would say that these relationships and how they are connected have become more important than the entities themselves. We will demonstrate examples of real-life graphs in our use cases in the following chapters with detailed instructions on how to build these networks and the core considerations you need to make for the graph design.

Graphs are fundamental to many systems we use every day. Each time you are online and receive a product recommendation, it is likely that a graph solution is powering this recommendation. This is why learning how to work with graph data and leveraging these types of networks is a fast-growing and key skill in data science.

Composite components of a graph

Networks are a tool to represent complex systems and the complex nature of the connections arising in today's data. We have already referenced how graphs are powering some of the big powerhouse recommendation systems in action today.

Graph methods tend to fall into four different areas:

- **Movement**: Movement is concerned with how things travel (move) through a network. These types of graphs are the drivers behind routing and GPS solutions and are utilized by the biggest players in finding the optimal path across a road network.

- **Influence**: On social media, this area specifies who the known influencers are and how they propagate this influence across a network.

- **Groups and interactions**: This area involves identifying groups and how actors in the network interact with each other. We will look at an example of how to apply community detection methods to find these communities through the node (the actor involved) and its connections (the edges). Don't worry if you don't know what these terms are for now; we will focus on these in the *Fundamentals of nodes, edges, and the properties of a graph* section.

- **Pattern detection**: Pattern detection involves using a graph to find similarities in the network that can be explored. We must look at this from the actor's (node's) point of view and find similarities between that actor and other actors in the network. Here, *actor* is taken to mean person, author profile, and so on.

In this section, we have explained the core components of a graph by providing simple working definitions. In the following section, we will delve deeper into these fundamental elements, which make up every graph you will come across in the industry. We will look at nodes, edges, and the various properties of a graph.

The fundamentals of nodes and edges and the properties of a graph

Graphs, or networks, are particularly powerful data structures for modeling and describing relationships between things, whether these things are people, products, or machines. In a graph, those *things* that we coined earlier are represented by *nodes* (sometimes known as *vertices*). Nodes are connected by *edges* (sometimes referred to as *relationships*). In a network, an edge represents a relationship between two things, indicating that, somehow, they are linked.

The following sections will look at the structures and types of graphs. First, we will start with undirected graphs before moving on to directed graphs. After that, we will look at node properties, then delve into heterogeneous graphs, and end by looking at schema design considerations.

Undirected graphs

To illustrate, a simple example is that of a real-life social network. In the following example, Jeremy and Mark are each represented by a node. Jeremy is friends with Mark, and the *friend* relationship is represented by an edge connecting the two nodes. The following diagram shows an **undirected graph**:

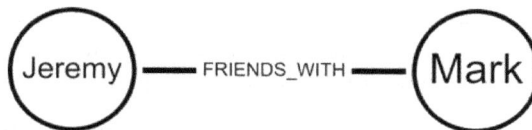

Figure 1.1 – Two friend nodes are linked together with a single edge

However, not all social networks are the same, and in some online social media platforms, relationships between users of a social network may not be mutual.

For example, on Twitter, one user can follow another, but this doesn't mean the inverse must be true. On Twitter, Jeremy may follow Mark, but Mark may not follow Jeremy.

Directed graphs

Here, a directional edge is used to show that Jeremy follows Mark, while the absence of an edge in the reverse direction shows that Mark does not follow Jeremy in return:

Figure 1.2 – Two friend nodes are linked together with a single edge

This type of graph is known as a **directed graph**. For reference, sometimes, undirected edges like those in *Figure 1.1* are shown as bidirectional edges, pointing to both nodes. This bidirectional representation is equivalent to an undirected edge in most senses and represents a mutual relationship.

Importantly, when creating a data model with directional edges, naming relationships appropriately becomes important. In our Twitter example, if the edge representing the interaction between Mark and Jeremy is *follows*, then the edge goes from the Jeremy node to the Mark node.

On the other hand, if the edge represents a concept such as *followed by*, then this should be in the other direction – that is, from Mark to Jeremy. This has particularly strong implications for some more complex graph modeling and use cases, which we will cover in *Chapter 2, Working with Graph Data Models*.

Node properties

While nodes and edges (directional or not) are the basic building blocks of a graph, they are often not sufficient to fully describe a dataset. Nodes can have data associated with them that may not be relational, so it would not be expressed as a relationship with another node.

In these cases, to represent data associated with nodes, we can use node properties (sometimes known as node attributes). Similarly, where an edge has additional information associated with it, in addition to representing a relationship, edge properties can be used to hold that data.

The following diagram shows a black line, indicating that Jeremy follows Mark but that Mark does not follow Jeremy – therefore, the black line indicates directionality:

followers: 130
location: London, UK **Jeremy** —— FOLLOWS ——▶ **Mark** followers: 2100
location: Dartmouth, UK

Figure 1.3 – Two friend nodes are linked together with a single edge

In the preceding model, node properties are used to describe the number of followers Mark and Jeremy have, as well as the locations listed in their Twitter bios. This kind of additional node information is particularly important for querying graph data when asking questions that involve filtering.

In our Twitter example, properties would need to be present in the graph if, for example, we wanted to know who followed users with above 1,000 followers. We will revisit answering graphical questions using nodes, edges, and properties in later chapters.

Depending on the dataset, there may be cases where different nodes have different sets of properties. In this case, it is common to have several distinct types of nodes in the same graph.

Heterogeneous graphs

Node types can also be referred to as layers, or nodes with different labels, though for this book, they will be known simply as types.

The following diagram shows the nodes representing Jeremy and Mark as people, where each node type has different properties, and there are multiple relationship types. Due to this, we can term these multiple relationships as heterogenous:

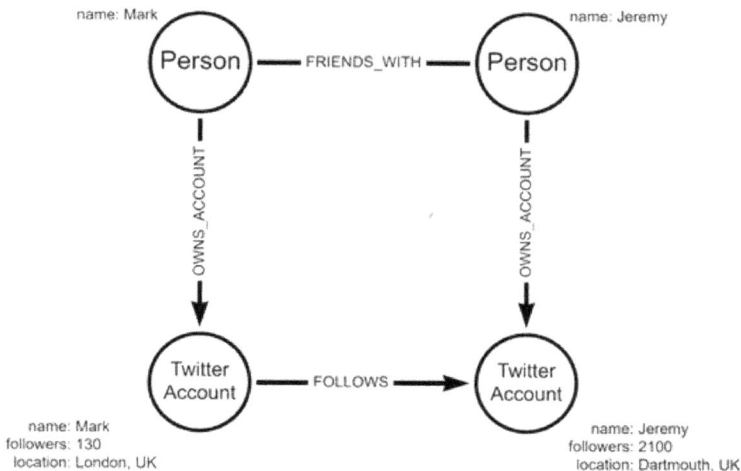

name: Mark **Person** —— FRIENDS_WITH —— **Person** name: Jeremy

OWNS_ACCOUNT

OWNS_ACCOUNT

Twitter Account —— FOLLOWS ——▶ **Twitter Account**

name: Mark
followers: 130
location: London, UK

name: Jeremy
followers: 2100
location: Dartmouth, UK

Figure 1.4 – Example of a heterogenous Twitter graph

Now, we have added nodes representing Mark and Jeremy as people, relationships representing their relationship outside of Twitter, and their ownership of their respective accounts. Note that since we have increased the number of node types, we also need new edge types to refer to the different interactions between different types of nodes.

Graphs with multiple node types are known as heterogeneous, multilayer, or multilevel graphs, though going forward we will use the term heterogeneous to refer to graphs with multiple types of nodes. In contrast, graphs with only one node type, as in the previous examples, are referred to as homogeneous graphs.

Schema design

At this point, it is reasonable to ask the question: *What features of a dataset should be nodes, edges, and properties?*

For any given dataset, there are multiple ways to represent data as a graph, and each is more suited to different purposes. Herein lies the trick to good graph modeling: a question or use case-driven schema design.

If we were particularly interested in the locations of Twitter users in our network, then we could move the location node property on the Twitter user nodes to create the LOCATED_IN relationship type. This is shown in the following diagram:

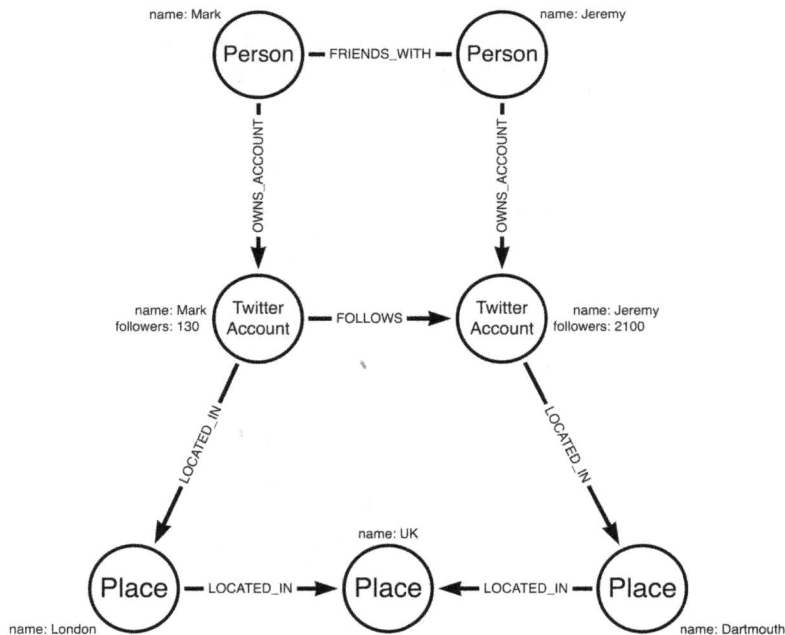

Figure 1.5 – The same graph but with the location property moved from a node property to a node type

If we were particularly interested in the locations of Twitter users in our network, then we could move the location node property on the Twitter user nodes to a separate node type and create the LOCATED_IN relationship type. We could even go one step further to represent the information we know about these locations, adding the country related to each location as a separate, abstracted node.

This graph structure models the same data in a different way, which may be more or less suitable or performant for particular use cases. We will explore the effects of schema design on the types of questions that can be asked, and performance, in later chapters.

In the next section, we will compare how graph data structures differ from traditional RDBs. This will expand on why GDBs can be more performant when modeled as a graph data problem.

Comparing RDBs and GDBs

RDBs have been a standard for data storage and data analysis across most industries for a very long time. Their strength lies in being able to hold multiple tables of different information, where some table fields are found across tables, enabling data linkage.

With this data linkage, complex questions can be asked of data in an RDB. However, there are drawbacks to this relational structure. While RDBs are useful for returning a large number of rows that meet particular criteria, they are not suited to questions involving many chained relationships.

To illustrate this, consider a standard database containing train services and their station stops, alongside a graph that might represent the same information:

Train	Stops at
GW1426	Truro
GW1426	Liskeard
GW1426	Plymouth
XC1200	Plymouth
XC1200	Bristol Parkway
XC1200	Cheltenham Spa
XC1200	Birmingham New Street
VT3160	Birmingham New Street
VT3160	Crewe
VT3160	Lancaster
VT3160	Carlisle
VT6200	Carlisle
VT6200	Glasgow Central

Figure 1.6 – Relational data structure of trains and their stops

In an RDB structure, it would not be difficult to retrieve all trains that service a particular stop. On the other hand, it may be a slow operation that returns a series of trains that can be taken between two chosen stations.

Consider the steps needed in a traditional RDB to find the route between Truro and Glasgow Central in the preceding table. Starting at Truro, we would know the **GW1426** train service stops at Truro, Liskeard, and Plymouth. Knowing that these stations can be reached from Truro, we would then need to find what train services stop at each of these stations to find our route.

Upon finding that Plymouth station is reachable and that a separate service runs to many more stations, we would need to repeat this process over and over until Glasgow Central is reached.

These steps essentially result in a series of computationally costly *join* operations on the same table, where one resulting row would give us the path between our stations of interest.

GDBs to the rescue

Using a graph structure to represent this train network puts greater emphasis on relationships between our data points, as illustrated in the following diagram:

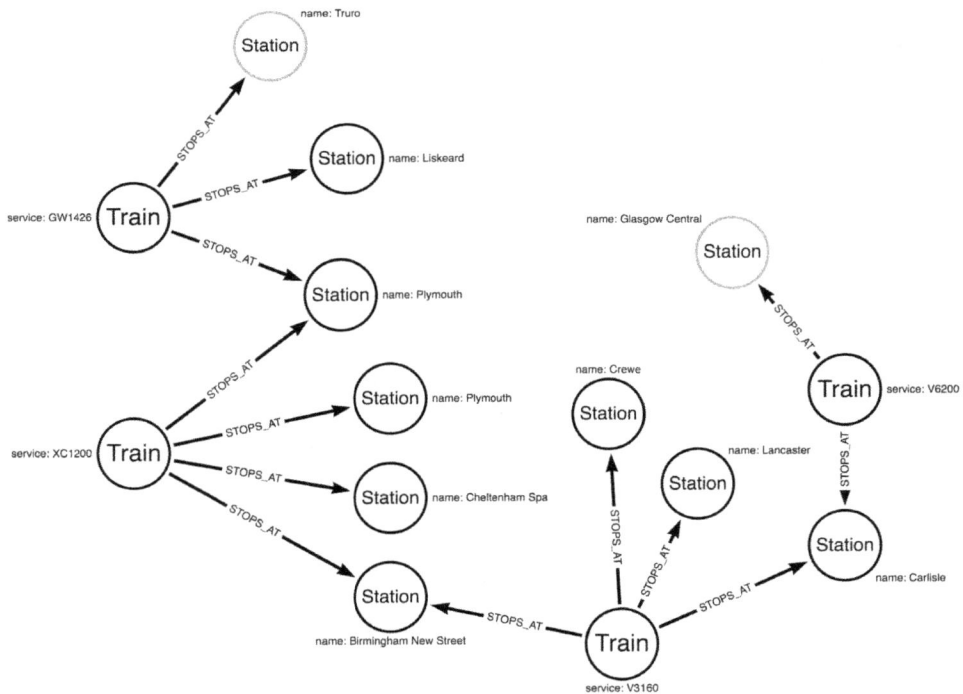

Figure 1.7 – Graph data structure of trains and their stops

Using a graph structure to represent this train network puts greater emphasis on relationships between our data points. Starting from Truro station, as in the RDB example, we find the train that services that station. However, when traversing the graph to find a possible route between Truro and Glasgow Central, at each station or train node we are considering fewer data points, and therefore fewer options.

This is in contrast to the RDB example, where repeated table joins are necessary to return a path. In this case, the complexity of the operations required over the graph representation is lower, which equates to a faster, more efficient method. Among many other use cases, those that require some sort of *pathfinding* often benefit from a graph data model.

In addition to being more suitable for specific types of queries, graphs are typically useful where a flexible, evolving data model is needed. Again, using the example of the train network, imagine that, as the database administrator, you have received a request to add bus transport links to the data model.

With an RDB, a new table would be required, since several bus services would likely serve each train station. In this new table, the names of each station would need to be duplicated from the existing table, to list alongside their related bus services.

Not only does this duplication increase the size of data stored, but it also increases the complexity of the database schema:

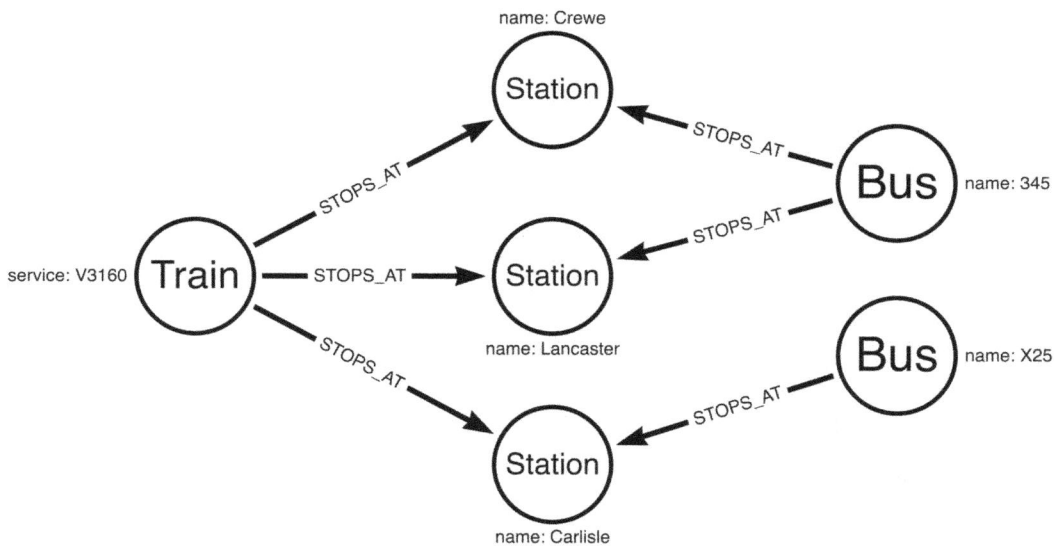

Figure 1.8 – Adding a new data type (buses) to the train station graph

Where the train station data is represented with a graph, the new information on buses can be added directly to the existing database as a new node type.

There is no requirement for a new table, and no need to duplicate each station node to represent the required information; the existing train nodes can be directly linked to new **Bus** nodes. This holds for any new data type that would require the addition of a new table in a traditional RDB.

In a graph, where new data could be represented in an equivalent RDB as a new column in an existing table, this may be a good candidate for a node property, as opposed to a new node type.

Here, an example suitable for being represented as a node property would be a code for each train station, where stations and their codes have a 1-to-1 relationship.

A comparison, in short, is captured in the following:

- RDBs have a rigid data format and a new table must be added for a new type of data. GDBs are more flexible when it comes to the format of the data and can be extended with new node types.

- RDBs can be queried via path-based queries – for example, how many steps between two people in a friend network, which involves multiple joins and can be extremely slow as the paths become longer. GDBs query paths directly, with no join operations, so information retrieval is more streamlined and quite frankly faster.

In summary, where the use case for a database concerns querying many relationships between objects – that is, paths – or when a flexible data schema is needed, a graph data model is likely to be a good fit to represent your data.

The use of graphs across various industries

Graph data science is prevalent across a wide array of industries.

The main areas where graphs are being used effectively are as follows:

- **Finance**: To look at fraud detection and portfolio risk.

- **Government**: To aid with intelligence profiling and supply chain analytics.

- **Life sciences**: For looking at patient journeys through a hospital (the transition of a patient through various services), drug response rates, and the transition of infections through a population.

- **Network & IT**: Security networks and user access management (nodes on a network represent each user logging into a network).

- **Telecoms**: Through network optimization and churn prediction.

- **Marketing**: Mainly for customer and market segmentation purposes.

- **Social media analysis**: We work for a company that specializes in platform moderation, online harm protection, and brand defense. By creating graphs to defend against attacks on brands, we can find vulnerable people or moderate the most severe type of content.

In terms of graphs in industry, they are pervasive due to the reasons we have already explored in this chapter. The ability to quickly link nodes and edges, and create relationships between them, is the reason why more problems in data science are being modeled as graphs or network science problems. In addition, the underlying data can be queried at a rapid rate. This can be done instead of using traditional database solutions, which, as we have already identified, are slow to query compared to GDBs.

Following this, in the next section, we will introduce the main two driving packages for graph analytics and modeling. We will show you the basic usage of the packages. In the subsequent chapters, we will keep building on why these packages are powerful.

Introduction to NetworkX and igraph

In this chapter, we will introduce two Python packages for creating in-memory graphs: NetworkX and igraph.

NetworkX lets you create graphs, perform graph manipulation, study and visualize their structures, and perform several graph manipulation functions when working with graphs. Their website (`https://networkx.org/`) contains details of the major changes to the package and the intended usage of the tool.

igraph contains a suite of useful and practical analysis tools, with the aim being to make these efficient and easy to use, in a reproducible way. What is great about igraph is that it is open source and free, plus it supports networks to be built in *R*, *Python*, *Mathematica*, and *C/C++*. This is our recommended package for creating large networks that can load much more quickly than NetworkX. To read more about igraph, go to `https://igraph.org/`.

In the following subsections, we will look at the basics of both NetworkX and igraph, with easy-to-follow coding steps. This is the first time you are going to get your hands dirty with graph data modeling.

NetworkX basics

NetworkX is one of the originally available graph libraries for Python and is particularly focused on being user-friendly and Pythonic in its style. It also natively includes methods for calculating some classic network analysis measures:

1. To import `NetworkX` into Python, use the following command:

    ```
    import networkx as nx
    ```

2. And to create an empty graph, g, use the following command:

    ```
    g = nx.Graph()
    ```

3. Now, we need to add nodes to our graph, which can be done using methods of the `Graph` object belonging to g. There are multiple ways to do this, with the simplest being adding one node at a time:

```
g.add_node(Jeremy)
```

4. Alternatively, multiple nodes can be added to the graph at once, like so:

```
g.add_nodes_from([Mark, Jeremy])
```

5. Properties can be added to nodes during creation by passing a node and dictionary tuple to `Graph.add_nodes_from`:

```
g.add_nodes_from([(Mark, {followers: 2100}), (Jeremy,
{followers: 130})])
```

6. To add an edge to the graph, we can use the `Graph.add_edge` method, and reference the nodes already present in the graph:

```
g.add_edge(Jeremy, Mark)
```

It is worth noting that, in NetworkX, when adding an edge, any nodes specified as part of that edge not already in the graph will be added implicitly.

7. To confirm that our graph now contains nodes and edges, we may want to plot it, using `matplotlib` and `networkx.draw()`. The `with_labels` parameter adds the names of the nodes to the plot:

```
import matplotlib.pyplot as plt
nx.draw(g, with_labels=True)
plt.show()
```

This section showed you how you can get up and running with NetworkX in a couple of lines of Python code. In the next section, we will turn our focus to the popular `igraph` package, which allows us to perform calculations over larger datasets much quicker than using the popular NetworkX.

igraph basics

NetworkX, while user-friendly, suffers from slow speeds when using larger graphs. This is due to its implementation behind the scenes and because it is written in Python, with some C, C++, and FORTRAN.

In contrast, igraph is implemented in pure C, giving the library an advantage when working with large graphs and complex network algorithms. While not as immediately accessible as NetworkX for beginners, igraph is a useful tool to have under your belt when code efficiency is paramount.

Initially, working with igraph is very similar to working with NetworkX. Let's take a look:

1. To import `igraph` into Python, use the following command:

    ```
    import igraph as ig
    ```

2. And to create an empty graph, g, use the following command:

    ```
    g = ig.Graph()
    ```

    In contrast to NetworkX, in igraph, all nodes have a prescribed internal integer ID. The first node that's added has an ID of 0, with all subsequent nodes assigned increasing integer IDs.

3. Similar to NetworkX, changes can be made to a graph by using the methods of a `Graph` object. Nodes can be added to the graph with the `Graph.add_vertices` method (note that a vertex is another way to refer to a node). Two nodes can be added to the graph with the following code:

    ```
    g.add_vertices(2)
    ```

4. This will add nodes 0 and 1 to the graph. To name them, we have to assign properties to the nodes. We can do this by accessing the vertices of the `Graph` object. Similar to how you would access elements of a list, each node's properties can be accessed by using the following notation. Here, we are setting the `name` and `followers` attributes of nodes 0 and 1:

    ```
    g.vs[0][name] = Jeremy
    g.vs[1][name] = Mark
    g.vs[0][followers] = 130
    g.vs[1][followers] = 2100
    ```

5. Node properties can also be added listwise, where the first list element corresponds to node ID 0, the second to node ID 1, and so on. The following two lines are equivalent to the four lines shown in *step 4*:

    ```
    g.vs["name"] = [Jeremy, Mark]
    g.vs[followers] = [130, 2100]
    ```

6. To add an edge, we can use the `Graph.add_edges()` method:

    ```
    g.add_edges([(0, 1)])
    ```

Here, we are only adding one edge, but additional edges can be added to the list parameter required by `add_edges`. As with NetworkX, if edges are added for nodes that are not currently in the graph, nodes will be created implicitly. However, since igraph requires nodes to have sequential IDs, attempting to add the edge pair (1, 3) to a graph with two vertices will fail.

Summary

In this chapter, we looked at why you should start to think graph, from the benefits of why these methods are becoming the most widely utilized and discussed approaches in various industries. We looked at what a graph is and explained the various types of graphs, such as graphs that are concerned with how things move through a network, to influence graphs (who is influencing who on social media), to graph methods to identify groups and interactions, and how graphs can be utilized to detect patterns in a network.

Moving on from that, we examined the fundamentals of what makes up a graph. Here, we looked at the fundamental elements of nodes, edges, and properties and delved into the difference between an undirected and directed graph. Additionally, we examined the properties of nodes, looked at heterogeneous graphs, and examined the types of schema contained within a graph.

This led to how GDBs compare to legacy RDBs and why, in many cases, graphs are much easier and faster to transverse and query, with examples of how graphs can be utilized to optimize the stops on a train journey and how this can be extended, with ease, to add bus stops as well, as a new data source.

Following this, we looked at how graphs are being deployed across various industries and some use cases for why graphs are important in those industries, such as fraud detection in the finance sector, intelligence profiling in the government sector, patient journeys in hospitals, churn across networks, and customer segmentation in marketing. Graphs truly are becoming ubiquitous across various industries.

We wrapped up this chapter by providing an introduction to the powerhouses of graph analytics and network analysis – igraph and NetworkX. We showed you how, in a few lines of Python code, you can easily start to populate a graph.

In the next chapter, we will look at how to work with and create graph data models. The next chapter will contain many more hands-on examples of how to structure your data using graph data models in Python.

2

Working with Graph Data Models

This chapter will move you toward taking what you have learned hitherto and moving from a business problem through to how to obtain the data and then to getting that data graph ready. In this chapter, the aim is to teach you the fundamental skills needed to start working with graph data models at pace.

It will focus on many of the key skills to get up to speed with working with graph data models and many of the attributes of a graph structure. In the following sections, the aim will be to get you familiar with igraph and how to use it to ingest data into your graph.

From there, we'll move on to building your understanding of how to model nodes and edges in a graph. This will culminate in working on a use case to cement and reinforce what you will learn in this chapter.

The use case will touch on the key techniques needed to model a graph structure and what is meant by degree centrality.

In this chapter, we're going to cover the following main topics:

- Making the transition from tabular to graph data
- Implementing the model in Python
- The most popular TV show – a real-world use case

Technical requirements

We will be using Jupyter notebooks to run our coding exercises; this requires `python>=3.8.0`, along with the following packages, which will need to be installed with the `pip install` command in your environment:

- `networkx==2.8.8`
- `igraph==0.9.8`
- `matplotlib`

All notebooks, with the coding exercises, are available at the following GitHub link: `https://github.com/PacktPublishing/Graph-Data-Modeling-in-Python/tree/main/CH02`.

Making the transition from tabular to graph data

To introduce the power of a graph data model, we will first focus on using a real social media dataset, from Facebook. This open source data contains information on Facebook pages, their name, and the type of page. Four types of pages are included, namely those for TV shows, companies, politicians, and governmental organizations. In addition, we have data on mutual likes between pages. If two pages *like* each other on Facebook, this is represented in our data.

It is at this stage that we can start to consider how best to model this dataset. To assemble a graph, we know from *Chapter 1, Introducing Graphs in the Real World*, that we need to have things represented by nodes, and relationships between those nodes represented by edges.

In the upcoming sections, we will look at examining data, thoughts, and considerations when designing efficient and effective schemas, and then we will get on to implementing the model in Python. Let's dive straight in.

Examining the data

We need to take a closer look at our data, to establish how we will translate the data into a graph format. Our data is supplied in the `.csv` format, so is tabular in nature.

We can first look into the first few lines of the Stanford dataset on a large page-to-page network (`https://snap.stanford.edu/data/facebook-large-page-page-network.html`) and a file from this dataset—namely, `musae_facebook_target.csv`—in an editor:

```
id,facebook_id,page_name,page_type
0,145647315578475,The Voice of China 中国好声音,tvshow
1,191483281412,U.S. Consulate General Mumbai,government
2,144761358898518,ESET,company
```

From this, we can observe that the headers and first few lines contain an *ID*, a *Facebook ID*, a *page name*, and a *page type*. This data will represent our node types and node attributes.

A separate file named `musae_facebook_edges.csv` contains relationships between the Facebook page nodes we looked into previously. Looking into the first few lines of these relationships in an editor, we see the following:

```
id_1,id_2
0,18427
1,21708
1,22208
```

The data shows that each line corresponds to an edge between two Facebook pages. Looking at the `.csv` file header, these pages are referred to by their IDs (`id_1` and `id_2`). This way of storing relationships in a tabular format is known as an *edgelist*. Simply, an edgelist is a data structure used to represent a graph as a list of its edges.

Designing a schema

We can now start to consider a schema for our data, based on the information we found in the CSV files.

In our Facebook data, we have pages linked together through mutual *likes* (likes on Facebook, or similar social media websites, where likes are shared on a mutually relevant bit of social media content). It is therefore sensible to model this data where the pages are our nodes and the mutual likes are the relationships between said nodes.

Because we are dealing only with Facebook page likes, we only need to consider one type of edge. It is therefore not necessary, in this case, to explicitly name them, as every edge is equivalent. In addition, because we only have information on mutual likes, as opposed to likes that are not reciprocated, it makes sense to consider the edges as *undirected* (we learned in *Chapter 1, Introducing Graphs in the Real World*, that an undirected graph is one where there is no implicit direction between the nodes and their edge connections).

Our nodes in this dataset can have different types, depending on the type of Facebook page they represent. We can consider the node's type as the type of page and the other information we have for each node as node attributes—namely, ID and page name. We can drop the Facebook ID from use in the graph schema since it doesn't relate to any other field and, without access to internal Facebook data, adds little to any later analysis—let's call this a redundant feature in our later analysis.

So, in this instance, we will be creating an undirected, heterogeneous graph (a special kind of information network, which contains either multiple types of objects or multiple types of links) with the schema depicted in the following diagram:

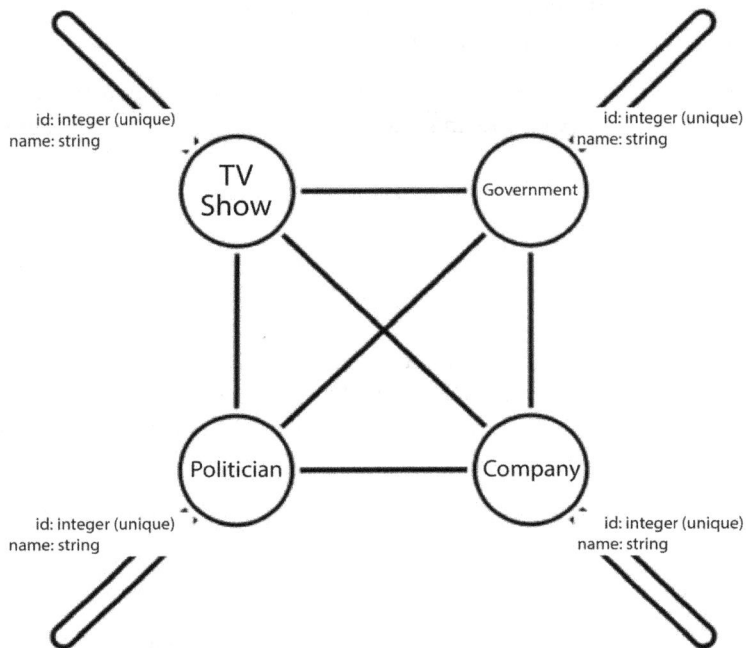

Figure 2.1 – Undirected heterogeneous graph

The schema represents the possibility of each type of node having an edge between them. Edges looping back to each type of node (known as *self-edges*) show that relationships can also exist between nodes of the same type. Finally, the data types for each attribute are listed, which are the same for each node: ID as a unique key integer, and name as a string.

Now, it is time to implement this model in Python. We will read our data from the supporting GitHub notebook (https://github.com/PacktPublishing/Graph-Data-Modeling-in-Python/blob/main/CH02/02.1_Implementing_model.ipynb).

Implementing the model in Python

In the following step, we will load in the data that we are going to be working with.

To begin creating this graph in Python, we can import the nodes from musae_facebook_target. csv, using the standard Python csv library:

```
import csv
with open('./data/facebook_large/musae_facebook_target.csv', 'r',
encoding='utf-8') as csv_file:
reader = csv.reader(csv_file)
```

```
data = [line for line in reader]
print(data[:10])
print(len(data))
```

Here, we open the CSV file with utf-8 encoding, as some node name strings contain non-standard characters. We use csv.reader to read the file, and convert this into a list of lists with a list comprehension (a special construct to encapsulate a loop inside a list to return a new list based on the loop logic, in essence to create a list from another list). Finally, we confirm that the CSV file is loaded correctly by examining the first few lines and checking the length of the imported list, which should be equal to 22,471, the number of rows.

Moving on, we will now extend our loaded-in data and add nodes and attributes to our graph.

Adding nodes and attributes

In igraph, we could add nodes one at a time to begin creating our graph, as we did in *Chapter 1, Introducing Graphs in the Real World*. However, as with many operations in Python, it is faster to add nodes listwise, in a single operation. The following steps take you through the process of adding nodes and their attributes:

1. To prepare our data for this, we need lists of node names, and each node attribute. We can prepare these lists using more list comprehensions:

    ```
    node_ids = [int(row[0]) for row in data[1:]]
    page_names = [row[2] for row in data[1:]]
    page_types = [row[3] for row in data[1:]]
    ```

    Note that the [1:] list slice on data is removing the csv header from each list, which we would not want to include as a node.

2. We need to confirm that the id row of our data increases sequentially. As mentioned in *Chapter 1, Introducing Graphs in the Real World*, igraph uses a sequentially increasing integer index for every node added to the graph. If our id column also uses this, adding nodes will be a simple process. To confirm that this is the case, we can compare the id column to a Python range():

    ```
    assert node_ids == list(range(len(node_ids)))
    ```

    This assert statement is making sure that a range() of 0 for the len() of the node_ids list is equivalent to the list of node IDs in our data. This assert statement should raise no AssertionError error, as they are identical.

3. This means importing our nodes into igraph, in this case, is as simple as creating a new, undirected, empty graph and telling igraph how many nodes we would like:

    ```
    import igraph as ig
    g = ig.Graph(directed=False)
    g.add_vertices(len(node_ids))
    ```

4. We can confirm how many nodes have been added by accessing the `vs` attribute of the `Graph()` object and checking that this is equal to the length of the `node_ids` list using another `assert` statement:

```
print(len(g.vs))
assert len(node_ids) == len(g.vs)
```

This will print from the console that the number of nodes is 22,470, one less than the number of rows in the original `.csv` file, which accounts for the removed header. Additionally, the `assert` statement will compare the length of both objects and raise an error if these values are not equal (expressed with the `==` equality symbol).

5. Now that nodes have been added, we can add our attributes to the nodes in a listwise operation, using the `page_names` and `page_types` attribute lists that were prepared earlier:

```
g.vs['page_name'] = page_names
g.vs['page_type'] = page_types
```

Here, we use the `vs` attribute of the graph to write the page names in order, from the node with ID 0 to node 22470. Because the order of our properties and IDs was preserved when preparing these lists earlier, this is the easiest way to quickly add all of our node attributes.

6. We can confirm that node attributes have been written to the graph with the following code to explicitly reference the `page_name` and `page_type` variables:

```
print(g.vs[0]['page_name'])
print(g.vs[0]['page_type'])
```

Once run, this will print the node name and type of the first data row in our original `.csv` file.

Adding edges

Hitherto, we have focused on adding nodes and their attributes. This section will focus on how to create edges. As we have already learned, these are relationships between nodes. The ensuing steps will take you from loading data to adding edges. Strap in:

1. Now that our nodes have been added to the graph, we can begin to connect them together. All the information we need to do this is contained in `musae_facebook_edges.csv`, so let's import this file:

```
with open('./data/musae_facebook_edges.csv', 'r') as csv_file_2:
  reader = csv.reader(csv_file_2)
  edge_data = [row for row in reader]
  print(edge_data[:10])
  print(len(edge_data))
```

As with the nodes earlier, we are importing the `csv` edge list using Python's inbuilt `csv` library (in *step 1* of the *Implementing the model in Python* section). This file contains no special characters, so we don't need to specify the encoding.

Again, we examine the first few rows of the imported list of lists by printing them, along with the number of rows, to get an idea of how many edges we are adding to the graph.

2. Notice that this file also contains a header that we do not want to inadvertently include as an edge in our graph. Also, in `igraph`, nodes are referred to by their integer ID, so we will need to change our list elements to integers, ready for edge addition. We can do this, and remove the header, using a list comprehension:

```
edges = [[int(row[0]), int(row[1])] for row in edge_data[1:]]
print(edges[:10])
```

We then confirm that the edge list has been converted to integers correctly, by again printing to examine the first 10 elements.

3. Now that the data is prepared, the edges can all be added to our graph at once with the `g.add_edges()` method:

```
g.add_edges(edges)
```

4. We can confirm that the edges have been added by accessing the `es` attribute of the graph, and counting them:

```
print(len(g.es))
```

This should be equal to the number of rows in the `.csv` file, minus one (171,002 edges).

5. Let's also confirm that an edge we know should be in the graph has been added correctly. Looking at the first non-header row of `musae_facebook_edges.csv`, we can see there should be an edge between node 0 and node 18427. We can access the first edge added to the graph using the `es` attribute and indexing:

```
first_edge = g.es[0]
```

6. This edge should be connecting nodes with IDs 0 and 18427. We can validate this by printing the `source` and `target` attributes of our newly created `first_edge` variable:

```
print(first_edge.source)
print(first_edge.target)
```

7. Finally, to relate this back to the real dataset, we can check which Facebook pages this edge represents, by accessing the node's `page_name` attributes:

```
print(g.vs[0]['page_name'])
print(g.vs[18427]['page_name'])
```

This shows us that the corresponding Facebook pages for these nodes are The Voice of China 中国好声音 and The Voice Global and that these Facebook pages share a mutual like.

Writing a generic graph import method

In the previous section, we created our graph from the datasets in many small stages. We may want to speed up this process the next time we import a similar graph, which we can do by writing some more generic Python methods.

Let's begin by considering the steps needed to create a graph from the Facebook mutual likes .csv files. Revisiting the previous section, we did the following:

- Created an empty igraph Graph() object

- Imported .csv files containing our nodes, node attributes, and edges

- Added nodes to our graph, with some tests

- Added edges to our graph, with more tests

The next series of steps will take you through how to create functions to speed up the process in the future, and so that you can use this code with your own projects with ease:

1. First, let's consider .csv imports. You may have noticed that we imported both previous .csv files with a very similar process, converting the rows in the .csv files to a list of lists. Let's instead define a function to do this for us:

```python
def read_csv(csv_path):
    '''
    Import a csv file.

    :param csv_path: Path to the csv to import.
    :return: A list of lists read from the csv.
    '''

    import csv
    import os

    assert os.path.exists(csv_path), \
        f'File could not be found at {csv_path}.'

    with open(csv_path, 'r', encoding='utf-8') as csv_file:
        reader = csv.reader(csv_file)
        data = [row for row in reader]

    return data
```

Included in the read_csv() method is an assert statement to make sure the specified file path exists, using the os Python standard library. A comma after the assert statement, followed by an f string, instructs Python to print the string to the console if the assert statement fails, helping in debugging. Using assert statements in this way is a useful tool for basic Python code testing.

2. Next, using our imported lists of lists, we are going to add nodes and edges to our graph, beginning with nodes. We will break down the function into multiple steps; firstly, we will add the doc settings to document the inputs into the function:

```
def add_nodes(g, nodes, attributes):
    '''
    Add nodes to the graph.

    :param g: An igraph Graph() object.
    :param nodes: A list of lists containing nodes and node
attributes, with a header. The first
                    element of each list in nodes should be the
node ID.
    :param attributes: A list of attributes corresponding to the
header (index 0) of the nodes list.
                    The names of attributes in this list will
be added to the graph.
    '''



    return g
```

3. We then use assert statements to throw errors if the conditions are not met. The first condition is looking for the id column of the column-separated values imported. The next assert statement checks that the nodes IDs are incrementing in a sequential and additive way. The final assert statement checks that the inputs into the graph are of type (list):

```
assert nodes[0][0] == 'id', \
        f'The first column in the imported csv should be the ID
header, "id". Instead, it '\
        f'is {nodes[0][0]}.'

    node_ids = [int(row[0]) for row in nodes[1:]]
    assert node_ids == list(range(len(node_ids))), \
        f'Node IDs should increase sequentially in the imported
csv, from 0 to the number of'\
        f' nodes-1, {len(node_ids)}.'

    assert isinstance(attributes, list), \
        f'Attributes to add to the graph should be a list.
Instead attributes is of type'\
        f' {type(attributes)}.'
```

4. The last parts of the function are to add vertices to our graph, loop through our attributes in our imported file, and make these attributes in the graph:

```
g.add_vertices(len(node_ids))

    headers = nodes[0]
    for attribute in attributes:
        attr_index = headers.index(attribute)
        g.vs[attribute] = [row[attr_index] for row in nodes[1:]]
```

This add_nodes() method builds upon the code from earlier in the chapter, where we first added nodes to the graph equal to the len() of the imported .csv file (without the header), then added attributes to those nodes. Here, a user-specified list of attributes to include is used to find the index element of those attributes in the csv header, before taking each element of that index from every list, in our nodes list of lists. The g graph now containing nodes and attributes is then returned.

Again, there are assert statements here to confirm that imported data is in the expected form. We test that the node attributes csv header loaded in contains an id field and that that field is in index [0] of the header. As previously mentioned in the chapter, we also assert that node IDs in the [0]th element of each row are sequentially increasing integers, which is a requirement for igraph to function as expected. Lastly, we assert that the user-specified attributes parameter is of type list. This is to ensure that the generic for loop for importing attributes functions is expected, for each attribute in attributes.

5. In this step, and now that nodes and attributes are added, we can add edges to the graph with another helper method:

```
def add_edges(g, edges):
    '''
    Add edges to the graph, where nodes are already present.

    :param g: An igraph Graph() object.
    :param edges: A list of lists containing edges, with a
header.
    '''

    assert len(edges[0]) == 2, \
        f'Each element in the imported edges csv should be of
length 2, representing an edge'\
        f' between two linked nodes. Instead, the first element
is of length {len(edges)[0]}.'

    edges_to_add = [[int(row[0]), int(row[1])] for row in
edges[1:]]
    g.add_edges(edges_to_add)

    return g
```

In the `add_edges()` method, as previously, we convert all rows after the header into pairs of integers, then use this list of lists to add edges to our graph in a listwise fashion. Then, the g graph, with edges added, is returned. Again, an additional `assert` statement has been added in this method, to ensure that the imported `.csv` file contains two columns, one for each node the edges connect. It is worth noting that although this dataset contains no edge attributes, these could be contained in an edgelist, which would result in the `assert` statement failing. For a graph with no edge attributes, however, there should be no reason for extra elements in each row.

6. Finally, we can now write a generic wrapper method to automate the individual steps in this process:

```
def graph_from_attributes_and_edgelist(node_attr_csv, edgelist_
csv, attributes):

    import igraph

    g = igraph.Graph(directed=False)

    nodes = read_csv(node_attr_csv)
    edges = read_csv(edgelist_csv)

    g = add_nodes(g, nodes, attributes)
    g = add_edges(g, edges)

    return g
```

Here, we take a `csv` node attribute, a `csv` edgelist, and a list of attributes to import from our `csv` node attribute, which will be used by the helper functions we've already defined. An empty, undirected `igraph Graph()` object is created, then nodes and edges are added to our new g graph, which is returned.

7. All that remains is to call our new `graph_from_attributes_and_edgelist()` function with the desired parameters, to create a g graph:

```
node_attr_path = './data/musae_facebook_target.csv'
edgelist_path = './data/musae_facebook_edges.csv'
attributes = ['page_name', 'page_type']

g = graph_from_attributes_and_edgelist(node_attr_path, edgelist_
path, attributes)
```

With this, our graph is now created from a single method call.

8. To confirm that our new graph is identical to the one in the previous steps, we can print some graph properties as we did earlier in the chapter and compare them. The following statements should print the same values as in the earlier examples:

```
print(g.vs[0]['page_name'])
print(g.vs[0]['page_type'])
```

```
first_edge = g.es[0]
print(first_edge.source)
print(first_edge.target)
print(len(g.es))
print(g.vs[0]['page_name'])
print(g.vs[18427]['page_name'])
```

Now that we are satisfied that our graph data model is set up as intended, we can begin to use it to answer network-based questions. Having the tools to examine the graph in detail will allow us to turn a critical eye to the dataset and the way we have represented it in our graph schema.

In the next section, we will take what we have learned here and apply it to a use case, acting under the pretense of a data scientist who has been hired by Facebook to apply graph data science techniques in action and to solve an actual use case.

The most popular TV show – a real-world use case

In this section, we will be taking on the very fortunate position or role of a Facebook data scientist to determine, among other things, what the most popular TV show in our dataset is. This will test the knowledge we have gained so far and will take you through a typical use case that gets asked of a graph data scientist.

In order to do this, we will first be taking a look into the general properties of the mutual likes graph. This will start with an examination of what the graph structure looks like, moving on to a few other considerations you may want to take into account, such as a concept known as degree centrality.

Here, you will put your newly acquired skills to work. We will first start by examining the structure of the graph, we will then perform the connectedness of the entities in the graph, and then we will look at the top degree nodes in the graph.

We will be looking at the following steps to achieve our *end goal* of finding the most popular television show, using the new knowledge we have acquired up to this point:

1. We start by doing some analysis of the structure of the data in our graph; this will focus on common data science techniques to visualize the distribution, such as a histogram of the graph.

2. Connectedness of the graph will be our next port of call. This is an important step, as it allows you to see how connected your components are in your graph. We will focus on our mutual likes dataset on Facebook to achieve this and will look at top degree node connectivity.

3. Finally, we will build out our initial recommendation engine to recommend the TV shows in this case.

This sounds fun, so let's get started and tame this graph problem like a snake charmer would.

Examining the graph structure

Now that we have our data in a graph model, we can consider some network-based analysis. A good place to start is examining some general properties of the graph, to get an idea of its structure.

It is common practice in network analysis to take a look at the degree distribution of a graph. Each node has a degree centrality, which in its simplest form is the number of nodes that it shares an edge with. Hence, the degree distribution is essentially a histogram of node-degree centralities, for a whole graph.

This will be detailed in the steps hereunder and relates to the graph we created in the previous section. In the supporting Jupyter notebooks, these functions have been saved in `graphtastic. utils` and can be imported easily by using `graphtastic.utils import graph_from_ attributes_and_edgelist`.

Handily, `igraph` has a built-in way to quickly construct and print a degree distribution for a given graph, using the `degree_distribution` method on a `Graph()` object:

```
histogram = g.degree_distribution(bin_width=5)
print(histogram)
```

The `bin_width` parameter can be changed to any integer and specifies how fine-grained the histogram plot is.

Our histogram plot shows us that in our mutual Facebook likes graph, there are 8,324 nodes that are connected to a maximum of 4 other nodes (note that the `(0, 5]` range notation shown on the left side of the printed histogram is exclusive of nodes with a *degree centrality* of 5). At the other end of the scale, our most connected node has a degree centrality of somewhere between 705 and 709, with the second most connected node having a degree centrality of between 675 and 679.

Let's plot these degree frequencies in a slightly more appealing format, using the `matplotlib` library:

```
import matplotlib.pyplot as plt
bins = 30
plt.hist(g.degree(), bins)
plt.xlabel('Node degree centrality')
plt.ylabel('Frequency')
plt.show()
```

This will give us the following chart:

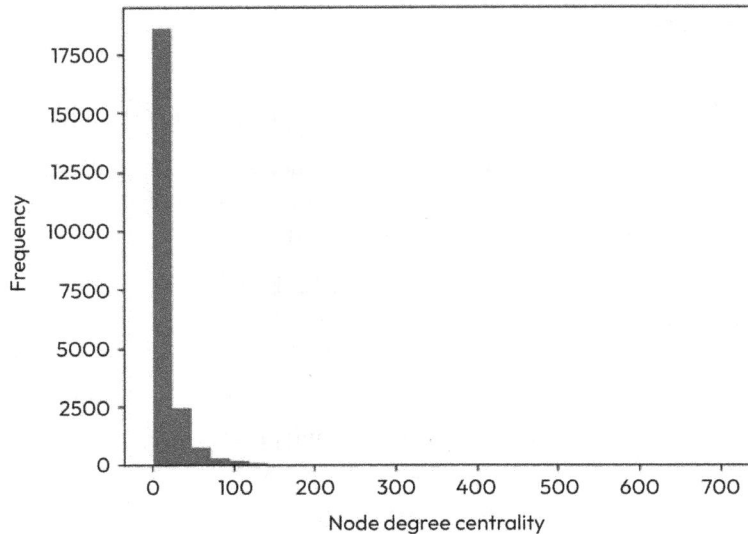

Figure 2.2 – Node degree centrality histogram

We will return to these degree distribution charts, as they are a particularly useful visualization of a graph's structure.

The type of graph structure we see here, where many nodes have few connections and few nodes have many connections, is very common. For reference, nodes that are highly connected in any given graph are known as *hubs* or *hub nodes*. These hub nodes are often responsible for a disproportionate level of connectivity between nodes, which gives rise to phenomena such as the *six degrees of separation* in social networks, where just six friends of friends can be used to connect any two people. We will explore these concepts in detail in later chapters, but for now, we'll focus on identifying nodes of importance in our Facebook graph.

Measuring connectedness

Not all graphs are fully connected, and it may be of interest to learn about this aspect of our Facebook mutual likes dataset. If any node in a graph cannot be reached from another node when traversing through edges, then a graph is fragmented. Each distinct part of the graph in this case is known as a connected component.

Let's use `igraph` to check how many connected components are in our Facebook mutual likes graph. We can use `igraph`'s inbuilt `clusters()` method to do this easily:

```
connected_components = g.clusters()
print(connected_components)
```

Our `print` statement will show us how many connected components are in our graph, and the membership of each, in terms of nodes. In this graph, we have only one connected component, indicating that the graph is fully connected.

Note that with our undirected graph, connected components are slightly simpler to understand than in a directed graph. For a directed graph, sometimes a part of a graph can only be reached by traversing in the wrong direction along an edge. If this is the case, then that part of the graph is known as a weakly connected component. A strongly connected component, in contrast, can be accessed by other nodes in the graph following the native edge direction. The `igraph` library allows you to specify the mode of the `clusters()` method as a parameter, which can be set to `weak` or `strong`. In our undirected graph case, we can allow `igraph` to default `mode` to strongly connected components.

Now that we have learned about the structure of our graph, which is always a good practice in graph applications, we can start to delve deeper into some specific elements and areas of our graph dataset.

Looking at the top degree nodes

The following steps will look at how to work with the top degree nodes in your network and the steps to implement this in Python:

1. To view the top degree centrality nodes, we first use `zip` to combine two tuples into a list wrapper; these tuples are `page_name` and the *degree of association* between the nodes. Next, we sort the degree and use an anonymous function (also known as a Lambda) to sort in a descending (reversed) fashion:

   ```
   degree = list(zip(g.vs['page_name'], g.degree()))
   sorted_degree = sorted(degree, key=lambda x: x[1], reverse=True)
   print(sorted_degree[:10])
   ```

   From the print to console, we can see that the *US Army* node has the highest degree centrality, with 709 mutual likes. To connect this back to real-world data, consider what this indicates about the *US Army* Facebook page. Not only is this a popular *liked* page among other government organizations, politicians, TV shows, and companies, but it also shows that the *US Army* page is active in liking these pages back in return.

2. If we want to take a look at top degree nodes of a certain type, then we need to adjust our `igraph` code. To find the top degree centrality TV show, we can use the `vs.select()` method with a parameter that specifies what page type we are looking for, `page_type_eq`. Then, as in the previous code snippet, we can zip the degrees and page names together—this time just for TV show nodes—order them, and print the results:

   ```
   tv_nodes = g.vs.select(page_type_eq='tvshow')
   tv_indices = [node.index for node in tv_nodes]
   ```

```
tv_degree = list(zip(g.vs[tv_indices]['page_name'], g.degree(tv_
indices)))
sorted_tv_degree = sorted(tv_degree, key=lambda x: x[1],
reverse=True)
print(sorted_tv_degree[:10])
```

This shows us that in our graph, the TV show with the highest degree is the *Today Show*, with 141 mutual likes.

Using select() to interrogate the graph

In the previous section, we used `vs.select()`, which is worth discussing in more detail, as it is a particularly powerful method. Its power stems from its flexible parameters, which are comprised of node types or attributes, and comparison operators.

In the prior example, we used the `page_type_eq` parameter, set to `tvshow`. This tells `vs.select()` to search for nodes that have a `page_type` attribute equal (designated by `_eq`) to `tvshow`. Here, `_eq` could be substituted for many other operators, as follows:

Select parameter element	Comparison operator
_eq	Is equal to
_ne	Is not equal to
_lt	Is less than
_gt	Is greater than
_le	Is less than or equal to
_ge	Is greater than or equal to
_in	Is in a given list
_notin	Is not in a given list

Table 2.1 – Dunder expressions for select()

So, using the previous table, if we wanted to find nodes of type `government` or `politician`, we could use the following code:

```
gov_pol_nodes = g.vs.select(page_type_in=['government', 'politician'])
```

Further to this, adding an underscore before a `Graph()` method, within a `select()` method, allows the calculation of a node property on the fly. For example, we can look for all TV show nodes with a degree of between `100` and `140` using the following code:

```
one_to_three_100_nodes = g.vs.select(_degree_ge=100,
                                      _degree_le=140,
                                      page_type_eq='tvshow')
print(one_to_three_100_nodes['page_name'])
```

Here, the `select()` parameters were layered to return a more specific set of just four nodes meeting our criteria. We also used degree in a `select()` method by preceding the `degree` keyword with an underscore. For example, to get a degree greater than 100, we used the magic method `_degree_ge=100`; this acted as our lower bound, and the upper bound was specified as `_degree_le=140`.

It is worth noting that this calculation of node and graph features on the fly with `select()` is most appropriate for simple calculations such as degrees. With some more computationally demanding network science calculations, it may be better to add the calculated node property as a node attribute rather than calculating it twice, as in the previous example with `degree`.

Compared to `degree`, which counts each node's edges, some algorithms involve more complex routines—for example, those that *walk* across paths in the graph. Algorithms that involve walking along paths typically involve far more operations and therefore take longer to compute than simple calculations such as node degree. More complex algorithms are available, some of which we will explore throughout this book.

To illustrate, the previous example can be rewritten as follows so that node degree is calculated only once, written to graph nodes as the `node_degree_` property, then queried by `select()`, rather than computing the `degree` for each comparison:

```
g.vs['node_degree'] = g.degree()
one_to_three_100_nodes = g.vs.select(node_degree_ge=100,
                                      node_degree_le=140,
                                      page_type_eq='tvshow')
print(one_to_three_100_nodes['page_name'])
```

The most efficient way to carry out these types of `select()` operations will differ for each use case, but the preceding considerations can be taken into account to aid in designing the best processes.

Up next, we will look at how we can use these operations over our popular nodes in a similar fashion.

Properties of our popular nodes

Knowing more about the `select()` method, we can now delve into exploring the properties of our most popular TV show node, and learn about its importance in the mutual likes Facebook graph.

We found earlier that the most popular TV show node, in terms of mutual likes, is the *Today Show*, with a degree centrality of 141. We can learn more about our top degree centrality node by examining its neighbors. In an undirected network, such as our Facebook mutual likes graph, nodes connected by an edge are known as incident nodes. Finding all incident nodes of the *Today Show* will reveal which Facebook pages share a mutual interest in each other, in our dataset.

1. To look into this, we will be using the `select()` method again, this time for edges. The `es.select()` method can find edges according to their attributes (if they have any), using the same syntax as in *Table 2.1*. However, our edges contain no attributes, and we are more interested in the nodes they link.

    As with the `vs.select()` method, `es.select()` has some special parameters that can be used to find edges that link nodes with particular criteria—again, each starting with an underscore.

    The following table shows the various dunder methods, also known as *magic methods*, to use with the `vs.select()` command. These can be accessed to perform the functions listed in the *Function* column:

Edge select parameter prefix	Function
`_incident`	Finds edges that are incident on a specific node, or list of nodes, ignoring edge direction.
`_source` (or `_from`)	In a directed graph, finds edges where a node or list of nodes are the edge sources.
`_target` (or `_to`)	In a directed graph, finds edges where a node or list of nodes are the edge sources.
`_within`	Finds edges where both nodes making up an edge are contained in a given list.
`_between`	Finds edges where both nodes making up an edge are contained in separate lists (these two lists are provided as a tuple).

Table 2.2 – es.select() special parameters

2. Now, because our mutual likes graph is undirected, let's use the `_incident` parameter in `es.select()` to select the edges incident to the *Today Show*. `es.select()` works with node IDs, so we need to first find the node ID of our TV show of interest:

    ```
    today_show_id = g.vs.select(page_name_eq='Today Show')[0].index
    print(today_show_id)
    ```

Here, similarly to earlier in the chapter, we use `vs.select()` to find the node with a page name equal to Today Show. Because `vs.select()` returns an iterable, we need to take the first element with `[0]` so that we can access the first element's `.index` attribute. Our `print` statement will show that our node's ID is 909.

3. Now, we can find edges that contain node 909 using `es.select()`. We specify the `_incident` parameter is equal to our `today_show_id` variable, and put it inside a list (note that `es.select()` requires lists of nodes for all special parameters in *Table 2.2*):

```
today_show_edges = g.es.select(_incident=[today_show_id])
```

4. Just as with `vs.select()`, this line returns an iterable containing edges. We can pull out the two nodes for each edge in `today_show_edges` using the `.source` and `.target` attributes of each edge in the iterable:

```
sources = [edge.source for edge in today_show_edges]
targets = [edge.target for edge in today_show_edges]
print(sources)
print(targets)
```

This will show us two lists of node IDs, all present in edges incident to the *Today Show*.

> **Note**
>
> Note that in our mutual likes graph, `source` and `target` are in reality equivalent, as the graph is undirected. Here, `source` and `target` are merely denoted by `igraph` for each edge, based on the index of each two-element node pair that was added previously with `add_edges()`.

5. Notice that node 909, representing the *Today Show*, is present multiple times in our lists. This is as expected because we asked `igraph` to return all edges containing it. However, for our purposes of examining the neighboring nodes of the *Today Show*, we need to remove it from our results. We can use `set()` to return a unique set of elements from the concatenation of our `sources` and `targets` lists, then remove node 909, corresponding to the *Today Show*:

```
neighbor_nodes = list(set(sources + targets))
neighbor_nodes.remove(909)
print(neighbor_nodes)
print(len(neighbor_nodes))
```

Our first `print()` statement should now show a list of unique node IDs. We can also print the number of unique `neighbor_nodes` list elements, which should be 141. Note that this is equal to the degree centrality of the *Today Show* calculated previously.

6. Now that we have our list of unique neighboring nodes, we can explore their properties to see what kinds of mutual connections the *Today Show* shares. Let's take a look at the `page_type` attributes of these neighboring nodes:

    ```
    neighbor_page_types = g.vs[neighbor_nodes]['page_type']
    print(neighbor_page_types)
    ```

7. A quick glance at the list we printed out shows us that there is a good mix of page types that share a mutual like with our TV show of interest. To count these types of pages, we can use the `Counter()` method from the native `collections` Python library:

    ```
    from collections import Counter
    page_type_dict = Counter(neighbor_page_types)
    print(page_type_dict)
    ```

    The `Counter()` method finds the frequency of the unique elements in our list and returns it as a dictionary. Printing this dictionary out, we can see that companies make up over half of the shared page likes with the *Today Show*, followed by other TV shows, government organizations, and finally, a single politician.

8. Let's see who this lone politician is. We can use the `zip()` method to join the node ID list and the page-type list together element-wise, and use the zipped iterable (a Python object that can be looped or iterated over) to locate the ID representing this politician:

    ```
    ids_and_page_types = zip(neighbor_nodes, neighbor_page_types)
    politician_id = [id_tuple for id_tuple in list(ids_and_page_
    types) if id_tuple[1] == 'politician']
    print(politician_id)
    ```

9. We find that the ID for this politician is `22243`, so to find the page name of this node, we can use `g.vs` to query the node attribute:

    ```
    politician_name = g.vs[22243]['page_name']
    print(politician_name)
    ```

    Upon the completion of preceding steps, this reveals that the only politician sharing a mutual like with the *Today Show* is *Aníbal José Torres*.

This concludes this chapter, and you should feel proud, as you have come a long way toward starting to build models in graph structures.

Summary

In this chapter, we looked at many of the concepts you need to learn when working with graph data models. We started off by looking at making the transition from tabular data files to building nodes, attributes, edges, and edge lists. From there, we then delved into considerations for designing a schema, focusing on a common type of graph in social networks—an undirected heterogeneous graph.

This stood us in good stead for then implementing the model in Python, which focused on the following key methods of building graphs with `igraph`. First, we looked at adding nodes and attributes to your graph—here, we started with the creation of nodes, then we added attributes for these nodes. Nodes in a graph can be thought of as properties in other object-oriented languages. Next, we looked at the creation of edges to connect your nodes or relationships to the nodes, and we discussed what is meant by an edgelist—a list of relationships (edges) describing connectivity between nodes. To end, we then consolidated this into a couple of helper functions that will allow you to build these connections really quickly in your projects. Transitioning from these fundamental building blocks, we then put you in a new position as a data scientist working for Facebook. The key business problem you had to solve here was to identify what is the current top-trending television program, as a use case.

In this use case, we looked at how to view the distribution of the graph with a histogram and expanded on what is meant by degree centrality—that is, the degree centrality of a node is simply the number of edges it has. In general, the higher the degree, the more important the node is. Simple as that. This then led to examining the top degree node in the business problem statement we had set.

Moreover, from this, we then paid special attention to the `select()` method and the power this has to interrogate your graph. This culminated in examining the properties of nodes to delve deeper into a part of the graph's structure.

In the next chapter, we will take what you have learned so far and take you through how you get out of the mindset of storing your data relationally. This will focus on why you should store your data in a graph database in fervent opposition to traditional relational database structures. This is a skill that is needed in this space, as we have many traditional data engineers being recruited to the market, but there is an absence in their skill sets of working with graph structures. I hope you are as excited as we are to get started with the next chapter!

Part 2:
Making the Graph Transition

Armed with what we learned from the previous part around the fundamentals, we can now move on to explain how and why graph databases are different to traditional relational database structures, and how and why you would want to use them. We will be working in MySQL and Python in the data model transformation chapter, which will culminate in building a recommendation engine to recommend a game to a user.

Once we have that chapter in our arsenal, we will move on to delve into how we can build a knowledge graph. This will involve getting our hands dirty with some data ingestion and cleaning, before we then create our knowledge graph and perform community detection over the top, to find medical abstracts that relate to a specific subject, as community detection's role is to find similar communities in entities, or in this sense, similar research based on a specific abstract text and what terms are mentioned in the text.

This part has the following chapters:

- *Chapter 3, Data Model Transformation – Relational to Graph Databases*
- *Chapter 4, Building a Knowledge Graph*

3
Data Model Transformation – Relational to Graph Databases

Up until this point, we have been getting you ready to work with graph data structures in a real-world environment. This will transition your knowledge even further, taking you from setting up your own MySQL database instances to building a recommendation system. This is an important step forward since many solutions out there in the wild are based on data being extracted from relational database environments, such as MySQL.

In this chapter, we will start with setting up your MySQL graph database and then move on to how to work with graph data and querying the database engine. Carrying on from there, we will look at path-based methods for carrying out your analysis. This will be followed by considerations of schema design for graph solutions and building a recommendation solution so that you can use a user's gaming history on the popular platform Steam, along with a graph to predict, or highlight, games that the specific user in question may be interested in. This will function very much like the popular streaming services that give you a prompt stating, "Because you watched this, you may also like this." Here, we will replace *watch* with played or downloaded.

In this chapter, we are going to cover the following main topics:

- Recommending a game to a user
- Using Jaccard similarity and path traversals in graphs
- From relational to graph databases
- Ingestion considerations
- Our recommendation system

Technical requirements

We will be using Jupyter Notebooks to run our coding exercises that require `python>=3.8.0`, along with the following packages, which will need to be installed in your environment with the `pip install` command:

- `igraph==0.9.8`
- `mysql==0.0.3`
- `mysql-connector-python==8.0.31`

All Notebooks, along with the coding exercises, are available at the following GitHub link: `https://github.com/PacktPublishing/Graph-Data-Modeling-in-Python/tree/main/CH03`.

Recommending a game to a user

In *Chapter 2, Working with Graph Data Models*, we showed how tabular node and edge data can be used to model and construct a graph with Python. We can use this graph to ask questions that would be difficult and inefficient using the original tabular data, thus demonstrating the power of a graph model.

In this chapter, we will be looking more closely, with examples, at the issues that arise when answering graph-like questions using a relational database. In *Chapter 1, Introducing Graphs in the Real World*, we touched on how path-based operations are inefficient when using tabular data, due to the requirement for repeated table joins.

However, in real situations, data is often not in the form of node properties and edge lists. A huge amount of data, across every sector, is stored in the form of relational data tables. Relational data is often stored and accessed using SQL, or a SQL-like storage system and query language (for example, MySQL).

In this chapter, we'll be using data from Steam, the online video game distribution service. We will be using data in two separate tables, each containing separate customer interactions. In one table, we have information on user purchases of games on the Steam platform, whereas in the other table, we have information on the total length of time a user has spent playing a game.

First, we will demonstrate the issues with using a relational database to ask a path-based question by creating a MySQL database from our datasets and attempting to perform some basic graph queries using SQL.

Installing MySQL

To demonstrate how we can work with relational databases, we will need to install one and move data across to it. We will be using MySQL, which is a freely available open source, SQL-compatible database.

For this section, we will be using MySQL version 5.7.39. Newer versions of MySQL are available, but loading data into MySQL tables in newer versions requires additional configuration. If you already have MySQL installed, you can skip the installation steps and proceed to the *Setting up a MySQL database* section.

Navigate to `https://downloads.mysql.com/archives/installer/` and select the appropriate MySQL 5.7.39 (`https://downloads.mysql.com/archives/get/p/25/file/mysql-installer-community-5.7.39.0.msi`) distribution for your operating system. Install MySQL with all default options (you can uncheck **Open Windows Firewall port for network access** if you wish – we will only be connecting to the database locally). When prompted to enter a password for the server, choose a dummy password for this chapter, since we will be connecting to the database using Python, and the password will be visible.

Should any issues arise during installation, consult the setup guide at `https://dev.mysql.com/doc/mysql-getting-started/en/` for operating system-specific tips.

Setting up a MySQL database

The following steps will aid you in setting up your MySQL database:

1. To begin setting up a MySQL database, first, navigate to the installation folder binaries. For a Windows machine, they are likely located at `C:/Program Files/MySQL/MySQL Server 5.7/bin`. Open a Command Prompt terminal here. Alternatively, open Command Prompt from the **Start** menu, and navigate to this folder that contains the `cd` commands:

   ```
   cd "Program Files/MySQL/MySQL Server 5.7/bin"
   ```

2. Once in a Command Prompt in the `bin` folder, access the MySQL shell by running the following command:

   ```
   mysql -u root -p
   ```

   When prompted for a password, enter the password that you set up during your MySQL installation earlier.

3. Now that we are in the MySQL shell, we can create a database, like so:

   ```
   CREATE DATABASE steam_data;
   ```

   This database now needs to have tables and data added to it. First, we need to move the `steam_play.csv` and `steam_purchase.csv` files over to an area where MySQL can access them. Copy and paste these `csv` files into `C:\ProgramData\MySQL\MySQL Server 5.7\Uploads`.

4. Now that MySQL can access our data, we can create our two tables. In this MySQL shell, we can prepare our tables with the following commands, each run separately:

```
USE steam_data;
CREATE TABLE steam_play (id VARCHAR(100), game_name
VARCHAR(255), type VARCHAR(10), hours FLOAT(10, 1), misc_column
INT);
CREATE TABLE steam_purchase (id VARCHAR(100), game_name
VARCHAR(255), type VARCHAR(10), game_purchased_flag FLOAT(2, 1),
misc_column INT);
```

5. We will come back to the structure of our data and its fields later in the next section, once it has been loaded into MySQL. For now, to populate the blank tables we have created, run the following lines:

```
LOAD DATA INFILE 'C:/ProgramData/MySQL/MySQL Server 5.7/Uploads/
steam_play.csv' INTO TABLE steam_play FIELDS TERMINATED BY ','
OPTIONALLY ENCLOSED BY '\"' LINES TERMINATED BY '\r\n';
LOAD DATA INFILE 'C:/ProgramData/MySQL/MySQL Server 5.7/Uploads/
steam_purchase.csv' INTO TABLE steam_purchase FIELDS TERMINATED
BY ',' OPTIONALLY ENCLOSED BY '\"' LINES TERMINATED BY '\r\n';
```

On a successful import, the MySQL shell window should print out how many records have been added. For the `steam_play` table, there should be 70,489 rows, while for the `steam_purchase` table, there should be 129,511 rows.

With our relational database set up, we are now ready to begin evaluating and analyzing the data.

Querying MySQL in Python

To transform our relational database into a graph, our first step must be examining the data and designing a sensible graph schema to represent it. As we did in *Chapter 2, Working with Graph Data Models*, let's examine the first few lines of the datasets.

From this point, we will be accessing data in MySQL from Python by using the `mysql.connector` driver. We can use the `mysql.connector.connect()` method to open an authenticated connection with our locally hosted database and query the data contained in its tables. The steps to get to your MySQL database instance, from Python, are captured hereunder:

1. To start, we'll need to import the driver and make a connection to our database. Connecting to `localhost` means that we are accessing a database on the local machine, while `root` means that we will be accessing the database as an administrator. Our database name is equal to the one we set up in the MySQL shell earlier. Replace `password` with the password you chose during the MySQL setup in the previous section:

```
import mysql.connector
PASSWORD = '<Your MySQL password upon creating MySQL instance>'
connection = mysql.connector.connect(
```

```
            host="localhost",
            user="root",
            passwd=PASSWORD,
            database="steam_data")
```

2. Now, we can specify some example SQL to query a table:

```
sql = 'SELECT count(*) FROM steam_purchase;'
```

3. We can run the SQL string in our variable using `connection.cursor()` and `cursor.execute()`. Then, we can retrieve and print the result using `cursor.fetchall()` and a `print` statement, before finally closing the connection with `connection.close()`:

```
cursor = connection.cursor()
cursor.execute(sql)
result = cursor.fetchall()
print(result)
connection.close()
```

4. Now, because we'll be accessing these tables many times, let's set up a reusable method for this process. We will just be changing the SQL queries to the same database so that we can abstract away the query into a new method parameter:

```
import mysql.connector
def query_mysql(query, password, host='localhost',
user='root',database='steam_data'):
    connection = mysql.connector.connect(
    host=host,
    user=user,
    passwd=password,
    database=database
    )
    cursor = connection.cursor()
    cursor.execute(query)
    result = cursor.fetchall()
    connection.close()
    return result
```

5. Now, we can call our new `query_mysql()` method to get the length of the `steam_purchase` table again, to check that it is functioning as expected:

```
result = query_mysql('SELECT count(*) FROM steam_
purchase;',password=PASSWORD)
print(result)
```

Our method returns the `result` variable, and printing this shows that the `steam_puchase` table contains 129,511 rows.

Examining the data in Python

Now that we can query data from our MySQL database through Python, let's begin to examine the data contained in our tables.

Follow these steps to examine your data in MySQL:

1. First, let's look at the `steam_play` table, which contains play time data for Steam users. We can take a look at the first few lines with another simple SQL query, using the method we defined in the previous section:

    ```
    result = query_mysql('SELECT * FROM steam_play LIMIT 4;',
    password=PASSWORD)
    for row in result:
      print(row)
    ```

2. Looking at the first few printed rows of `steam_play`, we can see that there are five columns:

    ```
    ('151603712', 'The Elder Scrolls V Skyrim', 'play', 273.0, 0)
    ('151603712', 'Fallout 4', 'play', 87.0, 0)
    ('151603712', 'Spore', 'play', 14.9, 0)
    ('151603712', 'Fallout New Vegas', 'play', 12.1, 0)
    ```

    According to the data's source, the first column contains a unique `user ID`. The second column contains the name of the game the user has played. The third column contains the `play` string in each row, which gives us little information. The fourth column shows the number of hours the row's user has been playing a game. Finally, the last column seems to contain only 0s; we can safely ignore this column going forward.

3. The other table, `steam_purchase`, contains information on user purchases. Again, we should check the first few lines of this dataset:

    ```
    ('151603712', 'The Elder Scrolls V Skyrim', 'purchase', 1.0, 0)
    ('151603712', 'Fallout 4', 'purchase', 1.0, 0)
    ('151603712', 'Spore', 'purchase', 1.0, 0)
    ('151603712', 'Fallout New Vegas', 'purchase', 1.0, 0)
    ```

    The `steam_purchase` table also seems to contain five columns. In the `steam_purchase` table, the first column again contains a unique `user ID`. As with `steam_play`, the second column contains a game's name. The third column always contains the `purchase` string. The fourth column in this table always contains `float 1.0`, indicating the purchase of that row's game, by the user. The last column, as in the previous file, contains all 0s.

    At a glance, we can see that there is data for user `151603712` in both the `steam_play` and `steam_purchase` tables. So, users in our datasets have data about both the purchase of games and play time. From a brief look into the data, we can see that there are plenty of columns that we won't need going forward, so we can start to exclude them from our analysis by querying specific rows.

In the next section, we will look at path-based methods for dealing with the tabular data we looked at in this section. This will allow us to get insights into what types of games users enjoy playing on Steam.

Path-based analytics in tabular data

Now that we have an idea of what our tables contain, we can ask some questions about our data. For example, we can ask, "What other games may a user enjoy, based on their previous purchase habits?" This type of question forms the basis of a recommendation system, used across the sales and marketing industry to drive additional customer purchases.

To answer a question like this simply, we will need to find the games a user has purchased, then find other users that have purchased the same games. Then, we will look at commonalities between those users to recommend a new game to our original user.

This type of system is often driven by a graph data model, due to the path-based operations required. The process of finding all games associated with a user, then users associated with those games, and finally the games those users associate with, represents a type of path-based query that graph databases are more suitable for than relational databases. In a relational database, we would have to repeatedly query the same table and perform a series of self-joins to find a series of relationships through users and games. We briefly explored these concepts in *Chapter 1, Introducing Graphs in the Real World*, but let's also use this as a more practical example to demonstrate the differences between database types.

The following diagram shows the relationship between a user's preferences and the games they play. We can use our graph recommendation engine to look at the games our user plays, and then look at what other users who play those games also play. Therefore, based on this tree, we can get an understanding of what games our (top node in the network) user may like based on similar users to them and the games they (all the other users) play:

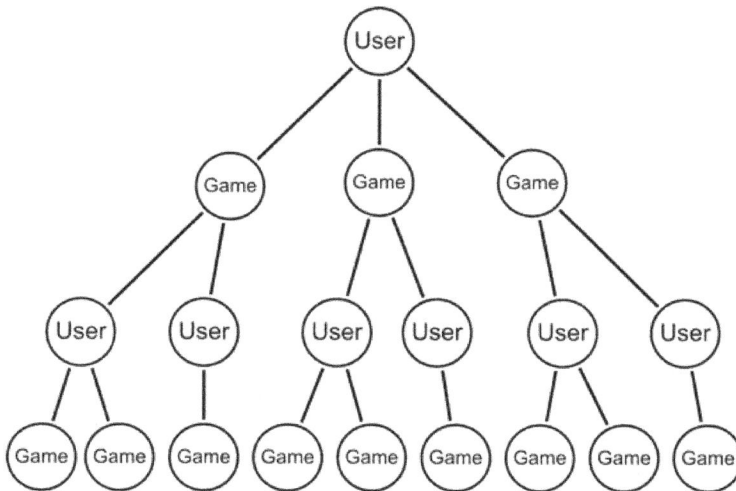

Figure 3.1 – Information required to make a game recommendation to a user

In the following steps, we will take you through how to query the graph to get the optimal information needed to form the recommendation of what a user might want to play, based on what we have told you previously:

1. First, we will need to query MySQL to find all games purchased by a specific user. Let's use the user at the top of the `steam_purchase` table as an example, 151603712. Making use of our query method again, we can query the `steam_purchase` table for this information:

    ```
    result = query_mysql('SELECT game_name from steam_purchase WHERE
    id = "151603712";', password=PASSWORD)
    print(result[:10])
    print(len(result))
    ```

2. From the `print()` statements, we can see that this user has purchased 40 separate games. Note that MySQL has returned the data as a list of tuples, where each tuple has an empty element. We will need to access the first element of each tuple and enclose each game in quote marks to find the users associated with these games. We will also need to add the results from this initial query to a new SQL query, as a string, so let's prepare this:

    ```
    games = ['"' + game[0] + '"' for game in result]
    games_string = ','.join(games)
    print(games_string)
    ```

3. Now, we can query the table again with these results to find the users that also purchased these games (not our original user):

    ```
    query_2 = f'SELECT id from steam_purchase WHERE game_name ' \
            f'IN ({games_string}) AND id != "151603712";'
    result_2 = query_mysql(query_2, password=PASSWORD)
    users = [user[0] for user in result_2]
    print(users[:10])
    print(len(users))
    ```

4. We have a list of 16223 users in our result, but this contains duplicates, so let's remove them with a `set()` operation:

    ```
    users = list(set(users))
    print(users[:10])
    print(len(users))
    ```

    Our print statements now show that we have 7728 unique users that play at least one of the same games as our originally selected user.

5. Now, we need to find new games to recommend to our selected user based on the purchases of our identified users. Let's set up the parameters for a new SQL query based on these requirements, in a similar way to the previous query:

    ```
    users = ['"' + user + '"' for user in users]
    users_string = ','.join(users)
    ```

```
query_3 = f'SELECT game_name from steam_purchase WHERE id IN
({users_string}) ' \
        f'AND game_name NOT IN ({games_string});'

result_3 = query_mysql(query_3, password=PASSWORD)
recommended_games = [game[0] for game in result_3]
print(recommended_games[:10])
```

6. Now, all we need to do is find the most popular games among the games returned, to make a recommendation to our original user. We can do this using the built-in `Counter()` method from the `collections` Python library:

```
from collections import Counter
game_frequency = Counter(recommended_games)
print(game_frequency)
```

This dictionary of game frequencies tells us that we could recommend the game *Unturned* to our specified user.

Taking data models into account, think about the operations involved in finding this game recommendation. Using a relational database, we had to repeatedly query the same table, with increasingly large results. This could also have been achieved with several self-joins of the `steam_purchase` table. Either of these methods is fairly inefficient as the same data is repeatedly read to build up an answer.

These types of questions are where graph data models and databases shine; the existence of native paths between related objects and entities means that graphs are ideal for path-based traversal of relationships. Next, let's consider how we might represent our data in a graph data model instead.

From relational to graph databases

Due to the poor performance of our relational database in answering graph-like questions, we may want to move our tabular data into a graph format.

First, we will consider a sensible graph schema for our data, based on the information we have available, before writing a pipeline to move data from MySQL into a Python *igraph* network. By doing this, we can benchmark how a graphical approach to our path-based question performs, in comparison to the same question we answered with SQL.

Schema design

In our tables, we have two types of entities, *users* and *games*, which have different *properties*. Because of this, it is wise to consider *users* and *games* as different node types.

For users, we only have a *unique ID* for each user. To add data to an **igraph** graph, we will need to add an increasing integer igraph node ID for each distinct node, as we learned in *Chapter 1, Introducing Graphs in the Real World*, and *Chapter 2, Working with Graph Data Models*.

On the other hand, for games, we are given the game's name as a *string*. We must also add an *igraph ID* to distinct game nodes in the same manner as for user nodes.

We have already considered the schema design for nodes, but we must also consider how we should represent relationships. For our purposes, we are interested in the interactions between *users* and *games*. We have information on games purchased by users, as well as the length of time a user has played a game for.

Because of this, it is sensible to consider these different interactions as different *edge types*. Purchasing a game is represented just by the existence of a row in the `steam_purchase` table, and essentially the relationship either exists or doesn't. We have no additional data to represent this interaction, so for game purchases, there will be no edge properties.

However, for relationships representing play time, we have information on how long a user played a game, in hours. In this case, we can use an edge property to represent the number of hours a game has been played by a user.

Taking all this into account, we can set out a schema for our graph, as follows:

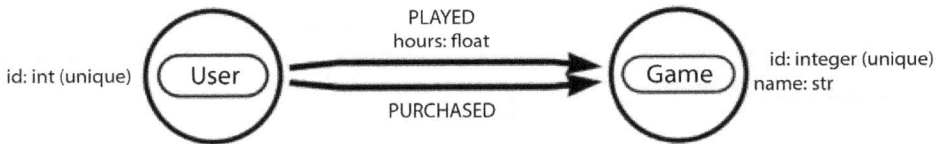

Figure 3.2 – Directed heterogeneous graph schema

Logically, since users either purchase or play games, in the graph schema, both the **PLAYED** and **PURCHASED** relationships are directional, from the `User` node to the `Game` node. For the remainder of this chapter, we will use this schema, but theoretically, it would make no difference if the relationships flowed from `Games` to `Users`, and instead had the names PLAYED_BY and PURCHASED_BY. The only downstream difference with this design would be that the direction of edges in any interrogation of the graph would need to be reversed.

Ingestion considerations

Now that we have decided on a schema for our graph, we can begin to move data from our MySQL relational database to an *igraph* graph. The subsequent steps detail how to achieve this:

1. The first thing we must do is extract the data from our MySQL database and move it over to Python. We can do this using the `query_mysql()` method we wrote previously in this chapter. Now that we know more about the data, and that we have designed a graph schema, we can extract only the columns we need to create our graph:

    ```
    play_query = 'SELECT id, game_name, hours FROM steam_play'
    play_data = query_mysql(play_query, password=PASSWORD)
    ```

```
print(play_data[:10])

purchase_query = 'SELECT id, game_name FROM steam_purchase'
purchase_data = query_mysql(purchase_query,password=PASSWORD )
print(purchase_data[:10])
```

In `play_data`, we have information on users, the games they have played, and the time they have spent playing each game. In `purchase_data`, we only need users and the games they have purchased.

Next, as stated in the process of schema design, to use `igraph`, we will need to add an increasing integer `igraph` node ID to both the `User` and `Game` nodes, starting from 0.

2. The following lines of code will generate a `set()` of unique user IDs and users in both the `play_data` and `purchase_data` lists. Then, a combination of a dictionary comprehension and the `enumerate()` method will generate a dictionary with keys containing Steam user IDs, and values containing our igraph IDs:

```
users = set([row[0] for row in play_data] + [row[0] for row in
purchase_data])
user_ids = {user_id: igraph_id for igraph_id, user_id in
enumerate(users)}
print(len(user_ids))
```

Printing the length of our dictionary with `len()` gives us the number of unique users, `12393`.

3. As with the users, we also need to generate igraph IDs for games. We can use a very similar process to the preceding one, but while making a small change to the `enumerate()` method parameters. We can use the second parameter in `enumerate()` to generate increasing integers, but rather than starting at 0, we can start at the highest igraph ID assigned to users using the `user_ids` dictionary's `len()`:

```
games = set([row[1] for row in play_data] + [row[1] for row in
purchase_data])
game_ids = {user_id: igraph_id for igraph_id, user_id in
enumerate(games, len(user_ids))}
print(len(game_ids))
```

As with users, our `print` statement shows the number of unique games in our datasets, `5155`. Using `enumerate()` with the second parameter should avoid any ID conflicts between users and games. Even though their node types are different, `igraph` still requires IDs for all nodes to be increasing integers from 0.

4. We can check that IDs have indeed been created as expected by examining the highest igraph IDs for users, and the lowest igraph IDs for games, using the `sorted()` method and console `print()` statements:

```
print(sorted(user_ids.values(), reverse=True)[:10])
print(sorted(game_ids.values(), reverse=False)[:10])
```

5. This will show that the highest generated ID for users is 12,392, while the lowest generated ID for games is 12,393, as expected. Let's further confirm that all the node's igraph IDs increase from 0 in increments of 1. We can do this by first concatenating and sorting both lists of ID values() from our ID dictionaries, to create the all_ids variable. Then, we can assert that all our IDs are equal to the range of integers from 0 to the length of all_ids:

    ```
    all_ids = sorted(list(user_ids.values()) + list(game_ids.
    values()))
    assert all_ids == list(range(len(all_ids)))
    ```

    Because this assert statement raises no exceptions, we can be confident that our generated IDs have been created correctly.

6. Now, we can begin to add nodes to our graph. First, we must import *igraph* and create an empty, directed graph using a Graph() object:

    ```
    import igraph as ig
    g = ig.Graph(directed=True)
    ```

7. Now, we can add nodes and node properties to the graph listwise. By sorting the user_ids and game_ids dictionaries, we preserve the order of the 0-indexed *igraph* ID to Steam ID relationships:

    ```
    user_ids = dict(sorted(user_ids.items(), key=lambda item:
    item[1]))
    game_ids = dict(sorted(game_ids.items(), key=lambda item:
    item[1]))
    ```

8. We can now take the keys from these dictionaries and convert them into lists, ready to be added as properties:

    ```
    steam_user_ids = list(user_ids.keys())
    steam_game_ids = list(game_ids.keys())
    ```

9. Now, we are ready to add nodes. We can add nodes equal to the length of both of our ID lists with add_vertices(); *igraph* will create nodes from ID 0 to the length of these combined lists, minus 1. We can confirm this by asserting that the len() property of all nodes in the graph is equal to the combined list length:

    ```
    g.add_vertices(len(steam_user_ids) + len(steam_game_ids))
    assert len(g.vs) == len(steam_user_ids) + len(steam_game_ids)
    ```

10. With nodes in our graph, we can add properties. Since it is most efficient to add properties to all nodes at once, let's create a list of Steam IDs containing user IDs and game names:

    ```
    all_steam_ids = steam_user_ids + steam_game_ids
    ```

11. Let's also use list comprehensions to create a list containing our node's types, which will be either user or game:

    ```
    node_types = ['user' for _ in steam_user_ids] + ['game' for _ in
    steam_game_ids]
    ```

12. With our lists prepared, we can now add properties listwise to all the nodes in our graph by accessing the vs attribute of our *igraph* Graph() object:

```
g.vs['steam_id'] = all_steam_ids
g.vs['type'] = node_types
```

13. To ensure our node properties have been added as intended, we can print some to the console. For a more thorough check, we can compare the number of game nodes in our graph to the number of unique games we counted in *step 6* of the *Path-based analytics in tabular data* section:

```
print(g.vs['steam_id'][:10])
print(g.vs['type'][:10])

game_nodes = g.vs.select(type_eq='game')
print(len(game_nodes))
```

Using the vs.select() method we learned about in *Chapter 2, Working with Graph Data Models*, we can see that the number of game nodes is 5155, which is the same number of games we counted in our dataset earlier.

14. Next, we need to add edges to our graph. Edges are contained in both the data from steam_purchase and steam_play, now contained in the purchase_data and play_data variables.

Let's generate the edges for both of these types of transactions by finding the igraph IDs for the users and games. These igraph IDs are contained in the user_ids and game_ids dictionaries we created earlier, so we can use a list comprehension to set up our igraph-compatible edgelists:

```
purchase_edges = [[user_ids[user], game_ids[purchase]]
                  for user, purchase in purchase_data]
play_edges = [[user_ids[user], game_ids[game], hours]
              for user, game, hours in play_data]
```

15. For play_edges, the number of hours is also included, so we can add this to our graph as edge properties. Let's add the PLAYED edges first, along with their hours attribute, in a listwise fashion, using more list comprehensions:

```
g.add_edges([(n, m) for n, m, _ in play_edges])
g.es['hours'] = [hours for _, _, hours in play_edges]
```

16. Now, we can add the edges representing the PURCHASED relationships. There are no attributes to add to our dataset that are specifically related to a game's purchase, so we can just use the following command:

```
g.add_edges(purchase_edges)
```

17. Finally, to complete our graph, we can add edge_type as an edge attribute to all edges:

```
edge_type = ['PLAYED' for _ in play_edges] + ['PURCHASED' for _ in purchase_edges]
g.es['edge_type'] = edge_type
```

18. As always, we should confirm that our data has been added correctly. Recall that earlier in this chapter, we examined the number of games purchased by a specific user, with ID 151603712, which was 40. We can check if this is the same in our newly created graph by first finding the .index attribute of the node with a steam_id of 151603712 by using g.vs.select(). Then, we can find all edges of the PURCHASED type that have a source of this user ID, using g.es.select(), with two parameters to narrow down our search:

```
user_id_ex = g.vs.select(steam_id_eq='151603712')[0].index
purchased_ex = g.es.select(_source_eq=user_id_ex, edge_
type='PURCHASED')
print(len(list(purchased_ex)))
```

This print statement confirms that the len() property of the edges with this user as a source is 40, as in the steam_purchase dataset.

Now that we've added all the nodes and edges to our igraph.Graph() object, we are ready to analyze its properties.

Path-based analytics in igraph

Graph data models are specialized for path-based analysis. Unlike in MySQL, which we covered earlier in this chapter, we do not need to make a series of queries to a database or perform a series of self-joins to find paths of related objects when using a graph. To demonstrate this, let's use the graph we have created, with our new schema, to again find games our specific user may enjoy.

Last time, we only used data from the steam_purchase table, but this time, our graph contains data from both the steam_purchase and steam_play tables, so we can use information from both to make our recommendations. We will make recommendations for the user with ID 151603712 again, but this time using a graph-based method.

Our user node igraph ID is stored in the user_id_ex variable, so we can use this going forward. Instead of repeated queries or joins, here, we will be finding paths using the get_all_simple_paths() method in *igraph*. The paths we are looking for are those in *Figure 3.1*, from a specified user to the games that similar users play. These paths contain three *hops* from our initial user to our destination, which are the game nodes for recommendation.

The following steps will show how we can achieve this:

1. Let's find these paths using get_all_simple_paths(). We need to specify the node to start paths from, as well as a cutoff for how long these paths should be. Not including the initial starting node, these paths are of length 3. We also need to specify the direction of the edges we are willing to travel in our paths using the mode parameter. Because all the relationships in our graph go from a user to a game, and we want to traverse multiple relationships in different directions to get our paths in this case, we made mode equal to all:

```
paths = g.get_all_simple_paths(user_id_ex, cutoff=3, mode='all')
print(paths[:10])
```

With our `print()` statement, we can take a look at some of the paths that have been found. Our `paths` variable contains the `igraph` IDs of nodes that are traversed from our original user node, as a list of lists.

> **Note**
>
> Some lists are not of length 4, which is what we are looking for to make recommendations. There is no sense in making recommendations of games our user has already purchased, as in paths of length 2, and no reason to recommend a user to our specified user, as in paths of length 3.

2. Because of this, we need to remove paths of length less than 4 from our `paths` list. We also only need the fourth element in each of these lists, which corresponds to a game we can base a recommendation on. We can achieve both of these requirements using a list comprehension with a conditional operator to ensure all path lengths are 4:

```
rec_game_ids = [path[3] for path in paths if len(path) == 4]
```

3. Now, we have a list of `igraph` IDs for nodes representing our games. We need the names of these games, so we will use another list comprehension to access the `steam_id` attribute of each node with `g.vs`:

```
game_names = [g.vs[game_id]['steam_id'] for game_id in rec_game_
ids]
```

4. The preceding code will give us a list of game names. However, this list contains games that our specified user has already played or purchased, so we don't want to recommend them. We can remove these games by first finding the neighboring nodes of our chosen user with the `neighbors()` method in igraph. We can then find the corresponding game names with a similar list comprehension as we used in the previous code snippet, looking for `steam_id` values with `g.vs`:

```
neighbors = g.neighbors(user_id_ex)
purchased_games = [g.vs[node_id]['steam_id'] for node_id in
g.neighbors(user_id_ex)]
```

5. Let's remove the games our user already plays with another list comprehension, comparing the lists:

```
game_names = [game for game in game_names if game not in
purchased_games]
```

6. As in the previous example of using MySQL to accomplish the same thing, let's take a look at the highest frequency games on the end of our paths by using Python's `collections` library and `Counter()`:

```
from collections import Counter
game_frequency = Counter(game_names)
print(game_frequency)
```

Looking at the start of the printed `Counter()` object, we can see the top three games we might want to recommend to our user are **Counter-Strike Global Offensive**, **Unturned**, and **Portal 2**.

In this section, we used a graph to perform a path-based analysis of our data. Where paths are involved, graphs are ideal data models to represent and query relationships between entities. We looked at simple ways to recommend games to users with our Steam data graph, but more sophisticated methods are typically used by recommendation engines in the real world.

Next, we will look at how our graph data model can help us implement a more savvy method for recommendations.

Our recommendation system

Now that we have our data in a Python graph, let's go one step further and design a more robust recommendation process, typically carried out with graph data.

Let's take on the role of a solutions engineer or data scientist and write a game recommendation system based on our Steam data. Recommendation systems are used heavily in customer-facing applications, to show the user a product that they may be interested in. Product recommendations are often based on what behaviorally similar users have played and purchased.

Generic MySQL to igraph methods

This time, we will write a set of reusable, generic methods to create an *igraph* graph from columns in a MySQL table. The functions will be designed to create a heterogeneous, bipartite, directed graph, given a set of column names.

Let's start by writing a main function, `mysql_to_graph()`. The method will need to accept a MySQL table name, the `table`, `source`, and `target` column names of that table, and a column of edge `weights`. In this case, we will use the `steam_play` table, where our `weights` are the number of hours each game (`target`) has been played by a user (`source`). We will sequence these methods in a stepwise way to make them easier to implement:

1. In our new method, we can generate a SQL query with our desired search criteria by using an `f string` and replacement. The names of the columns after `SELECT`, and the table to select `FROM`, can now be dynamically set using the parameters accepted by `mysql_to_graph`. Then, we can use the method we defined in *step 4* in the *Querying SQL with MySQL* section, called `query_mysql()`, to get a list of lists from our MySQL database:

```
def mysql_to_graph(table, source, target, weights, password):

    import igraph as ig
```

```
    sql_query = f'SELECT {source}, {target}, {weights} FROM
    {table}'

    data = query_mysql(sql_query, password=PASSWORD)
```

2. Now that we have data, we can use a series of list comprehensions to split the data into source nodes and target nodes. This helps us get the data in a sensible format for assigning *igraph* IDs. We will write a separate method, `create_igraph_ids()`, to create dictionaries of `{Steam ID: igraph ID}` pairs, after writing the main `mysql_to_graph()` method:

```
    source_nodes = sorted(list(set([source for source, _, _ in
    data])))
    target_nodes = sorted(list(set([target for _, target, _ in
    data])))

    source_igraph_ids = create_igraph_ids(source_nodes)
    target_igraph_ids = create_igraph_ids(target_nodes,
    len(source_igraph_ids))
```

3. Then, we need to generate an `igraph` edge list using the pairs in the created dictionaries, `source_igraph_ids` and `target_igraph_ids`. We can do this using another list comprehension, using `sources` and `targets` as keys. Lastly, before creating a graph, we must extract the edge `weights` from the list of lists returned by MySQL, ready to add to the graph edges later:

```
    edges = [(source_igraph_ids[source], target_igraph_
    ids[target])
                 for source, target, _ in data]
    weights = [weight for _, _, weight in data]
```

4. Now, all the data is in the correct format to be added to an *igraph* graph. First, we must create an empty, directed `Graph()` object using `ig.Graph()`. Then, we must add nodes with `g.add_vertices()` equal to the length of both of our node lists. `'Internal IDs'` – in our case, Steam IDs – are then added to the nodes by accessing the `g.vs` attribute of our graph, using the `source_igraph_ids` and `target_igraph_ids` dictionary keys. Node types are added, again using `g.vs`, by creating lists of our type strings, `source` and `target`, which in terms of the Steam data correspond to `user` and `game`, respectively. Finally, edges can be added from our `edges` list, containing the source and target `igraph` IDs, and the edge `weights` and hours played can be added listwise by accessing the `g.es` attribute of the graph. Our graph, `g`, is then returned so that we can analyze it in a separate function:

```
    g = ig.Graph(directed=True)
      g.add_vertices(len(source_nodes + target_nodes))
```

```
    g.vs['internal_id'] = list(source_igraph_ids.keys()) +
list(target_igraph_ids.keys())
    g.vs['type'] = ['source' for _ in source_nodes] + ['target'
for _ in target_nodes]
    g.add_edges(edges)
    g.es['weight'] = weights

    return g
```

5. In the previous `mysql_to_graph` method that we defined, we made a call to a separate user-defined function, `create_igraph_ids()`, which we will need to define separately. We can create *igraph* IDs for each node similarly to how we did earlier in the chapter – that is, by using a dictionary comprehension and making use of Python's `enumerate()` method. Then, all our `create_graph_ids` method needs as parameters is a list of node names and the index to `enumerate()` from:

```
def create_igraph_ids(nodes, from_index=0):
  igraph_ids = {internal_id: igraph_id for igraph_id, internal_
id
                  in enumerate(nodes, from_index)}
  return igraph_ids
```

We now have a reusable, generic method to create a graph from MySQL data describing any relationships where there is a source, target, and weighting for that relationship. Going back to our Steam use case, in our graph, we have users, the games they have played, and the length of time they have spent playing them. This is enough information for us to make suggestions about what games existing users might like to purchase next.

Earlier in this chapter, we made a very simple recommendation for a new game, based on whether users have played the same games as our specified user and what games they have played. However, this is a very simple example of a recommendation system. Using our graph, we can implement a more robust system that can be productionized to take a user ID as input and recommend games with a more sophisticated method, namely Jaccard similarity. Other similarity methods can also be applied using igraph, such as Dice similarity and inverse log-weighted similarity, which are also effective methods for comparing groups of nodes. Jaccard similarity was chosen for its simplicity and general good performance, but feel free to experiment with different similarity methods.

A more advanced recommendation system using Jaccard similarity

To recommend games more smartly, we are going to implement a solution based on node similarity. Node similarity compares the neighboring nodes of two nodes and returns a score. In our method, we will use Jaccard similarity, available in *igraph* as `similarity_jaccard()`. The score resulting from `similarity_jaccard()` will be equal to the count of two nodes' common neighbors, divided by the number of neighbors adjacent to at least one of the two nodes. The result will be a number between 0 and 1, where 0 means no similarity and 1 means the nodes have identical neighbors.

Relating to our use case, in our Steam graph, user nodes are adjacent to game nodes. So, user nodes that share a high Jaccard similarity with other user nodes play similar games. We can use this information to make new recommendations to our users. We will now work through the steps to simplify this process:

1. Let's define a new function, `make_recommenations()`. Our function will take an `igraph` graph, `g`, and a specific user to make recommendations to, `user`. We will take advantage of the weights on our graph edges by specifying a minimum number of hours that games need to be played to be involved in our recommendations, `min_hours`. This way, where users have purchased a game but played it for only a short amount of time, we can assume that they did not enjoy the game, and not use that information in recommending a new one:

    ```
    def make_recommendations(g, user, min_hours):
    ```

2. First, we need to find the node represented by our `user` parameter, using `g.vs.select()` to query our graph for the node with `internal_id` equal to `user`. This will return a list of one element, so we can access the first and only element with a list slice and find that node's `index` attribute, which will be the `igraph` ID:

    ```
    user_node = g.vs.select(internal_id_eq=user)
    user_node = user_node[0].index
    ```

3. Then, we will use another custom method, `prune_graph()`, to remove edges in our graph based on the number of hours that games have been played. We will come back to this method shortly, after defining the remainder of `make_recommendations()`:

    ```
    g = prune_graph(g, min_hours)
    ```

The modified graph can now be used to make recommendations. To make comparisons to other user nodes, we need to find nodes with `type` equal to `'source'`, which represents users in our previously defined `mysql_to_graph()` method. We can find nodes of the `source` type by using `g.vs.select()`. Then, we need to set up a list of lists containing pairs of nodes to compare. We want to compare our specified user to all other users in our graph, so we will write a list comprehension to create a list of lists, where each element is a two-element list of our chosen user's `igraph` ID and another user's `igraph` ID. We don't want to compare our selected user node with itself, so we will use a conditional `!=` in the comprehension to prevent this:

```
other_user_nodes = g.vs.select(type_eq='source')
pairs = [[user_node, other_user.index] for other_user in other_user_nodes if other_user.index != user_node]
```

Now, with our list of comparisons to make, we can run igraph's `similarity_jaccard()` to generate similarity scores for our pairs of nodes. In this case, since our edges run from users to games in a directed manner, we are interested in the "out" direction, which is specified in the `mode` parameter of `similarity_jaccard()`. Our similarity scores will be returned as a list, so they need to be linked to the node IDs related to the pair comparisons. We can do this using a list comprehension to take the compared user `igraph` ID in the second element of each list in `pairs` and link this to scores with `zip()`:

```
similarities = g.similarity_jaccard(pairs=pairs, mode='out')
node_similarity = [[pair[1], similarity] for pair, similarity in zip(pairs, similarities)]
```

We want to find the user most similar to our specified user, so we need to sort our `node_similarity` list by descending Jaccard similarity score. We can do this using Python's `sorted()` method, with an anonymous function to sort by the second element in each list in `node_similarity`. We will specify `reverse=True` to sort the list in descending fashion. Then, we can get the `igraph` ID of our most similar user by accessing the first element in our sorted list:

```
node_similarity = sorted(node_similarity, key=lambda x: x[1], reverse=True)
most_similar_node = node_similarity[0][0]
```

With the `igraph` ID of our similar user, we can look up the `igraph` IDs of the games this user has played with `g.neighbors()`, and access the corresponding Steam IDs of these games by looking up the `internal_id` node attributes using `g.vs`. We can do the same for our originally specified user so that we have two lists of games that similar users have played. Finally, let's use one last list comprehension to find all the games in our `game_recommendations` list that are not present in the original user's `owned_games` list, and return this list as `new_games`:

```
game_recommendations = g.vs[g.neighbors(most_similar_node)]['internal_id']
owned_games = g.vs[g.neighbors(user_node)]['internal_id']
```

```
new_games = [game for game in game_recommendations if game not
in owned_games]
return new_games
```

Next, we will return to the `prune_graph()` helper method we called in the `make_recommndations()` method. Here, we need a way to remove edges based on the edge weightings, which represent the number of hours a game has been played for. For `prune_graph()`, we take our graph, `g`, and the minimum number of hours necessary for a game to be considered in our recommendation system, `min_hours`, as parameters.

This method will use `g.es.select()` with `min_hours` as a parameter on `weight` to look up all the edges with a weight of less than our minimum play time. Then, `delete_edges()` can be used with the results of `select()` to trim away edges in our graph according to our criteria:

```
def prune_graph(g, min_hours):
  edges_to_remove = g.es.select(weight_lt=min_hours)
  g.delete_edges(edges_to_remove)

  return g
```

Let's test our new functions, which we created in the preceding steps. We can call our `mysql_to_graph()` function with our `steam_play` table, the source and target columns, `id` and `game_name`, and our edge `weights` column, `hours`. Then, using this graph, we can make a recommendation for a specific user by calling `make_recommendations()` with our graph, `g`, a user ID, such as `87907200`, and a minimum number of hours that our graph edges will represent – for example, `2`:

```
g = mysql_to_graph('steam_play', 'id', 'game_name', 'hours')
recommendations = make_recommendations(g, '87907200', min_
hours=0.5)
print(recommendations)
```

A list of recommendations will be printed for our user. Try experimenting with different user IDs (you can find them in the `steam_play` table's `id` column), and different numbers of `min_hours` for the same user. Note that in our more sophisticated system, the minimum number of hours can change the games that are recommended for a single user. This is because the structure of the graph changes when edges are removed, and similarities between nodes change.

In a production system that makes recommendations, the `min_hours` parameter could be varied and experimentally tested to find the ideal value to make useful game recommendations.

This concludes the more advanced example of our recommendation engine, which uses Jaccard similarity, and also concludes this chapter. I hope you have enjoyed getting to grips with transitioning data from relational to graph-centric data.

Summary

In this chapter, we compared and contrasted traditional relational databases and graph databases to perform path-based analyses. Our path-based analysis of choice was recommending a game to a user on the Steam publishing platform and was performed in both MySQL and *igraph*.

MySQL, and other relational databases, can be used to find paths between tables of related entities, such as users and the games they play and purchase. However, this involves performing self-joins on the same table or repeatedly querying the same table. On the other hand, graph databases and data models are natively set up for path-based queries, so we used *igraph* to recommend a game to a user based on paths between users and games in our graph.

Then, we covered how to move data over from MySQL to Python *igraph*, both step-by-step and with a generic set of methods that can be used for any directed, heterogeneous graph.

Finally, we set up a more sophisticated system to make game recommendations to users by using a graph data model. We based our recommendations on games similar users have played, using Jaccard similarity to estimate similarity. Our method allowed us to tune the results based on the edge weights in the graph, which corresponded to the play time for each user-game pair. This similarity-based recommendation system could be used in experiments to figure out how many hours a user should have played a game before it is allowed to influence the recommendations for Steam users.

In the next chapter, we will further concrete what you have learned up to this point. The core of the next chapter will be about using the graph to build a knowledge graph, where we will be looking at medical abstracts and using these documents to link terms and documents.

4

Building a Knowledge Graph

This chapter will extend your knowledge further and introduce knowledge graphs. While learning what a knowledge graph is, you will also get hands-on practice with cleaning data in preparation for ingesting into a graph. This will teach you about the hidden side of data science and graph modeling, in which you spend much of your time cleaning data and getting it ready to commence modeling.

Moreover, we will teach you the best methods of ingesting your data into a graph. After that, you will be ready to analyze your knowledge graph, which will be further extended by finding communities in your knowledge graph, with a technique known as community detection.

Community detection is commonly used to discover groups or clusters of similar items in your network. These methods can be utilized, for example, to find influential groups posting about a certain narrative on social media, or in the example we are going to utilize, to look for similar literature when comparing research abstracts.

To break this down in a structured way, we are going to be covering the following main topics:

- Introducing knowledge graphs
- Cleaning the data for our knowledge graph
- Ingesting data into a knowledge graph
- Knowledge graph analysis and community detection

Technical requirements

We will be using the Jupyter Notebook to run our coding exercises, which requires `python>=3.8.0`. In addition, the following packages will need to be installed, with the `pip install` command, in your environment:

- `igraph==0.9.8`
- `spacy==3.4.4`

- `scispacy==0.5.1`
- `matplotlib`

Alternatively, you could run `pip install -r requirements.txt`, in the supporting requirements file, to install all the supporting dependencies for this chapter.

For this chapter, you will also need to install a text corpus for some **Natural Language Processing (NLP)**. Go to `https://allenai.github.io/scispacy/` and download the `en_core_sci_sm` model. In a command prompt or terminal window, navigate to where this is downloaded and run `pip install en_core_sci_sm-0.5.1.tar.gz`.

All notebooks, with the coding exercises, are available at the following GitHub link: `https://github.com/PacktPublishing/Graph-Data-Modeling-in-Python/tree/main/CH04`.

Introducing knowledge graphs

In complex fields, such as science and medicine, the sheer amount of data and literature available on specific topics is hard to overstate. The same goes for knowledge management in established companies and industries where, over time, institutional knowledge in the form of textual information builds up, becoming too large to sensibly disseminate. In both of these cases, a knowledge graph may help to alleviate issues associated with too much disparate information.

The aim of a knowledge graph is to link together related information, text, and documents in a sensible and searchable way.

In the case of knowledge graphs using text, links in a graph often represent related documents or articles. Text processing and NLP are huge fields in themselves, so for the purposes of this chapter, we will be keeping methods for working with text simple. Of course, the quality of text data has a large impact on the preparation of data for knowledge graph ingestion. We will be using simple `.txt` files here, but documents (particularly from older sources) may be stored in image, PDF, or similar formats, making text extraction a large part of the challenge of connecting data:

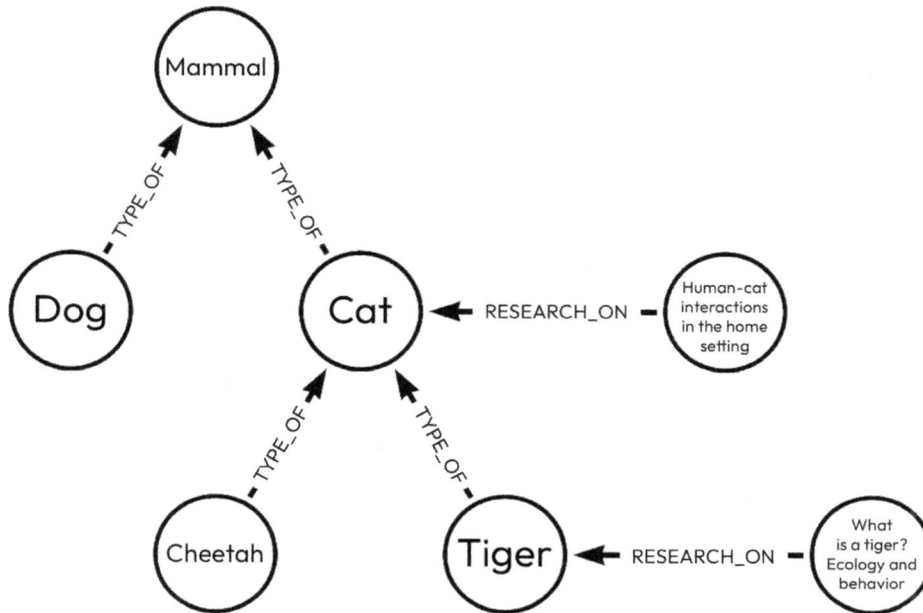

Figure 4.1 – An example knowledge graph excerpt

Knowledge graphs are also commonly associated with an ontology. An **ontology** is a collection of linked concepts, often related to a specific topic. Because of this, an ontology can also be thought of as a kind of graph, where concepts are nodes and links represent a relationship between those concepts.

Ontologies are regularly hierarchical in nature, where one broad concept may encompass several less broad concepts. For example, if we were to create a taxonomy of mammals, we might make a relationship between the concepts of *mammal* and *dog* and *mammal* and *cat*. In turn, because *cat* in itself is a broad concept, we may also make relationships from *cat* to *tiger* and *cat* to *cheetah*.

We can use ontologies in knowledge graph construction to locate concepts within documents; where similar concepts appear in two bodies of text, we may link a pair of documents together. Again, depending on the level of sophistication of the text processing being used, this could be as simple as matching words, or more complex, by using NLP tools such as lemmatization to aid in matching. In terms of knowledge graph creation, this can be thought of as a *top-down* approach – we know what terms we are looking for and how they are related, but we won't be finding any new concepts.

Flipping this idea on its head, we can also use text in documents to create an ontology within a knowledge graph. This is known as a *bottom-up* approach and contrasts with the previous example and its predefined ontology use. In a bottom-up approach, we can lean on the assumption that if concepts or terms are co-located (share a location with something else) in text, they are more likely to be related. For example, in a document about international travel, you are likely to see the terms *airport*, *airplane*, and so on. In the same document, you are far less likely to see terms, for example, associated with space travel, such as *rocket* or *moon*. Using these ideas, it is possible to use the co-occurrence of terms to link concepts and begin to construct a rudimentary ontology. This, of course, will not be perfect, like a hand-constructed ontology curated by experts might be, but the approach is far faster and easier to get off the ground with. Machine-constructed ontologies can also be further curated by experts if required.

In this chapter, we will be using ideas from both the *top-down* and *bottom-up* approaches to create a knowledge graph. To construct the graph, we will use publicly available research paper abstracts from PubMed and a corpus of medical terms. We can add value to both terms and abstracts by using the abstract's text to link co-occurring terms.

Now, we will look at how you clean your data prior to creating the knowledge graph.

Cleaning the data for our knowledge graph

Knowledge graphs typically contain relationships that represent commonalities between related documents and are built up using the content within those documents text. For this reason, a large part of knowledge graph construction is cleaning and preparing that text for later graph creation.

Let's begin by taking a look at the raw abstract data in `20k_abstracts.txt`. This data is displayed as in the following abstract style:

Aspergillus fumigatus

BACKGROUND IgE sensitization to Aspergillus fumigatus and a positive sputum fungal culture result are common in patients with refractory asthma.

BACKGROUND It is not clear whether these patients would benefit from antifungal treatment.

OBJECTIVE We are seeking to determine whether a 3-month course of voriconazole improved asthma-related outcomes in patients with asthma who are IgE sensitized to Aspergillus.

We can see that each abstract is given a reference number preceded by hashes and each sentence is preceded by a sentence type in capital letters. In addition, each abstract is separated by a newline.

It is common for text data to need processing before use, and this case is no exception. In our case, the abstract text has been prepared for another NLP application and contains information that we do not need, such as sentence types and reference numbers. For our purposes, we only need the text for each abstract, so let's next clean the data to get it into a more usable format.

In the subsequent steps, we will take you through the process of importing and cleaning the data that will then be used and aid in the construction of our knowledge graph:

1. First, we need to import the inbuilt `csv` module and open the file. We will need to specify that the format of our `.txt` file is tab delimited with the delimiter parameter in `csv.reader`.

We will also convert the data in this file into a list of lists using list comprehension and remove any blank lines with the != [] operator:

```
import csv
with open('CH04/data/20k_abstracts.txt') as c:
    reader = csv.reader(c, delimiter='\t')
    data = [line for line in reader if line != []]
```

With our data loaded, we can now convert it into a different format. We want to concatenate each of the sentences in an abstract into one whole abstract – at present the sentences are on different lines – as well as removing unnecessary data.

2. Because the logic for cleaning this data involves multiple steps, let's use a for loop to carry out our data cleaning in a readable way, rather than a highly complex list comprehension. We can first create an empty list that will later contain our cleaned data. We also need to initialize an empty abstract string that we can concatenate sentences into and build up a whole abstract:

```
clean_data = []
abstract = ''
```

3. Now, we can open our for loop and add some logic. We know the sentences begin from the second line, so we can slice our list of lists to process and begin looping through lines from data[1:]. We now need to use an if statement to process different lines in a different way. Where a line's length is only 1, we know that this just contains a reference number that we don't need. Because we start our loop from the second line of the raw data, we also know that a line of length 1 means that the sentences we have seen before make up one whole abstract. Applying this logic to our loop, when we see len(line) == 1, we can use append() to append an abstract to our clean data list, and initialize a new empty abstract string. If we have a line that is not of length 1, we can add the current line's second element to the abstract string to build up a complete abstract from several lines of text and ignore the sentence type annotation:

```
clean_data = []
abstract = ''
for line in data[1:]:
    if len(line) == 1:
            clean_data.append(abstract)
            abstract = ''
    else:
            abstract += ' ' + line[1]
```

4. Lastly, we just need to write our data back to the file so that we don't need to do this cleaning step every time our knowledge graph is constructed later. We can use the csv module again to write each abstract to a separate line. We can also take this opportunity to give each abstract a sequentially increasing integer ID, which *igraph* will require later, by using enumerate():

```
with open('CH04/data/20k_abstracts_clean.csv', 'w', newline='')
as d:
```

```
writer = csv.writer(d)
for i, line in enumerate(clean_data):
        writer.writerow([i, line])
```

This method will write a clean `abstracts` file to your directory and will look as in the following sample:

```
0," IgE sensitization to Aspergillus fumigatus and a positive
sputum fungal culture result are common in patients with
refractory asthma . It is not clear whether these patients would
benefit from antifungal treatment . We sought to determine
whether a 3-month course of voriconazole improved asthma-related
outcomes in patients with asthma who are IgE sensitized to A
fumigatus . Asthmatic patients who were IgE sensitized to A
fumigatus with a history of at least 2 severe exacerbations in
the previous 12 months were treated for 3 months with 200 mg of
voriconazole twice daily , followed by observation for 9 months
, in a double-blind , placebo-controlled , randomized design .
Primary outcomes were improvement in quality of life at the end
of the treatment period and a reduction in the number of severe
exacerbations over the 12 months of the study . Sixty-five
patients were randomized . Fifty-nine patients started treatment
( 32 receiving voriconazole and 27 receiving placebo ) and were
included in an intention-to-treat analysis . Fifty-six patients
took the full 3 months of medication . Between the voriconazole
and placebo groups , there were no significant differences in
the number of severe exacerbations ( 1.16 vs 1.41 per patient
per year , respectively ; mean difference , 0.25 ; 95 % CI
, 0.19-0 .31 ) , quality of life ( change in Asthma Quality
of Life Questionnaire score , 0.68 vs 0.88 ; mean difference
between groups , 0.2 ; 95 % CI , -0.05 to -0.11 ) , or any
of our secondary outcome measures . We were unable to show a
beneficial effect of 3 months of treatment with voriconazole in
patients with moderate-to-severe asthma who were IgE sensitized
to A fumigatus on either the rate of severe exacerbations ,
quality of life , or other markers of asthma control ."
```

Now that we have worked through the steps to get our data in a better, cleaner state, we can begin to design a method for graph ingestion. This is where your hard work pays off. As they say, life as a data scientist starts when you have cleaned your first dataset. Let's get ready to start ingesting data into our knowledge graph.

Ingesting data into a knowledge graph

There is a lot to consider before jumping straight into creating a knowledge graph from our cleaned abstract data. As with previous chapters, we must consider the structure of the graph we are aiming to produce first. We will then need to process our abstracts to extract terms of interest. Then, once we have terms, we can create a list of edges to import into *igraph*.

Getting the ingestion right into the knowledge graph is crucial and this all stems from how you conceptually and practically design your graph schema. The following section shows how to design your schema to make sure your knowledge graph works the way you expect it to.

Designing a knowledge graph schema

Before jumping straight into data ingestion, we must consider the structure of our knowledge graph. For our use case, we're interested in connecting related documents and concepts.

In terms of nodes, we have both abstracts and terms. Our abstracts have only an ID and text. Our terms will need to be similar, albeit the text is shorter. Due to this, our node properties are simple, with only two different properties needed per node.

> **Important note**
>
> It is worth noting that our abstracts are generally very large text fields, of over 1,000 characters. For our purposes in this chapter, adding the abstract text as a node attribute will not be an issue, due to the relatively small size of the overall graph. However, in a far larger graph of millions of nodes, such large attributes may vastly increase the in-memory size of the graph as a whole and impact performance. In the case of very large graphs, it often makes sense to store an ID that represents the attribute on the node itself, while holding the text data in a separate, keyed, non-graph database, for example, SQL. Accessing the text itself, rather than querying the structure of the graph, can then be handled by a separate, performant process.

The existence of two types of entities in our hypothetical graph, abstracts and terms, means that our graph is heterogeneous (containing multiple types of objects or multiple types of links). When we find terms in abstracts, it makes sense to link them to the abstracts that they are present in. This single type of relationship is enough to create a basic knowledge graph, in which entities are found in abstracts. Where the only type of link is between two different types of nodes, this is known as a bipartite graph.

We may also be interested in the frequency of terms in a particular abstract, to represent how strongly an abstract is related to a concept. This could be used to filter the graph in later analysis, similar to how this was performed in *Chapter 3, Data Model Transformation – Relational to Graph Databases*.

The following diagram shows an example of a bipartite knowledge graph relationship with a FOUND_IN edge between the term and the abstract. In essence, this says what terms are found in what abstracts:

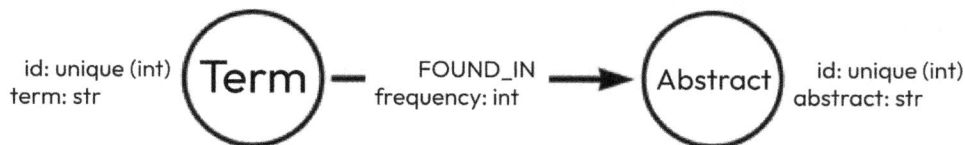

id: unique (int)   **Term** —   FOUND_IN   →   **Abstract**   id: unique (int)
term: str   frequency: int   abstract: str

Figure 4.2 – A bipartite knowledge graph

The preceding figure shows that we can set up a relationship between each term and a FOUND_IN property of the abstract, so we are essentially saying *get me a term that is found in the abstract, with a directional edge.*

Linking text to terms

Now that we know the graph schema we are aiming for, we need to isolate our nodes and edges, ready for graph construction. We already have our abstracts, which will make up one node type, but we have yet to identify terms.

Thinking back to the start of this chapter, our aim is to extract biomedical terms from abstracts to use as nodes in our graph. We therefore need a method to extract biomedical terms specifically. Luckily, as with many open source projects, much of the hard work has been done for us, in the form of the **scispacy** Python library, an extension to the **spacy** module.

The `spacy` module is typically used for no-fuss, quick NLP. In contrast to another popular NLP module, **Natural Language Toolkit (NLKT)**, *spacy* is a lot more user-friendly and quicker to get started with, at the cost of some more advanced configurability options. However, for our purposes, a simple module for NLP is perfect, so that we can focus on the resulting graph.

The `scispacy` extension is a library specifically for text processing in the biomedical field, which is ideal for our purposes. We will be taking advantage of a corpus of biomedical language that can be downloaded and integrated into *spacy* – see the *Technical requirements* section at the beginning of the chapter for specific instructions on how to do this.

We will now work through the steps to start ingesting our cleaned data into our knowledge graph:

1. With our requirements installed, we can begin to look at the terms, or entities, in our abstracts. Let's first reimport our cleaned data into Python as a list of lists for further processing:

    ```
    import csv

    with open('./data/20k_abstracts_clean.csv', 'r') as c:
        reader = csv.reader(c)
        data = [line for line in reader]
    ```

    Next, we need to load our corpus of biomedical language. For this example, we will use the medical abstracts corpora, commonly known as en_core_sci_sm, as these provide us with the nodes and edge lists to build our knowledge graphs. This library is part of the nlp library.

    We can do this using `scispacy` and `spacy` and create an `nlp` object variable using `spacy.load()`:

    ```
    import scispacy
    import spacy
    nlp = spacy.load("en_core_sci_sm")
    ```

2. Let's take a look at what biomedical language we can use in the `scispacy` module to find in our first abstract. We can access the first abstract with a list index, selecting the second element of the first row of our list of lists. Then, using our `nlp` object's inbuilt method, we can analyze

our text using the corpus we loaded previously. Now, we can print the entities extracted by `spacy` by accessing the `ents` attribute of our analyzed text:

```
text = data[0][1]
doc = nlp(text)
print(list(doc.ents))
```

We can see that technical-looking entities such as `IgE` and `asthma` are being extracted, which are the type of biomedical language terms we need to connect our abstracts to. However, we can also see entities such as `positive` and `severe`, which, while used in technical literature, are not specific enough to inform us about the contents of the abstract. Also, we see that some entities have capital letters. This would potentially prevent linking the same term across abstracts where the terms match but casing differs.

At this point, we could go straight ahead and construct our knowledge graph by building up the terms found in abstract relationships and adding them to *igraph*. However, due to the limitations we have identified, our graph will be more useful if we first preprocess the terms we have extracted.

3. Let's first extract all of the biomedical entities in each abstract, using a similar method to the previous approach, but now in a list comprehension. The second element of each row contains an abstract's text, so that is what we will feed into the `nlp()` method:

    ```
    abstract_entities = [[row[0], nlp(row[1]).ents] for row in data]
    ```

4. We can now deal with the casing issue we encountered when looking at the first abstract. We can write another list comprehension to convert each entity into a string term and then use the `lower()` method to convert each term to lowercase:

    ```
    abstract_entities = [
    [row[0], [str(ent).lower() for ent in row[1]]
    ] for row in abstract_entities]
    print(abstract_entities[:5])
    ```

    Now, we see that the extracted terms are all lowercase, which means when we use them to create nodes later, we won't have more than one node for terms such as `Asthma` and `asthma`.

5. Next, let's focus on the issue of what type of biomedical language *scispacy* is extracting as entities. We identified that some extracted technical terms will be useful to connect abstracts, while some are likely to be highly common terms among otherwise unrelated abstracts, such as `positive`. In many NLP applications, the number of extracted entities that make it through to further processing is limited. This is commonly approached by using the frequency of entity occurrence in documents. The extracted term `positive` is likely to appear many times, and for a knowledge graph, this means connecting many unrelated documents, with no real benefit.

6. To look into this issue, we can first examine the frequency of our extracted entities across all of our abstracts. First, we isolate the entities from the abstract IDs by using a list comprehension to grab the second element in every row of our data:

```
all_entities = [row[1] for row in abstract_entities]
```

7. Now, `all_entities` contains a list of lists, where each list contains many terms. We want to look at the frequency of terms across all abstracts, so we will need to join these lists into one large list. To do this, let's use Python's inbuilt `itertools` module, which contains many useful features for working with lists with complex structures. For our case, we need to use `itertool.chain.from_iterable()` to convert our lists of lists into one list:

```
import itertools
entities = itertools.chain.from_iterable(all_entities)
```

8. With all our terms in one list, we can count the frequency of them using another inbuilt Python library, `collections.Counter()`, which will convert our list into a dictionary of `{term: frequency}` key-value pairs. Then, we can sort the resulting dictionary in reverse order, with the `sorted()` method, sorting by the second element of each item in `entity_freq.items()` using an anonymous function:

```
from collections import Counter
entity_freq = dict(Counter(entities))
entity_freq = dict(sorted(entity_freq.items(),
    key=lambda item: item[1], reverse=True))
print(entity_freq)
```

Our `print` statement shows that the highest frequency terms are `patients`, `treatment`, `study`, and `groups`, followed by many other generic terms found in the research literature. These terms will not provide any value for our knowledge graph, as we will be connecting many unrelated abstracts. Looking further down the printed frequencies, the lower-frequency terms are much more likely to be useful to us.

9. At this point, we need to select a cutoff point for what high-frequency terms we will allow in our knowledge graph. There is too much data to do this term by term, so choosing a threshold, or a method for threshold selection, is likely to be arbitrary. For the purposes of this chapter, we will remove any terms with a frequency of above `100`, recognizing that this will remove some useful terms, and preserve some lower-frequency generic terms. When designing processing for a real knowledge graph, this frequency cutoff is something that might be modified in conjunction with some downstream analysis to examine the effect on the resulting graph and identify an optimum threshold. Let's see how many terms we will remove by setting an upper-frequency threshold of `100`. We can use a dictionary comprehension with a conditional to limit our `entity_freq` dictionary to high-frequency entities and print the resulting dictionary's length:

```
high_freq = {ent: value for ent, value in entity_freq.items() if
value > 100}
```

```
print(len(high_freq))
print(len(entity_freq))
```

Our first `print` statement shows that we will be removing 199 terms from our graph with this upper threshold. Our second `print` statement shows that the total number of unique terms extracted, before removing any, is 47,667, so our upper threshold of `100` results in removing around 0.4% of terms.

Before removing our high-frequency entities that will be taken forward to knowledge graph construction, we must also consider very low-frequency terms. Terms only found in one abstract won't connect abstracts and therefore have limited use in a knowledge graph intended to create relationships between related documents.

10. We can examine how many terms occur only once in our entire set of abstracts with a similar dictionary comprehension to the previous one used for high-frequency terms. Here, we replace the `value > 100` conditional with `value == 1` to get a dictionary of terms with a frequency of `1`:

```
low_freq = {ent: value for ent, value in entity_freq.items() if
value == 1}
print(len(low_freq))
```

This shows that there are 29,364 terms that occur only once. This is magnitudes larger than the number of highly common terms, which is fairly typical for NLP pipelines. Looking back at our total number, we can calculate that terms with a frequency of `1` represent around 61.6% of unique extracted terms. Due to the large number of low-frequency terms, choosing not to include them in our downstream graph construction will improve the overall performance during knowledge graph analysis later.

11. We can now implement the thresholds we have selected, by first creating a list of terms we do not want to extract. Here, we use a list comprehension with conditions set to select the entity strings of those that occur either more than 100 times or only once:

```
removed_terms = [ent for ent, value in entity_freq.items() if
value > 100 or value == 1]
```

12. With our list of terms to exclude, we can now trim down the entities associated with each abstract in our `abstract_entities` variable. Let's use a list comprehension again to select terms that are not in the `removed_terms` list while retaining their relationship to each individual abstract. Then, we can print the first abstract's newly trimmed-down entities to confirm our method is working as expected:

```
abstract_entities = [[row[0], [ent for ent in row[1] if ent not
in removed_terms]]
                        for row in abstract_entities]
print(abstract_entities[0])
```

Comparing the printed entities to those printed at the start of this section, we can see that some of the very common terms have been removed, as well as some highly specific terms unlikely to be in another abstract.

While the methods we have used for text processing here are fairly simple, NLP pipelines can also be highly complex and sophisticated. Designing preprocessing workflows for text can be a bit of an art and generally benefits from extensive knowledge of the subject and analysis of the text data before any implementation. We could do more to improve the preprocessing of our abstracts and terms, but in the interest of focusing on graph data modeling, the next step will be adding our data to a graph as nodes and edges.

Constructing the knowledge graph

Now that our data is cleaned and we have abstracts associated with our terms, we are ready to begin constructing a knowledge graph. This will be highlighted in the following steps, with the first step being the creation of the nodes and edges from the data we already processed in the preceding sections:

1. When we initially processed our raw abstract data earlier in the chapter, we created an increasing integer ID for each sequential abstract. These can now be used as *igraph* IDs in node creation. However, we do not have node IDs for terms, as until terms were extracted from the abstracts, we didn't know how many nodes we would be adding to our graph.

    Let's next create node IDs for each term. We will need a list of unique terms, which we can access from the `abstract_entities` variable, in the first element of each sublist. Then, as we did previously in the chapter, we can use `itertools.chain.from_iterable()` to concatenate every list in our `terms` list of lists:

    ```
    terms = [abstract[1] for abstract in abstract_entities]  # get
    just ents no abstract IDs
    unique_terms = list(set(itertools.chain.from_iterable(terms)))
    ```

    Now, we need to find all unique terms and assign each one an integer ID. These IDs must also start from the last ID we assigned to an abstract, plus 1, so that each node has a unique *igraph* ID irrespective of its type. To do this, we can use a dictionary comprehension in tandem with `enumerate()` to create a dictionary with `{term: ID}` pairs for each unique term. Using the `len()` of data as the second parameter in `enumerate()`, which is equal to the number of abstracts, assures that the first ID assigned to a term is the next integer after the highest ID given to an abstract previously:

    ```
    term_ids = {term: i for i, term in
        enumerate(unique_terms, len(data))}
    ```

2. Let's make sure that IDs have been assigned to terms by looking for the ID of `ige`:

    ```
    print(term_ids['ige'])
    ```

Great, now that we have all the node information we need for our graph, we need to construct an edgelist to represent the interactions between terms and abstracts. All the information we need to do this is already held in the `abstract_entities` variable, but we need to convert abstracts and terms into integer IDs ready for import into an `igraph` graph. We will need to go through each list in our `abstract_entities` list of lists and replace strings with the corresponding integers. To do this, let's open a `for` loop and unpack each list into `abstract_id` and a `terms` sublist. We will also need to make a new empty list to hold the `igraph`-compatible edges:

```
edgelist = []
for abstract_id, terms in abstract_entities:
term_freq = dict(Counter(terms))
```

In our schema, we added an edge attribute to our FOUND_IN relationships. This is `frequency`, which will represent the number of times a term is used in a single abstract and act as a sort of weighting for how relevant a term is to its source.

To find the frequencies of each term in an abstract, we can again use the `collections.Counter()` method. This will create a dictionary of `{term: frequency}` pairs we can use to add a weight to each edge. The dictionary data structure in Python always follows a key-value relationship, allowing you to add to an existing index, reference an index, or remove an index.

3. Now, we need to loop through each term in the sublist associated with the current abstract and assemble an edge from integer IDs. For each term, we append a list representing the edge to the *edgelist* list. Each list contains the integer representing the current term, taken from the `term_ids` dictionary we created previously, the abstract ID cast as an integer, and the frequency of the term in the abstract, taken from the `Counter()` dictionary. We can then print the first few edges in `edgelist` to check that they are structured as expected:

```
for term, freq in term_freq.items():
        edgelist.append([int(term_ids[term]),
            int(abstract_id), freq])

print(edgelist[:10])
```

4. Let's also confirm that an edge we know should be present exists in the edgelist. In our first abstract, the term `ige` is used four separate times. This means the weighting of our edges should be equal to 4. We can use an `assert` to make sure an edge exists from the ID of `ige` to the node with ID 0, representing our first abstract, and ensure its weight, in the third list element, is as expected:

```
assert [term_ids['ige'], 0, 4] in edgelist
```

5. It's graphing time – now that we have our nodes and edges in the correct format, let's go ahead and add them to an *igraph* graph. We can import *igraph* and create a directed graph with `igraph.Graph()`, specifying the `directed` option:

    ```
    g = igraph.Graph(directed=True)
    ```

6. We first need to add nodes to our graph. This is a simple case of adding nodes equal to the number of terms and abstracts we have, using the `add_vertices` method:

    ```
    g.add_vertices(len(term_ids) + len(data))
    ```

7. We can add our abstract and term text to the nodes as attributes, by accessing the `vs` attribute of our graph, g. We can do this listwise, by creating one list of both abstract text and term text, taken from our cleaned `data` list, and the `items()` in our `term_ids` dictionary, respectively:

    ```
    text = [abstract[1] for abstract in data] +
        [ent for ent, _ in term_ids.items()]
    g.vs['text'] = text
    ```

    Let's briefly make sure that the `text` attribute of the node representing the term `ige` is in fact equal to `ige`, by printing it:

    ```
    print(g.vs[term_ids['ige']]['text'])
    ```

8. We also need to add the node type to nodes in our graph. We have two types of nodes, abstracts and terms. Because the IDs for abstracts were assigned first, we know that IDs from 0 to `len(data) - 1` are for abstracts, and the subsequent node IDs represent terms. Due to this, we can add the node types listwise, by creating two lists of strings using two list comprehensions, before adding these strings to the `type` node attribute in `g.vs`:

    ```
    types = ['abstract' for _ in data] +
        ['term' for _ in term_ids.items()]
    g.vs['type'] = types
    ```

9. Again, let's make sure that this operation has succeeded as we expect, by printing the type of the `ige` node. This should be equal to `term`:

    ```
    print(g.vs[term_ids['ige']]['type'])
    ```

10. With all of our nodes in place, we can now add our edges to the graph. To do this, we need to first create a pairwise edge list without the edge weightings and a separate list of edge weight attributes. We can accomplish both of these tasks using list comprehensions:

    ```
    edges = [[source, target] for source,
        target, _ in edgelist]
    frequencies = [freq for _, _, freq in edgelist]
    ```

11. Finally, to finish setting up our knowledge graph, we can add these edges with the `add_edges()` method and assign the attributes by adding the `frequency` property to `g.es`:

```
g.add_edges(edges)
g.es['frequency'] = frequencies
```

With that, our knowledge graph is set up and ready for analysis. Next, we can use the graph to answer interesting questions about the knowledge contained in our thousands of biomedical abstracts.

Knowledge graph analysis and community detection

Before we begin to delve deeper into our knowledge graph, it makes sense to get an understanding of its structure. Information on our graph's structure will frame further analysis that we carry out. This analysis will be pivotal and we will examine how to examine the knowledge graph structure by looking at which components are connected; conversely, disconnected components would mean that there are abstracts in our knowledge graph that are standalone terms and abstracts that are separate from our main knowledge of medical abstracts. From there, we will look at common terms and methods to identify abstracts of interest. Let's get started by examining our knowledge graph structure.

Examining the knowledge graph structure

The next series of steps in our process will be to examine the knowledge graph structure:

1. Let's first find the number of nodes and edges in our graph, since in this chapter, we have constructed our graph not from discrete data points but from text. We can find the number of nodes by printing the `len()` of the `g.vs` attribute and the number of edges by printing the `len()` of the `g.es` attribute:

```
print(len(g.vs))
print(len(g.es))
```

This shows us that we have 20,603 nodes and 71,463 edges in our knowledge graph.

2. It would also be useful to know whether our graph is fully connected, particularly in the case of knowledge graphs. A disconnected graph would mean that there are technical areas in our groups of abstracts that never use the same phrases or biomedical terms. We can find connected components by using the `g.clusters()` method. We have the choice between setting a parameter, `mode`, to `strong` or `weak`. Strongly connected nodes have to have undirected edges or directed edges in both directions between them to be considered connected as part of a cluster. The impact of this on our directed graph, with edges only from terms to abstracts in one direction, would be a completely disconnected graph. Since the strongly connected components algorithm overestimates the disconnectedness of a bipartite graph like our knowledge graph, we will use the `weak` option. We can print the result to examine the number and structure of the clusters:

```
connected_components = g.clusters(mode='weak')
print(connected_components)
```

Our printed result shows that we have just one weakly connected component, containing all nodes in our graph. Considering that some term nodes we created, even with the high-frequency filter, were quite generic, this is an expected outcome. Even very disparate fields are likely to use common scientific language, and this is reflected in the number of components.

If we were using documents containing terms we expected to be unrelated and creating a knowledge graph from them, then connected components could be a useful indicator of whether term frequency thresholds are set correctly during entity extraction. When designing a pipeline for data ingestion into a knowledge graph, these thresholds could be varied to reach an expected number of weakly connected components.

3. Another element of structure we can examine is the degree distribution of nodes in our knowledge graph. The degree of a node is the number of neighboring nodes, or the nodes that share an edge with our node of interest. Looking at the degree distribution across our entire graph will help us to understand how abstracts and terms are connected on a large scale. Since we have a heterogeneous graph containing two types of nodes, it makes sense to examine the degree distribution of each node type separately. This is especially important in a bipartite graph, as we know that terms only connect to abstracts, and vice versa. We might expect these degree distributions for different types of nodes to be quite different, given the large number of biomedical terms that we are extracting from each abstract.

To create our distributions, we first need to use the `vs.select()` method again to select only nodes of a specific type, beginning with nodes we have labeled `abstract`. We can do this using the custom `type_eq` parameter, where `type` specifies our node attribute `type` that we created earlier, and the `_eq` suffix specifies that it must be equal to the string `abstract`. We can use a very similar `select()` method to get a list of `term` nodes:

```
abstract_nodes = g.vs.select(type_eq='abstract')
term_nodes = g.vs.select(type_eq='term')
```

4. To find the degree of our `abstract` and `term` nodes, we can use *igraph*'s `degree()` method. It is important to remember that our graph is directed and `degree()` has a `mode` parameter that specifies in which direction edges should face in order to be counted for `degree`. However, since the default value of `mode` is `degree`, we can leave the `mode` parameter out this time:

```
abstract_degree = g.degree(abstract_nodes)
term_degree = g.degree(term_nodes)
```

5. Our `abstract_degree` and `term_degree` variables contain lists of node degrees. We can plot these in a histogram using the `matplotlib` module, with `pyplot`. After importing the module as `plt`, let's first plot a histogram of values in `abstract_degree` by using `plt. hist()`, with a number of bins to divide our data into and an `edgecolour` of `black`, in order to tell each bin apart. We can then set the `xlabel()` and `ylabel()` of our chart, before finishing by drawing the chart with `plt.show()`:

```
import matplotlib.pyplot as plt
plt.hist(abstract_degree, bins=20, edgecolor='black')
```

```
plt.xlabel('Abstract Node Degree')
plt.ylabel('Frequency')
plt.show()
```

The following figure shows the frequency of associated terms by their degree:

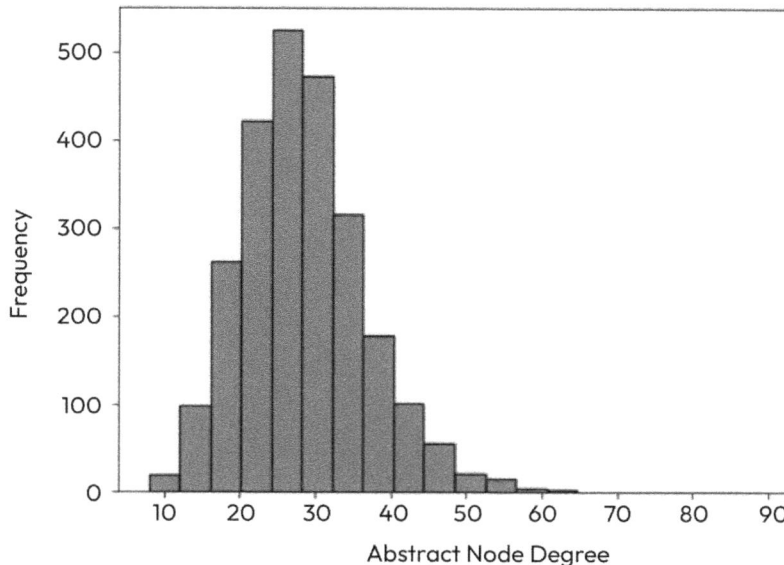

Figure 4.3 – Degree distribution of abstract nodes in the knowledge graph

We can see from our histogram that the majority of our several thousand abstract nodes have around 25-35 associated terms, while a handful have over 65. The degree of abstract nodes here is closer to a normal distribution than many examples of other graph degree distributions.

6. We are going to repeat this process for our term nodes, as this will allow us to look at the distributions in a juxtaposed and side-by-side fashion:

```
plt.hist(term_degree, bins=20, edgecolor='black')
plt.xlabel('Term Node Degree')
plt.ylabel('Frequency')
plt.show()
```

This code generates our chart for **Term Node Degree**, observable in *Figure 4.4*:

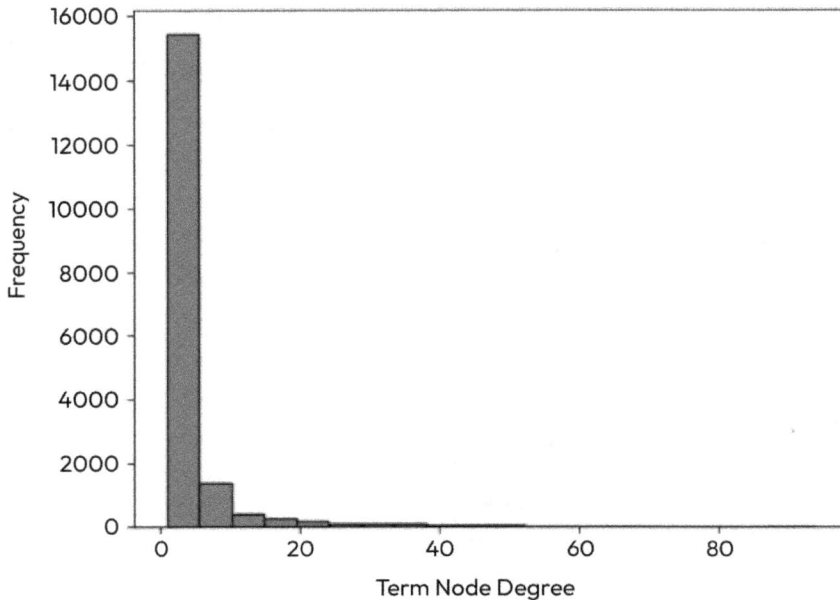

Figure 4.4 – Degree distribution of term nodes in the knowledge graph

It is immediately clear that our term nodes have a very different degree distribution from our abstract nodes. The vast majority of terms are connected to between 1 and 10 abstracts, and the shape of our distribution is heavily skewed, with a very long tail, as is typical in many graph degree distributions. Very few terms have a degree of over 50.

Thinking back to the thresholds we applied earlier when preparing data for our knowledge graph with entity extraction, these charts can further aid in parameter tuning in a graph construction pipeline. As thresholds for term frequency are set, these distributions are likely to dramatically change and serve as good insight into our graph's structure. The vastly differing degree distributions of our two types of nodes, abstracts and terms, show that in heterogeneous graphs, it can pay to analyze node types separately. The different distribution shapes for our node types would likely have been lost if not plotted independently.

Now that we have a baseline understanding of our graph's structure, we can delve into some more specific analysis and knowledge graph use cases. Our examination of graph structure will help us to put further results into context.

Identifying abstracts of interest

With our knowledge graph assembled, we can now use it to interrogate the information contained in our abstracts. Knowledge graphs provide several advantages over a more classical, searchable database. In an abstract database, we could search for a particular term and find all abstracts associated with it. However, from there, if we want to find themes in those abstracts or associated concepts, it would be down to the user to do this analysis manually. This often also relies on the database user being an expert in the subject area covered by the documents in the database, in order to find the commonalities and insights from the raw text.

In our knowledge graph, we have extracted scientific terms, using a corpus of known biomedical language. We have done this in an unbiased way, without needing expertise in the specific field. Our terms now connect abstracts that share their use, and it is likely that those abstracts in turn contain other common terms or related concepts.

The following steps will show how we can set up our Python logic for the identification of the abstracts that we are interested in:

1. Let's examine a concept in our knowledge graph, by starting with a chosen term. If we wanted to find all abstracts that use one term, we could use the `vs.select()` method. For example, let's find all biomedical abstracts in our knowledge graph containing the term `yoga`, by making use of `select()`'s `text_eq` parameter. The `vs.select()` method always returns a list of nodes, though we know that there should only be one `yoga` term node, so we can select the first and only element using a list index. Then, we want the *igraph* node ID to use in further analysis, so we can use the `.index` attribute to access this:

    ```
    yoga_node_id = g.vs.select(text_eq='yoga')[0].index
    ```

2. Once we have the node ID for the term `yoga`, to find the associated abstracts, we can identify its neighbors. In *igraph*, we can do this by using the `neighbours()` method and adding our `yoga` node's ID as a parameter:

    ```
    yoga_abstract_nodes = g.neighbors(g.vs[yoga_node_id])
    ```

3. This returns a list of neighboring node IDs, which, due to our bipartite graph structure, will all be abstract nodes. With our list of neighbor IDs, let's find the abstract text associated with each node using a list comprehension to access the `text` node attributes, making use of `g.vs`:

    ```
    yoga_abstracts = [g.vs[neighbor]['text'] for neighbor in yoga_
    abstract_nodes]
    print(yoga_abstracts)
    ```

4. Printing these results shows that there are six abstracts associated with the term `yoga`. Now, if this was the result from, for example, a search engine, we would need to read each abstract and understand the concepts within them in order to find biomedical themes associated with yoga.

However, because our technical terms have been extracted and converted into a knowledge graph, we can use the graph to locate terms that are associated with these abstracts.

To do this, we need to use the `neighbors()` method again, this time using the node IDs of the abstracts containing the term `yoga`, contained in the previously assigned `yoga_abstract_nodes` variable. We want to find neighbors for a list of nodes, which we can perform in a list comprehension:

```
related_term_nodes = [g.neighbors(node) for node in yoga_
abstract_nodes]
```

5. This will return a list of lists, containing the node IDs of each abstract node's neighbors. To get a list of all unique terms, we will need to first flatten our list of lists. As we have done previously, we can use `itertools.chain.from_iterable()` to achieve this, first importing the inbuilt `itertools` Python library and calling the method on `related_term_nodes`:

```
import itertools
related_term_nodes = itertools.chain.from_iterable(related_term_
nodes)
```

6. Then, we need to find the `text` node attribute associated with each of the term nodes in our flattened list. We can use `g.vs` to find the `text` attributes, contained within a `set()` to remove duplicates:

```
related_terms = set(g.vs(related_term_nodes)['text'])
print(related_terms)
print(len(related_terms))
```

This completes the steps to find the related terms for our specific term to look up. Printing `related_terms` shows us all biomedical terms that were extracted from the abstracts containing the term `yoga`. From this, we can find terms and concepts related to research on yoga, such as *mental health*, *visceral fat*, and *chronic stroke*. In total, there are 168 unique terms that were associated with these 6 abstracts.

In our graph, all of our edges are explicitly representing terms found in abstracts. In some more advanced knowledge graphs, you may find that relationships reflect the context between words, phrases, or concepts that nodes represent. For example, rather than `yoga` linked to an abstract that also contains `mental health` through FOUND_IN relationships, the term `yoga` might be connected to `mental health` via a contextual link, such as USED_TO_TREAT. Creating contextual links requires mining text for context, and it can be notoriously difficult to infer context. Sometimes, this may not be present in the data and it certainly goes beyond the scope of this chapter.

However, with more complex NLP approaches to generate nodes and edges for graph construction, more advanced and nuanced knowledge graphs can be created.

Identifying fields with community detection

In the previous section, we used our biomedical knowledge graph to identify abstracts containing a specific term, and through these abstracts found terms related to our original term of interest. This can be thought of as establishing a related set of information, or perhaps a concept, or *field*.

We can access these groups of nodes from a starting point if we know the term of interest. But what if we wanted a more general method to examine the fields that might be contained in our abstracts? We might ask the question *are some of our abstracts related to specific scientific research areas?*

Without a starting point, we could look to the structure of the graph to answer questions like these. Where abstracts and terms are related, there should generally be more edges between them. For example, if a group of scientific articles is written by scientists that study the brain, you would not necessarily expect them to contain much of the same language as articles containing research on the function of the liver. We can use these assumptions to attempt to split the graph into strongly connected parts, with a common language, with a group of methods known as community detection.

Community detection algorithms typically find regions of a graph that are highly interconnected, compared to other neighboring regions. These methods split a connected graph into parts, known as communities.

For the purposes of this section, we will be using the multilevel method for community detection. Multilevel community detection, also known as the Louvain method, splits a graph into communities by gradually assigning each node to neighboring communities and calculating the modularity of communities in the graph. Modularity can be thought of as the interconnectedness (the state of being connected) of groups of nodes. The algorithm aims to vary the community nodes belonging to different communities until modularity is as high as possible or a minimum threshold for the amount of modularity change is reached. The end result is a graph split into distinct communities.

It is worth noting that in contrast to connected components of a graph, which we examined in the previous section, communities can be connected through edges. The difference is that while communities can still be linked to each other, they are likely to be less strongly linked than the nodes residing in a community.

The multilevel community detection algorithm is just one method for splitting a graph into communities to find high-level structural information and doesn't require setting too many parameters, while being fairly easy to understand. Some methods are highly effective and more complex but scale poorly to large graphs (e.g., walktrap, which uses random walks as the driver for going up and down the connected paths). Other methods run extremely quickly, even on millions of nodes, but often provide less useful results (e.g., label propagation). Others still provide consistent, identical results for each run on the same graph, while many community detection methods, including the multilevel method, can generate different results each time they are run, due to the random initialization and iteration of their algorithms. Different methods are suitable for different graph structures, and a discerning graph specialist will use and compare several before settling on one method for a particular use case. Many options are available in *igraph*.

The following diagram shows terms and abstracts that have different communities, that is, bodies of research that relate to a specific subject. These could be medical abstracts about certain conditions, such as cardiovascular and oncological conditions, for example:

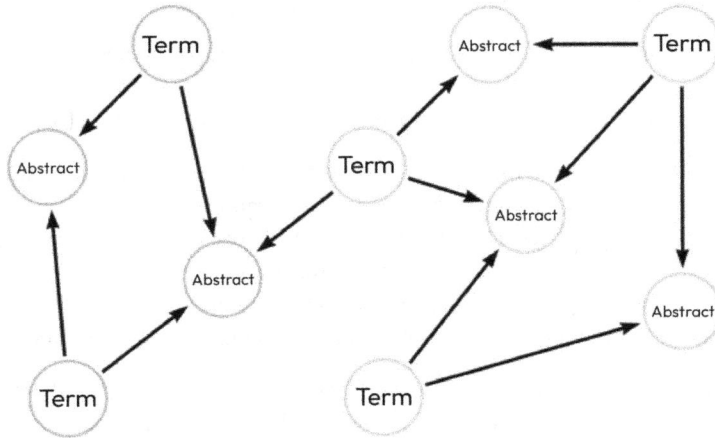

Figure 4.5 – Example of two distinct concepts, split into communities

As we have done in previous examples, we will now highlight the steps to run the multilevel community detection algorithm on our knowledge graph:

1. Let's try to run multilevel community detection on our knowledge graph to find some areas of related abstracts and terms. First, we will need to convert our directed graph into an undirected representation of the same graph. This is because in *igraph*, the multilevel algorithm is not configured to run over directed edges. Because our graph only contains one type of edge, and these edges always run from terms to abstracts, we do not lose any information in this conversion. In *igraph*, the easiest way to convert a graph into an undirected format is using the `as_undirected()` method:

    ```
    g_u = g.as_undirected()
    ```

2. Our new graph, `g_u`, now contains the undirected version of our knowledge graph. We are now ready to perform community detection, so let's use *igraph*'s `community_multilevel()` method to run the algorithm over our graph. There are some optional parameters for `community_multilevel()`, but for now, we can run the method without these:

    ```
    community_membership = g_u.community_multilevel()
    print(len(community_membership))
    ```

The `community_membership` variable contains a list of *igraph*-specific `VertexClustering` objects, which each contain a community label and the nodes that belong to that community.

Printing the length of `community_membership` will show how many communities the graph has been split into. Because the multilevel algorithm has a random seed component, this number may be slightly different with each run, though the structure of the communities found should stay relatively stable. If the parameters for thresholding in the graph construction steps are kept the same, you can expect somewhere in the region of 20 communities.

3. Next, let's take a look at the size of these communities. If we loop through the `VertexClustering` elements in `community_membership` using `enumerate()`, we can print the community ID and the size of each community using an `f print` string:

```
for i, community in enumerate(community_membership):
size = len(community)
    print(f'Community: {i}, size: {size}')
```

Communities are likely to have very different sizes because each is separated according to the algorithm's recurring attempts to maximize modularity, rather than any other measure. If a small community exists, its nodes are likely to be highly interlinked compared to neighboring nodes in other nearby communities.

4. Let's take a look at the membership of a single community to get an idea of whether this approach can be used to find related research terms and fields. We can convert our `VertexClustering` elements into a list of lists containing only node membership by simply casting the community detection result as a `list()`. We can also look into the nodes in the smallest community by using `sorted()`, with the `len()` of each element used as the `key` parameter, before taking the first element of the resulting sorted list:

```
smallest_community = sorted(list(community_membership), key=len)
[0]
print(smallest_community)
```

The `print` statement shows the node IDs of the smallest community. To understand what concept or field these terms represent, we next need to find the term nodes in this community and the text attributes that these nodes hold.

We can find term nodes as we have done several times in this chapter, by calling the `vs.select()` method. We can use `select()` with only the list of community nodes returned by the `g.vs` attribute and specify that we only want to find `term` nodes by specifying this in the `type_eq` parameter:

```
community_nodes = g.vs[smallest_community].select(type_
eq='term')
```

5. Then, we can find the text node attributes for these term nodes by specifying the `text` property on our `community_nodes` versus `object`, before printing the terms:

```
community_terms = community_nodes['text']
print(community_terms)
```

Voilà! That is all you need to do to get your first community detection algorithm off the group. However, due to the random nature of the multilevel community detection algorithm, the smallest community can contain different terms for each run.

This can aid in checking the terms that belong to this community and can be very helpful to answer questions, or key business problems, such as: are they related in any way? Are some generic, while others are specific and related? This kind of approach can be used to find relationships between groups of abstracts, or indeed any other types of documents, where you might not expect them.

In addition, community detection, like other elements of graph structure, has another use in setting thresholds and parameters for knowledge graph construction. If we expect a strongly linked set of abstracts from a particular field to be represented in the complete knowledge graph, then does it appear? If not, perhaps thresholds and methods used, such as entity extract and graph construction, should be modified. Often, working alongside specialists or domain experts in the document contents or area of knowledge a graph is trying to represent can help in data modeling and pipeline construction for knowledge graphs.

This brings this chapter to a close. We have taken you through everything you need to know to create a knowledge graph, handle the data in the right way, and separate entities into communities that are connected to find terms.

Summary

This chapter has taken you on a rollercoaster ride through how to develop knowledge graphs with the powerful *igraph* package. Firstly, we delved into the data preparation phases of knowledge graph construction, by looking at separating each *abstract* and then saving this into a separate cleaned abstract file.

Moving on, we looked at the steps needed to design the graph schema in the right way. This involved using popular NLP libraries such as *spacy*, plus a package we downloaded, and pip installed, the *scispacy* library for biomedical NLP tasks. Following this, we looked at extracting terms from our dataset and setting bounds on the frequencies of entities to include or exclude.

Once we had the foundations in place, we swiftly moved on to constructing a knowledge graph, from the ground up. This involved performing many of the key data modeling tasks we have been looking at in the chapters up until now. Furthermore, we made sure the graph contained the abstracts and terms we needed for later analysis.

We then moved on to analysis, via the creation of simple visualizations in `matplotlib`, looking at the distribution of abstracts and terms, relating to their degree centrality (number of relationships to neighboring nodes).

This segued into identifying abstracts of interest and using community detection to identify fields of research. Here, we used a multilevel community detection approach and proposed other options to investigate, such as label propagation and random walk methods. Using the community detection model, we were able to separate distinct groups or clusters by using this algorithm. We then looked at the nodes we generated to look at the specific terms contained within those community nodes. This then led us to extract the textual entities for those communities.

Concluding this chapter, we summarized some key points about community detection and knowledge graphs. This kind of approach can be used to find relationships between groups of abstracts, or indeed any other types of documents, where you might not expect them.

We hope you found this chapter useful and that it can serve as a blueprint for projects you might want to build a knowledge graph for, as well as helping you to explore community detection.

In the next chapter, we will be looking at how you can store your graph in memory and how to query it.

Part 3:
Storing and
Productionizing Graphs

Building production-grade systems is a breeze with this part. We start by working with graph databases and expose the use of Neo4j to store our databases for fast and efficient processing and information retrieval. Once we have the data stored, we then move on to create a route optimization solution, using the flexibility of the node to edge connections, and the speed at which they can be queried in a graph database.

Logically, the transition is then to move on to designing production-quality pipelines that can be evolved effectively to meet the change in the underlying data. The focus of these sections is to make Python work in harmony with Neo4j and to make sure we have built pipelines along the way that can be changed, morphed, and evolved over time.

This part has the following chapters:

- *Chapter 5, Working with Graph Databases*
- *Chapter 6, Pipeline Development*
- *Chapter 7, Refactoring and Evolving Schemas*

5
Working with Graph Databases

This chapter introduces you to in-memory graph databases. We will show you the steps of how to work with a very popular graph database, Neo4j. We will take you through the process of how to download this software to use on your own machine and explain why Python can become slow when trying to deploy your graph databases and models at scale. Following the setup phases, we will explore how to create relationships in this *in-memory* graph database application and then how to query them with a popular query language, Cypher.

Then, we will look at the various ways you can store information in Neo4j and use Python to interact with the application. We will take a slight detour to look at alternatives to Neo4j, such as Memgraph, and how they can be used. But the focus of this chapter will mainly be on Neo4j, as it does not require you to configure your machine to work with Docker and microservices.

Finally, we will look at a use case of how Python and Neo4j can be utilized together, in harmony, for large-scale and large data analytics, in a rapid and repeatable fashion. This will culminate in using our newly acquired Neo4j and Python skills to tackle a real-life use case. The use case for this task will be using graph networks to map out optimal travel routes between cities, and we will replicate functionality used in most common mapping software, such as Google Maps.

The following are the topics we are going to cover in this chapter:

- Using graph databases
- Storing a graph in Neo4j
- Optimizing travel with Python and Cypher
- Moving to ingestion pipelines

Technical requirements

We will be using Jupyter Notebook to run our coding exercises, which requires `python>=3.8.0`, along with the following packages, which will need to be installed with the `pip install` command into your environment:

- `igraph==0.9.8`

- `geopy==2.3.0`

- `neo4j==5.5.0`

For this chapter, you will need to start by going through the following steps:

1. Install Neo4j Desktop, which is free. Primarily, we will be using Neo4j for its long-term graph database storage, though Neo4j Desktop installs a desktop graph browser alongside this. To install Neo4j Desktop, go to `https://neo4j.com/download-center/#desktop` and fill out some details. Make a note of the activation key as you will need this during installation and select the relevant operating system installation for your machine.

2. Once Neo4j is installed, open Neo4j Desktop and create a new database (this can be achieved by navigating to the database tabs in the application and using the **Add** dropdown to create a new local DBMS) with a unique name, for example, `Python DB`. For the purposes of this chapter, use a password for this database that you are comfortable with writing in open code – we will be using `testpython`. In a real Neo4j setup, you would likely want to mask this password through the use of encryption, but that is beyond the scope of this chapter.

These steps will be covered in greater detail in the next section, so hold your horses for now.

All notebooks, with the coding exercises, are available at the following GitHub link: `https://github.com/PacktPublishing/Graph-Data-Modeling-in-Python/tree/main/CH05`.

Using graph databases

In all the previous chapters, we have been creating graphs in memory as part of Python scripts. This is fine for analytical work, or when creating proof-of-concept applications, but for workflows that need to scale, or for long-term storage, Python and *igraph* will not be enough.

In production systems that involve graphs, a graph database acts as a persistent data storage solution. As well as holding large amounts of data, graph databases are typically designed to perform a large number of read and write operations efficiently and concurrently. They are likely to be part of any production pipeline that relies on huge amounts of graph data processing, such as in a recommender system for a large online retailer.

As well as holding data, graph databases allow basic queries to be carried out on the data they hold. Many of these databases can be queried with at least one of several common graph query languages, such as **Cypher**, **GraphQL**, or **Gremlin**. In this chapter, we will be using some basic Cypher to read and write data to a graph database. Neo4j has an extensive list of Cypher queries and their uses; see `https://neo4j.com/developer/cypher/`.

It is worth noting that while these query languages are powerful in terms of accessing and writing data, they do not currently offer the breadth of analyses and algorithms that a package such as *igraph* offers. In this chapter, we will be interfacing Python with a graph database, to demonstrate how *igraph* might be used in a complex analysis pipeline.

Neo4j as a graph database

The graph database we will be using here is Neo4j, a commonly used high-performance database with a free local version. Neo4j can be queried using Cypher, which, of the graph query languages, is arguably the easiest for new users and so perfect for this introduction. For a more in-depth understanding of the usage of Cypher, see the documentation: `https://neo4j.com/developer/cypher/`.

Neo4j has analogous concepts to all of the graph concepts we have come across in previous chapters. In the Cypher documentation, while nodes are still named nodes, edges are more often referred to as relationships, and node and edge attributes are known as properties.

We have encountered several graphs with multiple types of nodes in heterogeneous graphs, and in Neo4j, these types of nodes have distinct *labels*. Labels are used heavily in the Cypher query language to access particular nodes and patterns; we will return to this concept when reading and writing to the graph database.

To get up and running with working with Neo4j, we need to carry out the following steps:

1.   Neo4j can be installed using the instructions in the *Technical requirements* section of this chapter. This is shown in the following screenshot:

Figure 5.1 – Neo4j database setup

2. Click **Start** on the new database to get it running, and the example database will be stopped, as Neo4j only supports one concurrent database running in the Desktop edition. The example database can now be deleted.

3. The Desktop edition of Neo4j comes bundled with the Neo4j Browser. Click **Open** next to our newly created database to open a Neo4j Browser window. Primarily, we will be focusing on using Neo4j for its function as a database, over its ability to visually display networks. From here, we can also create a new user, whose credentials we will use to access the database from Python. In the command line at the top of the window, enter the following:

    ```
    :server user add
    ```

4. A window containing fields to complete for a new user will appear. In the username field, add `admin`. For the password, again, we will use `testpython`. For roles, select both **admin** and **PUBLIC** from the drop-down menu, so that the new user will have full access to the database, both read and write.

5. Finally, click **Add User** to create our new admin user.

Now, with Neo4j installed and our Neo4j database created and configured, we will next need to learn how to interact with it, through the **Cypher** query language.

The Cypher query language

Cypher is an open source query language compatible with several graph databases, including Neo4j. It shares some similarities with more common query languages, such as SQL, but is designed with graphs in mind, as opposed to tabular data. Much of Cypher's design is centered around matching node and edge patterns in a graph, using a special syntax that almost looks like *drawing* network paths.

When we want to refer to a node using Cypher, we enclose it in parentheses. Similarly, to denote a specific edge, square brackets are used. Nodes and edges are linked with dashes and arrows, like so:

```
(node) - [edge] -> (node)
```

This pattern would match nodes in a graph that are connected to other nodes, in a directed fashion. In practice, we are likely to be much more specific about the nodes we create or return.

We can begin by executing some simple Cypher queries in the Neo4j Browser window, before we start to query Neo4j directly from Python. Let's start by creating some nodes:

1. The CREATE function can be used at the start of a line to instruct Neo4j to create new nodes. To create a new node of the Person type with the name Jeremy, we open parentheses and use a colon to designate the type of the node. This is followed by opening curly braces to add the name attribute to this node, with the value Jeremy. We can follow this pattern to create two Person nodes:

    ```
    CREATE (:Person {name: "Jeremy"})
    CREATE (:Person {name: "Mark"})
    ```

2. These nodes have now been added to the database but are currently disconnected. We can connect these nodes by searching for them in the database with the MATCH function, followed by another CREATE function. This time, we are supplying temporary variables to our matched nodes by adding Jeremy and Mark before the colon in each MATCH. Then, we create a new edge between Jeremy and Mark by referring to their variables in parentheses, with a -[:FOLLOWS]-> relationship to denote that Jeremy follows Mark on a social media platform:

    ```
    MATCH (jeremy:Person {name: "Jeremy"})
    MATCH (mark:Person {name: "Mark"})
    CREATE (jeremy)-[:FOLLOWS]->(mark)
    ```

3. When dealing with a large amount of data, we may get duplicate information or need to update a database rather than create new items. The MERGE function exists to handle these scenarios and combines the functions of both MATCH and CREATE. When MERGE is used, a match takes place to check whether the pattern specified already exists in the graph database. If there is a match, no write operation takes place. If there is no exact match, the pattern is used in a CREATE function to add to the graph. The following line will have no effect, since a Person node with the name Jeremy already exists:

    ```
    MERGE (:Person {name: "Jeremy"})
    ```

4. However, if we run this MERGE function call, we will create a new Person node named Sophie, because the node is not already present in the graph:

    ```
    MERGE (:Person {name: "Sophie"})
    ```

    The MERGE function also works with edges and longer path patterns.

5. We have covered the basics of writing to a Neo4j database, but let's briefly look at how to retrieve information from the graph with read operations. We have already used MATCH, and we can continue to use it to find nodes or edges that match certain patterns and features to report back on. Then, we can use RETURN to retrieve that information. The following code will find all Person nodes and return them to the Neo4j Browser window:

    ```
    MATCH (n: Person)
    RETURN n
    ```

6. As well as accessing whole nodes, we can access node or edge attributes using ., as you would access an attribute of a Python object. To return just the name attribute of the nodes in our graph, we can run the following:

    ```
    MATCH (n: Person)
    RETURN n.name
    ```

7. Cypher also has methods for the basic analysis of results, including aggregations such as `count()`, `sum()`, and `max()`. For example, we can count and return the number of nodes in our database as follows:

```
MATCH (n)
RETURN count(n)
```

8. Finally, we can remove data from our database using DETACH DELETE. Here, we match all nodes in the database and remove edges attached to them, before deleting the nodes themselves:

```
MATCH (n) DETACH DELETE n
```

Neo4j can be used in this manner to create nodes and relationships, as well as querying the database and examining parts of the graph. However, typically, in real-world cases, read and write operations need to be triggered by an external process, rather than typed directly into the Neo4j Browser window. In addition, visualization becomes less useful, as graphs stored in databases become large and cannot display every node and edge. With practicality in mind, for the rest of this chapter, we will mostly be interacting with the Neo4j database from Python.

Querying Neo4j from Python

With Neo4j installed, we are ready to connect to the database through Python. To do this, we will be using the `neo4j` Python module, which contains everything we need to connect to the database and send queries to it from a Python script. We will iterate through this in the following steps:

1. Let's start by creating a driver object for the Python-to-Neo4j connection. We will first need to import the `GraphDatabase` class from the `neo4j` module. Then, to create the driver, we will need to supply the `uri`, `username`, and `password` parameters to the `GraphDatabase.driver()` function:

```
from neo4j import GraphDatabase
driver = GraphDatabase.driver(uri='bolt://localhost:7687',
                              auth=('admin', 'testpython'))
```

Our `uri` parameter is the address of our local running instance of Neo4j. If the Neo4j database is being hosted on a separate server, then this would be substituted for the appropriate **Internet Proxy (IP)** address and port. Our username and password for the database we set up have also been passed as a tuple into the `auth` parameter.

2. Now, we need to create a session in order to send queries to the Neo4j database, using the `session()` method of our `driver` object:

```
session = driver.session()
```

3. With our session set up, we are now ready to query the database. For this example, we will add the query parameter to be used to create the graph relationship to our Neo4j session:

```
query = 'CREATE (:Person {name: "Jeremy"})-[:FOLLOWS]->(:Person
{name:"Mark"})'
result = session.run(query)
driver.close()
```

These lines of code won't return anything, since we have performed a write operation on the Neo4j database. However, we can confirm that it was successful by either opening the Neo4j Browser or using a read query from Python. For this first query, we will demonstrate both, beginning with the browser.

4. Go back to the Neo4j Browser for our Python DB database and run the following query from the command line at the top of the window:

```
MATCH (n) RETURN n
```

This query essentially matches every node in the database and returns it for viewing. The nodes and relationships we added in Python will be displayed:

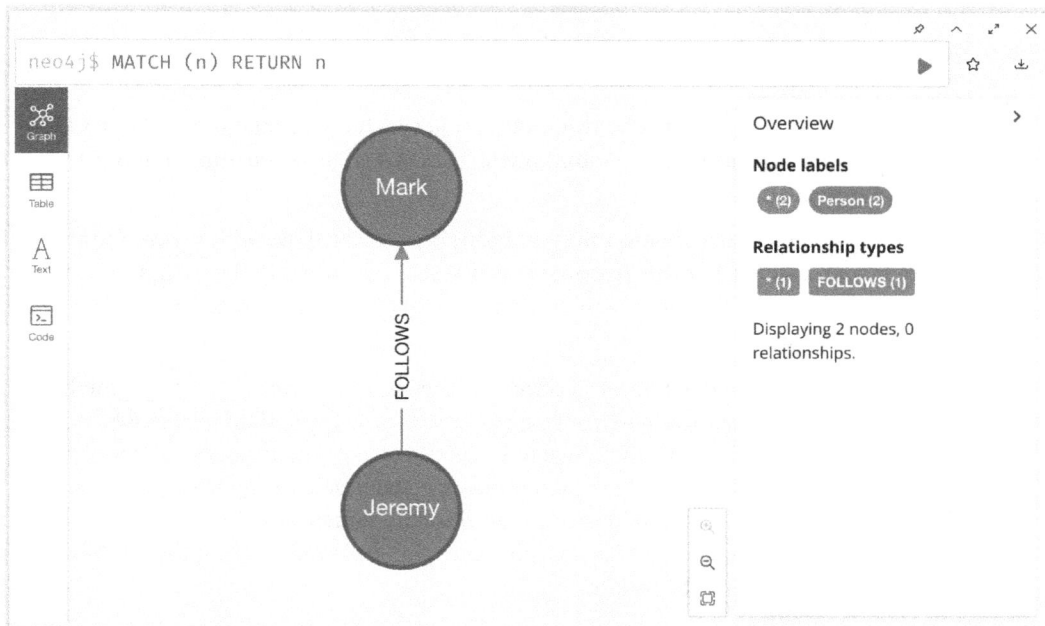

Figure 5.2 – Neo4j Browser result

5. Alternatively, we can write read queries in Python to confirm that our write operation ran as intended. To establish a session, we will use the same code framework as for the previous write query:

```
driver = GraphDatabase.driver(uri='bolt://localhost:7687',
                              auth=('admin', 'testpython'))
session = driver.session()
```

6. Now, instead of writing to the graph database, let's define two read queries. One query will match all `Person` nodes in the graph, while the other will match all FOLLOWS edges:

```
node_query = 'MATCH (n:Person) RETURN n'
edge_query = 'MATCH ()-[e:FOLLOWS]->() RETURN e'
```

7. Now, we can run both queries, before closing the connection. Accessing the `data()` method of `run()` transforms the results into a more consumable format that can more easily be handled in Python:

```
node_result = session.run(node_query).data()
edge_result = session.run(edge_query).data()
driver.close()
print(node_result)
print(edge_result)
```

Printing our results shows that we have two results for *n*, which each contains one of our added `Person` nodes. We also see that we found one FOLLOWS edge, confirming that our write process ran as intended.

At this point, you may notice that to interface Python with Neo4j, we will be running these types of queries regularly. For this reason, we will create a reusable Python class to handle connections and queries to the database, removing the need to manually connect to the database every time we run a query.

8. Let's define a Python class named `Neo4jConnect`. The class will have a `__init__` method, which will be called automatically when `Neo4jConnect` is instantiated. Because we will always want to connect to the database when we call `Neo4jConnect`, we can handle the driver connection here, using `uri`, `user`, and `password` parameters supplied to the class. We will also define a `close()` method in the class, to close the connection. A `query()` method will complete the class, which will take a Cypher query and execute it using the established connection, before returning the result:

```
class Neo4jConnect:
    def __init__(self, uri, user, password):
        self.driver = GraphDatabase.driver(uri, auth=(user,
password))
    def close(self):
        self.driver.close()
```

```
def query(self, query):
    session = self.driver.session()
    result = session.run(query)
    return result
```

9. Let's ensure that our class is functioning as intended by rerunning the read queries we executed previously. Now, we can create a `connection` object of the `Neo4jConnection` class, which handles authentication and the driver. Queries can now be run by accessing the `query()` method of the `connection` object, and the connection can be closed with the `close()` method:

```
connection = Neo4jConnect('bolt://localhost:7687', 'admin',
'testpython')

node_cypher = 'MATCH (n:Person) RETURN n'
edge_cypher = 'MATCH ()-[e:FOLLOWS]->() RETURN e'

node_result = connection.query(node_cypher).data()
edge_result = connection.query(edge_cypher).data()

connection.close()
print(node_result)
print(edge_result)
```

Printing `node_result` and `edge_result` displays the same results as we obtained previously, showing that our class is implemented correctly. For the remainder of this chapter, we will continue to use the `Neo4jConnect` class to read and write to Neo4j.

Next, we will look at a practical use case for a graph database, and use Python and Cypher to query the database and perform complex analyses.

Storing a graph in Neo4j

With our graph database set up, and our methods for interacting with Neo4j written, we can start to use Python and Neo4j to store and explore our graph data.

In this section, we will be looking at an air travel network between the US and Canada and analyzing its properties to find efficient routes between locations.

Preprocessing data

To begin, let's take a look at our data (sourced from Stanford University: https://snap.stanford.edu/data/reachability.html). We have two files, reachability_250.txt and reachability-meta.csv.

If we open `reachability-meta.csv` and take a look at the first few lines, we'll find a list of information about cities in the US and Canada:

```
"node_id","name","metro_pop","latitude","longitude"
0,"Abbotsford, BC",133497.0,49.051575,-122.328849
1,"Aberdeen, SD",40878.0,45.45909,-98.487324
2,"Abilene, TX",166416.0,32.449175,-99.741424
3,"Akron/Canton, OH",701456.0,40.79781,-81.371567
```

The file contains node attributes for our city nodes, keyed by the node ID. We have city names, the cities' populations, and their respective latitudes and longitudes. This CSV file can be loaded into Neo4j as it is, so we don't need to do any preprocessing.

However, our other file, `reachability_250.txt`, is not a CSV, which Neo4j prefers for imports. Opening `reachability_250.txt` and examining the first new lines, we can see that this contains a list of edges:

```
# Directed graph: reachability.txt
# Transportation reachability of cities in the United States and
Canada
# (edge from i to j if the estimated travel time from i to j is less
than a threshold)
# Edges are weighted by similarity (more negative --> more dissimilar)
# Nodes: 456 Edges: 27677
# FromNodeId ToNodeId Weight
57 0 -84
113 0 -90
235 0 -170
```

According to the data source, the graph is directed. Each edge represents travel between two cities, represented by node IDs. The edge weighting is a measure of travel time between the two cities, where more negative values refer to further distances. There are also six lines of information that we will need to remove.

In the next steps, we will look at starting to clean and preprocess this data so that it is graph ready.

To preprocess this information ready for Neo4j import, let's convert it to CSV format and remove the header lines. We can also make the distance measures non-negative to simplify the weightings. All of this preprocessing can be handled with the Python `csv` module and some list comprehensions, as we have done in previous chapters:

```python
import csv
with open('./data/reachability_250.txt', 'r') as txt:
    reader = csv.reader(txt, delimiter=' ')
    edges = [edge for edge in reader][6:]
    edges = [[edge[0], edge[1], int(edge[2])*-1] for edge in edges]
```

```
with open('./data/reachability.csv', 'w', newline='') as c:
    writer = csv.writer(c)
    for edge in edges:
        writer.writerow(edge)
```

This time, our data source is already in a sensible graph format, with a node attributes file and an edge list. The source also gives us information on a graph schema. The graph contains directed edges, and these edges are always between cities, making it a homogeneous graph. Our node attributes are the same types for each node, making the schema for this air travel graph fairly simple:

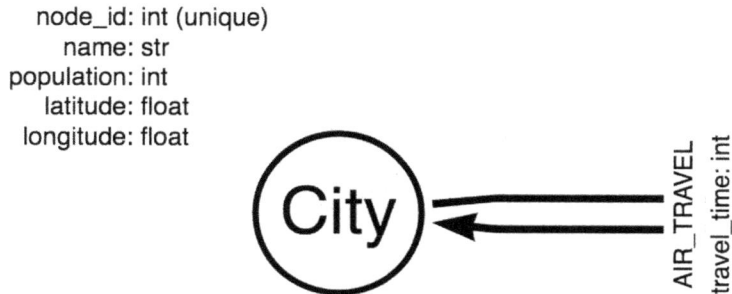

Figure 5.3 – US and Canada air travel graph schema

With our data in the correct format for Neo4j import and our air travel schema finalized, we can move on to creating the graph in the Neo4j database.

Moving nodes, edges, and properties to Neo4j

We will be using Python to write to our Neo4j database. We will need to first write some Cypher queries that we will later get Python to send to Neo4j.

At this stage, we should also make sure that our Neo4j database is empty; if not, the MATCH (n) DETACH DELETE n query can be run in the Neo4j Browser window before starting.

Our Cypher scripts will read data from CSV files, which on a local installation of Neo4j should be in a specific folder that Neo4j can access. Follow these steps to get the data into Neo4j:

1. In the main Neo4j application window (not the Browser window for the current database), click the **...** icon next to our newly created database.

2. From there, choose **Open folder** then **Import**, to open the /import folder in your operating system's file browser.

3. Copy reachability.csv and reachability-meta.csv to this import folder.

4. Now that Neo4j can read the files, let's write some Cypher to access their content. We can use LOAD CSV WITH HEADERS to load the reachability-meta.csv data, and the as function tells Neo4j to run the remaining code for each csv line, where each line is now named row. The headers are read in and can be used to access the corresponding csv columns, which we reference in CREATE to build nodes with the correct properties. Node IDs and population numbers are turned into integers with toInteger(), while our latitude and longitude attributes are converted into floats using toFloat(). When run from the Neo4j Browser, the following script will load the node attributes file:

```
LOAD CSV WITH HEADERS from 'file:///reachability-meta.csv' as
row
CREATE (city:City {
    node_id: toInteger(row.node_id),
    name: row.name,
    population: toInteger(row.metro_pop),
    latitude: toFloat(row.latitude),
    longitude: toFloat(row.longitude)
})
```

5. Next, we will use Cypher again to load in the edges file. Unlike our node properties file, reachability.csv doesn't contain headers, so we use LOAD CSV to import the data into Neo4j. Our two MATCH functions find the corresponding nodes for our edge using slice notation (e.g., [0]) to refer to the csv columns. We can also use Cypher's toInteger() function to convert our node attributes into integers, for both matching and merging. This identifies the nodes that we loaded in the previous step. Then, a MERGE step adds an :AIR_TRAVEL edge between these nodes, with travel_time added as an attribute from the third csv column:

```
LOAD CSV from 'file:///reachability.csv' as row
MATCH (from:City {node_id: toInteger(row[0])})
MATCH (to:City {node_id: toInteger(row[1])})
MERGE (from)-[:AIR_TRAVEL {travel_time: toInteger(row[2])}]-(to)
```

6. With our data loaded into Neo4j, we should now confirm that it is as expected and try to access it from Python. To perform Cypher queries in Python, we will again be using the Neo4jConnect class we prepared earlier in this chapter. This can be imported from the custom package we have made for this chapter, namely graphtastic (apologies for the cheesy naming), in the GitHub repository (https://github.com/PacktPublishing/Graph-Data-Modeling-in-Python/blob/main/CH05/) and can be implemented in Python code as so:

```
from graphtastic.database.neo4j import Neo4jConnect
```

7. Let's write some simple Cypher queries inside Python to test that our data import was successful and that our graph can still be accessed. As before, we establish a connection with the Neo4jConnect class and run some Cypher using connection.query(). Our Cypher here simply matches

all nodes, and `count (n)` aggregates those nodes into a single sum. We can then close the connection and print the result:

```
connection = Neo4jConnect('bolt://localhost:7687', 'admin',
'testpython')
cypher = 'MATCH (n) RETURN count(n)'
result = connection.query(cypher).data()
connection.close()
print(result)
```

The result should show that there are 456 nodes in our graph, which is the same number of rows in `reachability-meta.csv` minus one row for the header.

8. Next, let's ensure that an edge we know should be present in Neo4j was added correctly. We can use the same pattern as in the node-counting example to run a Cypher query from Python, but this time with alternative Cypher code. The edge on the first line of `reachability.csv` is between node ID 57 and node ID 0. This time, for our test, let's create a list of two elements to represent this edge. We will refer to these elements in our Cypher query:

```
edge_test = [57, 0]
```

9. Now, we can write some Cypher as a Python string, which will accept attributes from `edge_test` using f-string replacement. We can use a `MATCH` function to match a whole edge, assigning n and m as our nodes and r as our relationship. Double curly braces are used around the node attributes we want to match, to escape Python's f-string behavior in these areas. Where we do want replacement is where we reference the `node_id` attributes of each node, using values in `edge_test`. We can then add a `RETURN` statement to return the names on both nodes and the travel time between them, as attributes of the nodes and edge assigned to n, m, and r. Due to the amount of string modification going on here, let's also print our Cypher query to see how Neo4j will receive it:

```
cypher = f'MATCH (n:City {{node_id:{edge_test[0]}}})' \
         '-[r:AIR_TRAVEL]->' \
         f'(m:City {{node_id:{edge_test[1]}}}) ' \
         'RETURN n.name, m.name, r.travel_time'

print(cypher)
```

10. The f-string replacement and escaped characters will be resolved into a valid Cypher query, ready to be sent to Neo4j. We can send this query in the same manner as we have previously:

```
connection = Neo4jConnect('bolt://localhost:7687', 'admin',
'testpython')
result = connection.query(cypher).data()
connection.close()
print(result)
```

From the `print` statement, you should see that we matched one edge, from Calgary, AB, to Abbotsford, BC, with a travel time of `84`. Try changing the node IDs in `edge_test` and rerunning to check for a few more edges present in `reachability.csv`.

At this point, you may be starting to see some of the power that comes from using Python and Cypher concurrently, where conditions and parameters in Cypher can be set dynamically through the use of f-strings, or other string replacement methods. Of course, this is useful not only in checking that data has been ingested correctly but also in downstream analysis in Python and pipeline construction. In the remainder of this chapter, we will use these methods to do some static analysis in both Cypher and *igraph*, using data streamed from Neo4j. We will be focusing on data ingestion and analytics pipelines involving both Neo4j and Python in *Chapter 6, Pipeline Development*.

Optimizing travel with Python and Cypher

With our graph fully loaded into Neo4j, and our methods for querying data using Cypher and Python set up, we are ready to perform some more complex analysis. At the start of this section, we will use Cypher to answer questions and return answers in Python. Later, we will be doing more complex analysis, by sampling graph data from Neo4j and working with the sample in *igraph*.

Let's begin by delving into the structure of our graph and asking some questions of our data to understand it better. The following steps will look at finding some relationships in the data:

1. The first query we will run will find out the highest population by city and we are going to return the name of the city and the city's population as the result. ORDER BY will order by the population of those nodes (n). For those **SQL** people out there, these commands will look very familiar, and you will find the transition to Cypher much easier than those who have never used SQL. Anyway, back to the task at hand:

```
cypher = 'MATCH (n) ' \
         'RETURN n.name, n.population ' \
         'ORDER BY n.population ' \
         'DESC LIMIT 1'
connection = Neo4jConnect('bolt://localhost:7687', 'admin',
'testpython')
result = connection.query(cypher).data()
connection.close()
print(result)
```

2. Our results show us that the city with the highest population is *New York*. Another simple task we could ask of our graph is what cities we can travel from New York to in a relatively short travel time. For this, we can make use of the WHERE function, which again has a similar effect to its SQL counterpart. When used after a MATCH statement, we can filter the matched nodes by their travel time property with a WHERE function, before returning the names of the cities easily reachable from New York. As always, we then execute the query against the Neo4j database using Python:

```
cypher = 'MATCH (n:City {name: "New York, NY"}) ' \
         'MATCH (n)-[r:AIR_TRAVEL]->(m) ' \
         'WHERE r.travel_time < 100 ' \
         'RETURN m.name'

connection = Neo4jConnect('bolt://localhost:7687', 'admin',
'testpython')
result = connection.query(cypher).data()
connection.close()

print(result)
print(len(result))
```

These first analyses are fairly simple and could be achieved using a relational database. Let's now move on to some questions best tackled with a graph data structure and graph database, such as calculating paths.

Our graph contains flights available between cities in the US and Canada, but to make some journeys, connections will need to be made, involving stops along the way. As an example, let's look at how we might travel from San Diego, CA, all the way north to St. John's, NL.

3. We will begin, as many Cypher queries do, by using MATCH statements. First, we match the cities of interest, to find their corresponding nodes. Next, we match a path between these nodes using the [*..3] wildcard in place of specific edges or edge types. This notation allows paths to be matched up to a length of three hops from the starting node, n. We also assign these whole matched paths to the variable p. The last operation we need to do is return the paths, p, as well as the relationship details with travel time information with relationships (p), and map this to the rels variable:

```
cypher = 'MATCH (n:City {name: "San Diego, CA"}) '\
         'MATCH (m:City {name: "St. Johns, NL"}) '\
         'MATCH p=(n)-[*..3]->(m) ' \
         'RETURN p, relationships(p) as rels'

connection = Neo4jConnect('bolt://localhost:7687', 'admin',
'testpython')
result = connection.query(cypher).data()
connection.close()
```

```
print(result)
print(len(result))
```

In the next section, we will look at extending this to look at making travel recommendations around what route to take. This is a more complicated question, but luckily we can use Dijkstra's algorithm (https://isaaccomputerscience.org/concepts/dsa_search_dijkstra?examBoard=all&stage=all). This will be explained in the upcoming section.

Travel recommendations

Many systems working with travel recommendations and optimizations will use graph technology behind the scenes. When you use a taxi application such as *Uber*, optimized paths are calculated between your starting point and your destination, taking into account traffic, speed limits, and anything else that might affect your journey. In this example, these parameters can be thought of as edge weights, and road junctions as nodes. The distances between all sections of your journey, or all the time taken to traverse each road section, are taken into account to get you from A to B efficiently.

In our dataset, we have information on air travel between cities in the US and Canada, and this includes travel times between cities, measured in units of time. This information can be used in exactly the same way as with travel by road in the previous example, to find the most efficient air travel routes between cities.

To abstract this problem, we can look at a classical graph theory method likely to be used by many travel optimization solutions. Dijkstra's algorithm is commonly used to find optimized paths in weighted graphs.

We can demonstrate Dijkstra's algorithm with a simple example. In *Figure 5.3*, if we wanted to get from city A to city D, we would need to plan a route with a stop at more than one city. The route involving the fewest steps is to go from A to C, then on to our destination, D. At first glance, this would seem to be the most efficient, as the length of this path is the shortest. However, adding up the travel time weights for the edges traversed results in a sum of 176. On the other hand, traveling via a different path, from A, to B, to C, and finally to D, results in a total travel time of 127, which, despite the extra steps, is shorter overall:

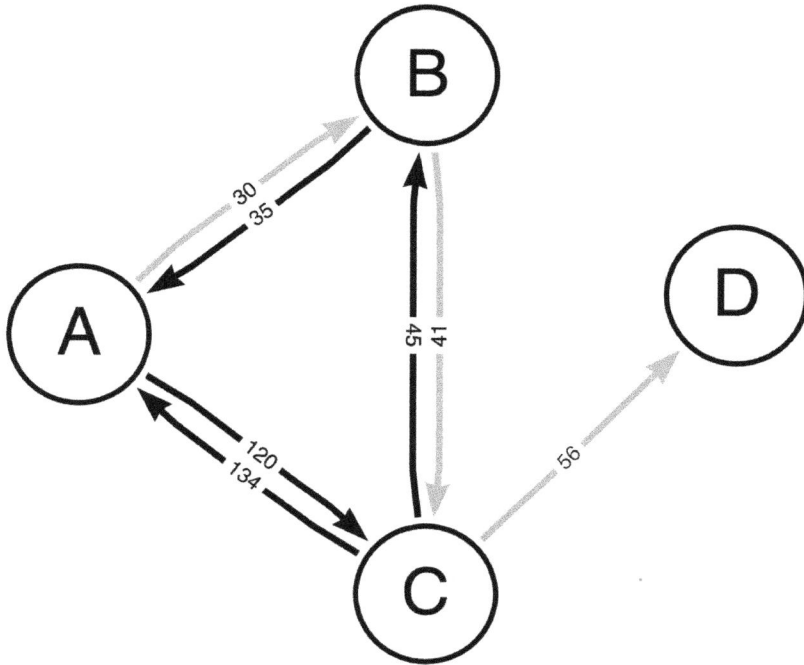

Figure 5.4 – Optimized air travel using Dijkstra's algorithm

To find the quickest path between our cities of choice, let's return to using Python and igraph. The first stage will be to parse our results from the most recent Cypher query into a better format for working in Python. When working with *igraph*, remember that we need to define node attribute lists, edge lists, and igraph IDs for each node. This will be achieved in the following steps:

1. Looking back, our query to find paths between San Diego and St. John's returned both paths and relationships. We can first separate the paths in our query results with a list comprehension, separating the results for p from the dictionary previously returned by query.data():

```
paths = [path['p'] for path in result]
```

2. Each of the paths in our path list contains both nodes and [:AIR_TRAVEL] separating connected nodes. For the purposes of defining node attribute lists and IDs, we don't need any information on the adjacency of nodes or the [:AIR_TRAVEL] strings. So, we can flatten the paths into a list of nodes using a double list comprehension, with an if statement:

```
nodes = [node for path in paths for node in path if node !=
'AIR_TRAVEL']
```

3. This node list now contains duplicate nodes, where nodes were present in more than one path. Let's use a clever temporary dictionary comprehension to create a temporary dictionary, where the keys are the node IDs, to filter out duplicate nodes. The `.values()` method will convert our nodes back into a list of dictionary node objects:

```
node_attributes = {node['node_id']:node for node in nodes}.
values()
```

4. We are now in a place to generate lists of node attributes to add to our set of properties to be used in our travel time graph. We can also create a dictionary with newly created *igraph*-ascending integer IDs, and map these to the original `node_ids` using `enumerate()`, as we have done in previous chapters. The following code allows us to achieve this:

```
node_ids = [node['node_id'] for node in node_attributes]
names = [node['name'] for node in node_attributes]
populations = [node['population'] for node in node_attributes]
latitudes = [node['latitude'] for node in node_attributes]
longitudes = [node['longitude'] for node in node_attributes]
igraph_ids = {node['node_id']: i for i, node in enumerate(node_
attributes)}
```

5. With our node attributes and *igraph* node IDs set up, it's time to create an edge list. Edges are in the paths we extracted from Neo4j's `query.data()` result, where adjacent nodes are separated by the `:AIR_TRAVEL` string. Distances can be extracted from the *result* by accessing its `rels`:

```
travel_time_paths = [path['rels'] for path in result]
print(travel_time_paths)
```

6. Now, the next step is to extract adjacent nodes from each path and assign the corresponding `travel_time` edge attributes. This is a more complex operation and so will take place in a `for` loop.

7. First, we create empty lists for `edge_list` and `edge_attributes`. In a `for` loop, we will iterate through zipped `paths` and `travel_time_paths`, which are lists of the same length. For each `path`, we will take the `node_id` attribute and remove the `AIR_TRAVEL` strings, resulting in a path containing only node IDs. We will do the same with travel times, resulting in a list of edge attributes. Next, we use `zip()` to zip `clean_path` with itself, offset by 1 using `[1:]` – essentially generating pairs of nodes representing each edge. We in turn use `zip()` to zip this with travel times, which will now be of equivalent length to our edges. Finally, we can iterate through this `zip()` object to append each edge to our edgelist and add travel times in the same manner, in the corresponding indices. This ensures we can add edge attributes to *igraph* in a listwise manner later:

```
edge_list = []
edge_attributes = []
for path, times in zip(paths, travel_time_paths):
```

```
    clean_path = [node['node_id'] for node in path if node !=
'AIR_TRAVEL']
    travel_times = [rel['travel_time'] for rel in times]
    for n, time in zip(zip(clean_path, clean_path[1:]), travel_
times):
        edge_list.append([igraph_ids[n[0]], igraph_ids[n[1]]])
        edge_attributes.append(time)
```

8. With our node attributes, edge list, and edge attributes prepared, we can now create our
    graph. As always, we create a blank graph using `igraph.Graph()`, and in this case specify
    `directed=True`. It is especially important to specify a directed graph in this example,
    since travel time to and from two cities can differ depending on the direction. Next, we set
    `add_vertices()` equal to the number of `node_ids` and add the corresponding node
    attributes. Then, we add our edges with `add_edges()` and add edge attributes to these edges
    in the same manner as we would add node attributes:

```
import igraph
g = igraph.Graph(directed=True)
g.add_vertices(len(node_ids))
g.vs['node_id'] = node_ids
g.vs['name'] = names
g.vs['population'] = populations
g.vs['latitude'] = latitudes
g.vs['longitude'] = longitudes
g.add_edges(edge_list)
g.es['travel_time'] = edge_attributes
```

Our graph is now assembled in Python and represents the subgraph making up paths from
San Diego to St. John's. Let's take a look at some edges and confirm that the edges also exist in
Neo4j and our code has worked as expected.

9. We can print edges of adjacent node IDs (as they are in Neo4j) by accessing `g.vs[edge.
    source]['node_id']` and `g.vs[edge.target]['node_id']` in each edge, along
    with `travel_times` of each edge, by using a list comprehension. Printing this will show us
    a list of edges that should be present in Neo4j:

```
print([[g.vs[edge.source]['node_id'], g.vs[edge.target]['node_
id'], edge['travel_time']] for edge in g.es])
```

10. We select one edge between node ID `294` and node ID `401` and confirm that it exists in the
    Neo4j database by running a small query in the Neo4j Browser (head over to the Neo4j Browser
    and run the following Cypher statement). We can simply match the path between these nodes
    and return the nodes to confirm that our Neo4j-to-Python *igraph* code has worked as intended.
    Let's now head over to the Neo4j Browser and execute this Cypher statement:

```
MATCH (n:City {node_id:294})-[:AIR_TRAVEL]->(m:City {node_
id:401})
RETURN n, m
```

11. Head back over to Python and now, we're ready to do some more complex analysis in *igraph* and find the shortest travel method from San Diego to St. John's. With our graph set up, this is actually fairly simple in terms of code. We can first specify the nodes we want to find paths between using `g.vs.select()`, and name them `source` and `target`. To run Dijkstra's algorithm, we can call *igraph*'s `get_shortest_paths()` method between our source and target cities. As long as we specify our weight parameter as `travel_time`, *igraph* will use travel times as an edge weight in the path calculation and return the minimum distance path:

```
source = g.vs.select(name_eq='San Diego, CA')
target = g.vs.select(name_eq='St. Johns, NL')
shortest_path = g.get_shortest_paths(source[0], target[0],
weights='travel_time')
```

12. The result of `get_shortest_paths()` will contain *igraph* integer IDs, so let's get the names of each city in the path corresponding to these nodes and take a look at them:

```
shortest_path = [g.vs[node]['name'] for node in shortest_path]
print(shortest_path)
```

13. We can see that the most optimal path in terms of travel time is to go via Chicago and then Montreal. To get the distances of each of these steps, we can specify an optional parameter, `output='epath'`, in `get_shortest_paths()`, which returns edge IDs. Then, we can access the travel times associated with these edge IDs with a list comprehension and take a look. We can also carry out a sum to find out the total travel time:

```
short_path_rels = g.get_shortest_paths(source[0], target[0],
weights='travel_time', output='epath')
short_path_distances = [g.es[edge]['travel_time'] for edge in
short_path_rels]
print(short_path_distances)
shortest_travel_time = sum(short_path_distances[0])
print(shortest_travel_time)
```

So, we can use this method to find optimal travel routes between the cities in our dataset. However, what if we wanted to look at other features of our edges to recommend specific paths between cities? For example, the physical distance between our nodes might be of interest. Again, calculating this is something more suited to Python than a graph database, so let's take a look at how this might be done.

14. We can first extract edges and latitudes and longitudes from our *igraph* graph by accessing `g.es` and `g.vs` and performing comprehensions. We will be using the node IDs to match nodes with their corresponding edges:

```
edges = [[g.vs[edge.source]['node_id'], g.vs[edge.target]['node_
id']] for edge in g.es]
latitudes = {node['node_id']: node['latitude'] for node in g.vs}
longitudes = {node['node_id']: node['longitude'] for node in
g.vs}
```

15. Next, we need a function to calculate distances from latitudes and longitudes. Let's define a function, `find_distances()`, which will take a list of edges and two dictionaries, `latitudes` and `longitudes`, each keyed by node ID. We can use the `geopy` module to import `geodesic()`, which will calculate the distance between two `lat`/`long` coordinate points. For each edge, we make a tuple of latitude and longitude for both the source and target, in `loc_1` and `loc_2`. We can find the distance using `geodesic()` and provide these points as parameters, before converting the distance into kilometers by accessing the km attribute. The distance between each pair of connected nodes is appended to a list and returned:

```
from geopy.distance import geodesic
def find_distances(edges, latitudes, longitudes):
    distances = []
    for n, m in edges:
        loc_1 = (latitudes[n], longitudes[n])
        loc_2 = (latitudes[m], longitudes[m])
        distance = geodesic(loc_1, loc_2).km
        distances.append(int(distance))
    return distances
```

16. Now, we can call our method on our prepared edges, latitudes, and longitudes, and apply the distances to each edge in our graph using `g.es`:

```
distances = find_distances(edges, latitudes, longitudes)
g.es['distance'] = distances
```

17. With distances added to *igraph*, we can find the shortest path between San Diego and St. John's in terms of physical distance instead, using the same process as earlier:

```
source = g.vs.select(name_eq='San Diego, CA')
target = g.vs.select(name_eq='St. Johns, NL')
shortest_path = g.get_shortest_paths(source[0],
    target[0], weights='distance')
shortest_path = [g.vs[node]['name'] for node in shortest_path]
print(shortest_path)
short_path_rels = g.get_shortest_paths(source[0],
    target[0], weights='distance', output='epath')
short_path_distances = [g.es[edge]['distance'] for edge in
short_path_rels]
print(short_path_distances)
shortest_travel_time = sum(short_path_distances[0])
print(shortest_travel_time)
```

This gives us a different answer, with a path through `Chicago` then `Toronto`.

In a travel recommendation system, customers may be interested in other features of their proposed travel routes. In the scenario that physical distance was of interest, we might want to precompute these distances and add them to a graph database that serves a web application.

This way, they would not have to be recalculated each time a recommendation is made. We can do this for our graph of air travel in the US and Canada, by first extracting all edges, nodes, latitudes, and longitudes from the Neo4j database, with some simple Cypher, before running these queries against Neo4j:

```
edges_cypher = 'MATCH (n)-[:AIR_TRAVEL]->(m) ' \
               'RETURN n.node_id, m.node_id'
nodes_cypher = 'MATCH (n) ' \
               'RETURN n.node_id, n.latitude, n.longitude'
connection = Neo4jConnect('bolt://localhost:7687', 'admin',
'testpython')
edges = connection.query(edges_cypher).data()
lat_longs = connection.query(nodes_cypher).data()
connection.close()
```

18. We can then use a similar approach as for our subgraph example to calculate physical distances for all of our edges, reusing our custom `find_distances()` method. These can be written to a CSV file, ready for import into Neo4j:

```
edges = [[edge['n.node_id'], edge['m.node_id']] for edge in
edges]
latitudes = {node['n.node_id']: node['n.latitude'] for node in
lat_longs}
longitudes = {node['n.node_id']: node['n.longitude'] for node in
lat_longs}
distances = find_distances(edges, latitudes, longitudes)
distances = list(zip(edges, distances))
import csv
with open('chapter05/data/distances.csv', 'w', newline='') as c:
    writer = csv.writer(c)
    for edge in distances:
        writer.writerow(edge)
```

19. Now, as we did before when we first assembled our graph in Neo4j, we can move the created `distances.csv` file into Neo4j's `import` folder. Some simple Cypher, using what we have learned in this chapter, will import all our new `distance` edge attributes into Neo4j. The only new function here is `SET`, which updates a given feature for a specified node or edge:

```
LOAD CSV from 'file:///distances.csv' as row
MATCH (n:City {node_id: toInteger(row[0])})
MATCH (m:City {node_id: toInteger(row[1])})
MATCH (n)-[r:AIR_TRAVEL]->(m)
SET r.distance = toInteger(row[2])
```

Now, let's move on to the next section!

Moving to ingestion pipelines

In this chapter, we have created a static Neo4j graph, queried and analyzed it, and updated its features. This type of solution might be used in a production environment, where it might be used to serve up results in an application.

However, there are elements of this type of process that we are yet to cover. In a production system, nodes and edges may be read and written to a graph database regularly, often in small batches. Complicated processing might take place outside of Neo4j, before data is ingested, using Python or other languages. Think about how many options a real travel optimization or recommendation service actually offers – each of these has to be embedded into a graph database pipeline.

In *Chapter 6*, *Pipeline Development*, we will look at an example of a complex graph data pipeline and explore how to make it reliable and efficient.

Summary

We have covered so much in this chapter, and now you should have a good understanding of the power of *in-memory* databases, such as Neo4j. We started our quest for knowledge by looking at how you can set up your Neo4j instance, where we did all the configuration to install a local version of Neo4j and get up and running quickly.

Following on from this, we looked at how you can then start to perform queries against the Neo4j database, using a query language known as Cypher. For some of you, this will have been your first exposure to Cypher, and we took you through how this language is similar to other query languages, such as SQL. To get a better understanding of how to use Cypher, a good resource is the Neo4j website (`https://neo4j.com/developer/cypher/`).

Upping the ante, we then started to look at how you store data in your Neo4j graph database, using a combination of Cypher and Python's `cypher` package, to start interacting with your graph database.

This culminated in exploring a use case of recommending the best route to travel on and analyzing optimal paths between two points. Here, we introduced Dijkstra's algorithm (`https://isaaccomputerscience.org/concepts/dsa_search_dijkstra?examBoard=all&stage=all`) and used it to calculate the shortest path between two points. This emulated a pipeline and everyday applications you use, such as Google Maps or Uber's routing systems. Here, you worked hands-on with Python, Cypher, *igraph*, and Neo4j. To end on a crescendo, so to speak, we then started to explain how we are going to look at scaling up ingestion pipelines in the next chapter and will expand on the examples provided in this chapter.

You have come a long way since the first chapter, so well done for making it this far. We look forward to taking you through how to create production-ready graph pipelines, which will be the focus of the next chapter.

6

Pipeline Development

This chapter will involve you, as a progressing graph data scientist, getting directly involved in building production-grade schemas. Here, we will teach you everything we have acquired from our years of experience as graph practitioners.

The use case for our pipeline design in this chapter will be to develop a schema that can be used to look at customers purchasing habits, with the ultimate aim of building a recommendations system that can be used as new (unseen) data is added to the graph. This will function very much like a streaming service, where, instead of *You might like this film* recommendations, you will be given recommendations on products you are likely to buy. We will look at querying methods looking at product similarity, alongside a popular similarity matching method called Jaccard similarity.

Again, you will be working extensively with Neo4j and Python to integrate and build the pipeline seen in many production environments. I hope you are excited to get started, as we are. Let's list what the core sections will be:

- Graph pipeline development
- Designing a schema and pipeline
- Making product recommendations – using methods of similarity to recommend products

Technical requirements

We will be using Jupyter notebooks to run our coding exercises, which require `python>=3.8.0`, along with the following packages that will need to be installed with the `pip install` command in your environment:

- `neo4j==5.5.0`
- `Faker==17.0.0`

For this chapter, you will also need Neo4j Desktop installed. Please see the *Technical requirements* section of *Chapter 5, Working with Graph Databases*, if Neo4j is not yet installed, as it will be needed to follow along with the tutorials in this chapter.

All notebooks, with the coding exercises, are available at the following GitHub link: `https://github.com/PacktPublishing/Graph-Data-Modeling-in-Python/tree/main/CH06`.

Graph pipeline development

In the last chapter, we learned how to interface Python with a Neo4j database. We harnessed Neo4j's long-term graph storage solution to set up a more realistic, production-like system, which could be queried to find air travel routes, according to several parameters.

We set the graph database up by writing a large amount of data to it using static queries. At the point of setting up the database, we knew what data we wanted it to hold, and we wrote Cypher queries to get our data in, in bulk. The focus of the resulting graph was on delivering read query results to, for example, a frontend web application. These read queries were executed against the database only when we had a question to ask of the data.

However, in reality, these graph database systems often serve as the backend to applications that frequently and automatically send queries to a graph database. These queries may not only be driven by direct user behavior but also executed to collect and compute information passively.

For example, consider how a financial transaction graph might be stored by a financial services company, in order to look for suspicious activity. For this type of use case, the company would want to detect suspicious behavior as it was happening, rather than wait for a bulk upload of data, by which point fraudulent activity may have already occurred. In this scenario, there would likely be components in a data pipeline outside of just a graph database such as Neo4j, interacting in small queries, in order to write data and look for certain patterns of interest.

In terms of write queries, rather than writing to a graph in bulk, as we did in the last chapter, small transactions of information from many users could be written to the graph, often simultaneously. In a graph database, there are some extra considerations to take into account for a system that performs in this way, which we will cover in this chapter.

In the following sections, we're going to set up a new Neo4j graph database and look at some ways in which large numbers of small read and write queries can be handled, by mocking up users and user interactions for an online retailer. As previously, we will be using Neo4j and Python to do this, making the most of the advantages of each.

A graph database for retail

In this section, we will be designing a backend system to handle requests resulting from a web application or a mobile app. In a worked example, we will explore the steps needed to onboard a retailer with a method to make product recommendations to customers. We will be building the backend database for a system for an online electronics retailer, where customers can browse, compare, and purchase products, while receiving recommendations on what they might be interested in viewing.

For this complex system, as in production database setups, we will need to consider several elements, and how they will interact. We will need to initialize a graph database to accept queries and simulate user interactions with our application that trigger queries against the data.

Designing a schema and pipeline

Let's tackle each of the elements we need to set up one at a time. For our backend system, we will need a graph database, so the first stage is setting up a new, blank Neo4j database.

Setting up a new database

As we did in *Chapter 5, Working with Graph Databases*, let's start up Neo4j Desktop. Once we have loaded up the desktop, we need to follow these steps to add a new database:

1. In the main Neo4j window, select **Add**, and choose **Local DBMS**.
2. Choose a name for the new database, for example, `Store DB`.
3. Use a generic password too, for example, `testpython`. We will need to use this password in open code in this example, so make sure not to use a sensitive keyphrase. In a real production system, any authentication to this database required by third-party scripts would likely use a password secret system, to prevent exposure of this password in plain text and code.
4. Next, click **Create**, and wait for the new graph database to be created.
5. Once the graph database is created, make sure you can connect to it through Neo4j Desktop, by clicking **Start** next to the new database name. The database will be shown as **Starting**. Again, wait for the database to load, before clicking **Open**, to open a new Neo4j Browser window, connected to our new database.
6. We will need to create a new admin user, in order to access the graph database from Python. In the Neo4j command line at the top of the window, run the following:

    ```
    :server user add
    ```

7. In the resulting window, add a username and password. For our example, we will be again using `admin` as the username, and `testpython` as the password. The same applies to this password as to the database password: don't use a password you would be uncomfortable typing in open code (strongly typed and visible to all if committing to a repository such as GitHub).
8. Next, add the user roles **PUBLIC** and **admin** from the drop-down roles list. Then, select **Add user** to create the **admin** user. We will be using these credentials to access the database later.

With our database set up, we now need to decide what type of data is going to be held there. The first stage, as always, is to consider and design a schema.

Schema design

What data do we want to hold on our customers? What will help us to recommend products to them?

Let's take a look at the products that our online electronics retailer sells. We can get a rough idea of the information we have by opening up `products.csv`, and examining the first few lines:

```
productID,name,brand,mainType,subType
1001,WX100 In-ear Headphones,Hans,Audio,Bluetooth Headphones
1002,WX-B210 Bluetooth Headphones,Hans,Audio,Bluetooth Headphones
1003,Hans-3 Bluetooth Headphones,Hans,Audio,Bluetooth Headphones
1004,J9 Bluetooth Headphones,JLB,Audio,Bluetooth Headphones
1005,J8-I In-ear Headphones,JLB,Audio,Bluetooth Headphones
1006,J-basics Wired Headphones,JLB,Audio,Wired Headphones
```

From the structure of this data, it looks like each product our retailer currently offers is listed on a separate `csv` row. We have a product ID for each one, a name, and a product brand. We also have a level of categorization for each product, in the `mainType` and `subType` columns. So, we have three distinct types of entities to hold in our graph, which can be represented by the node types `Product`, `Brand`, and `Type`. Each unique product has a type and a brand that we could represent with the named edges `HAS_TYPE` and `HAS_BRAND`, respectively.

For each main type, there are several subtypes of products. We can think of these descriptive classes as a sort of ontology, a concept we explored more thoroughly in *Chapter 4, Building a Knowledge Graph*, where we dealt with knowledge graphs. In this case, we can consider connecting subtypes to the main types of products in our graph, and represent classes of products at different granularities. One way to do this would be to create more `HAS_TYPE` relationships between subtypes and the main types.

This data will form the backbone of our database, containing links between products, brands, and their types. The schema of our graph will develop as we consider different elements, and will become more complex, but to begin, let's design a data model for our products alone:

productID: int (unique)
name: str

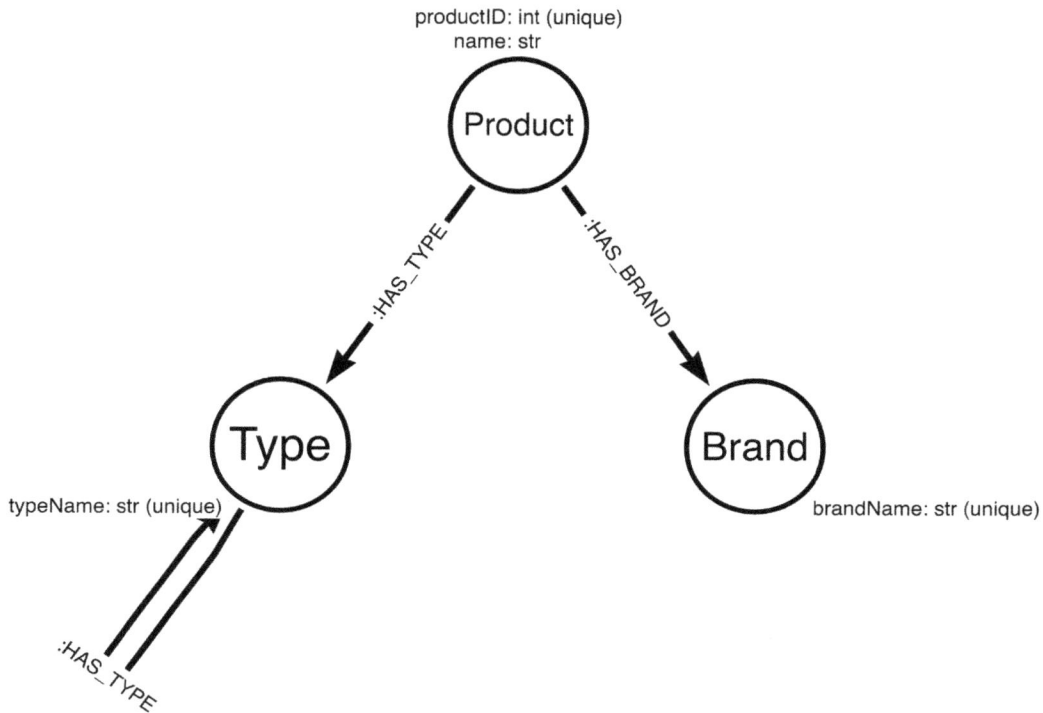

Figure 6.1 – Product graph schema

Figure 6.1 illustrates a schema for our products, but we may want to store customer information too. We can learn what types of products a customer is interested in by keeping track of their past purchases. To store customers, we will need to give each a unique customer ID, as well as store other useful information about them, such as their name and address.

To store these features, we can create customer nodes, with **ID**, **name**, and **address** as node attributes. For purchases, we can create relationships with products. For each purchase, we can store a **date** and **time** on the edge, to distinguish between multiple purchases of the same item by the same customer.

Figure 6.2 shows an extended schema, containing both product and customer information:

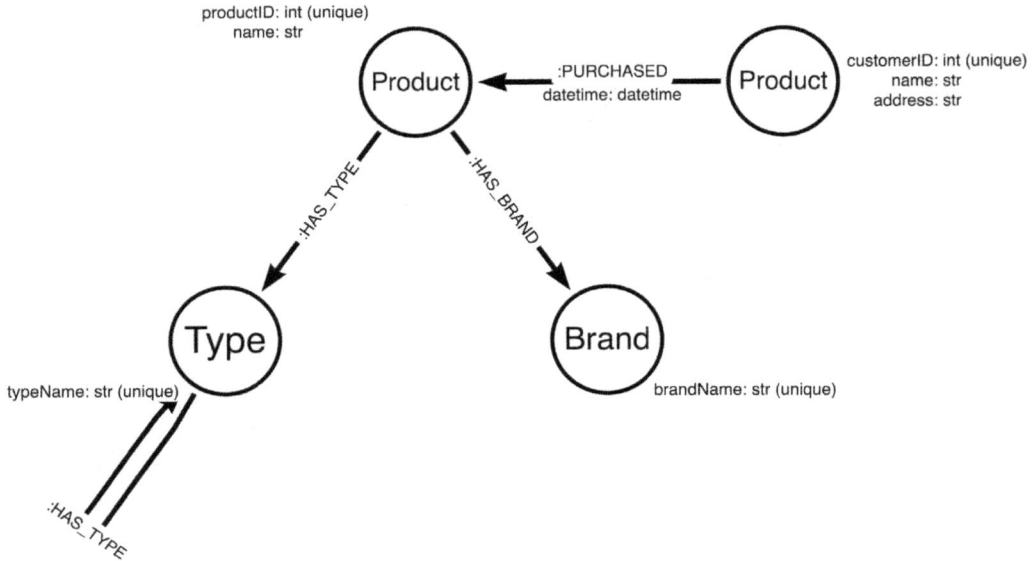

Figure 6.2 – Adding customer purchases to the graph schema

Representing all the features of our products, and the features of customers that interact with them, results here in a directed heterogeneous graph. The fact that customers can make multiple purchases of the same item will result in the potential for more than one edge between a pair of nodes, meaning that our network is classed as a multigraph.

The information in our graph schema is such that if we want to find what types or brands of products a customer tends to purchase, we can traverse paths in our graph to find an answer. We will come back to this idea later, when making product recommendations. We may also want to add to this schema later, to capture additional information about our customers. Thankfully, a heterogenous graph schema is more flexible than a relational database, as we explored in *Chapter 1, Introducing Graphs in the Real World*, and allows for additional types of nodes and edges to be added when required, without affecting the data currently modeled.

Now that we have a plan for representing data in our graph database, we can start to create processes to store it.

Adding static product information

As we mentioned previously, the products on offer in our online store will form the backbone of our graph data. We have a list of products already on offer, as well as extra information on them, in `products.csv`.

To get started, let's populate our graph database with product information:

1. Neo4j can easily access data in a given database's import folder, so let's first move products. csv (this will be stored in the supporting GitHub repositories data folder at https:// github.com/PacktPublishing/Graph-Data-Modeling-in-Python/tree/ main/CH06/data) to that location. From the main Neo4j Desktop window, click the three dots ... next to **Store DB**, or whatever name you have used for this chapter's database.

2. From the pop-up list, choose **Open folder**, then click on **Import**. This will open the database's import folder in the file browser of your operating system. Copy and paste, or drag products. csv into this folder to give Neo4j access to it in Cypher queries.

3. With our data in the correct location, we can start to think about how to turn this tabular CSV into nodes and edges, according to the graph schema we have specified. For the initial transfer of data, we can use the Neo4j Browser and the command line, by opening up the Browser window for our **Store DB** database.

4. Next, let's write some Cypher to load this data. As we did in *Chapter 5, Working with Graph Databases*, we can use the LOAD CSV WITH HEADERS function to read our data into Neo4j. We specify the filename and location in the /import folder by using FROM 'file:/// products.csv', and read one line at a time with AS row.

5. From there, we start to add nodes to our graph with MERGE. We add nodes with the Product, Brand, and Type types, and add their node attributes using the row.column syntax. We use the aliases p, b, m, and s for each type of node added or matched with MERGE in order to easily add edges next. We can use even more MERGE functions to now add the HAS_BRAND and HAS_TYPE and relationships, including the relationships between the main types and sub-types:

```
LOAD CSV WITH HEADERS FROM 'file:///products.csv' AS row
MERGE (p:Product {productID: toInteger(row.productID), name:
row.name})
MERGE (b:Brand {brandName: row.brand})
MERGE (m:Type {typeName: row.mainType})
MERGE (s:Type {typeName: row.subType})
MERGE (p)-[:HAS_BRAND]->(b)
MERGE (p)-[:HAS_TYPE]->(s)
MERGE (s)-[:HAS_TYPE]->(m)
```

> **Important note**
> It is important to remember that using MERGE, rather than CREATE here, ensures that duplicate nodes are not created for each row. Using CREATE could potentially be manageable for Product nodes, of which one per CSV row is added, but for Brands and Types, the CREATE function would add Brand and Type nodes with identical names to the graph, as well as creating extraneous edges.

6.   Before moving on to the next stage, we should confirm that product data has been correctly added to our graph using some simple Cypher queries, executed in the Neo4j Browser. Looking at our data in `products.csv`, we can use the first row to validate our graph data. We can first write Cypher to confirm that the product with ID 1001 has the correct node attributes, and run this in the Neo4j Browser:

```
MATCH (n:Product {productID:1001})
RETURN n.productID, n.name
```

This should show us that this node has the name `WX100 In-ear Headphones`.

7.   Let's now confirm that relationships were added correctly. We can find the brand of these headphones using another `MATCH` function, and `RETURN` the connected `Brand` nodes:

```
MATCH (n:Product {productID:1001})-[:HAS_BRAND]->(m)
RETURN m.brandName
```

This will show that these headphones are of the `Hans` brand.

8.   Finally, let's make sure product types and connected sub-types are as expected. In this case, we need to traverse (travel across or through) several edges to find the subtype, and then the main type of the product with productID 1001. This can be done over two `MATCH` functions for clarity:

```
MATCH (n:Product {productID:1001})-[:HAS_TYPE]->(subtype:Type)
MATCH (subtype)-[:HAS_TYPE]->(maintype:Type)
RETURN n.name, subtype.typeName, maintype.typeName
```

We should see in the resulting table that the subtype of these headphones is **Bluetooth Headphones**, with a main type of **Audio**.

These are all the steps needed to complete the process of getting your data into your Neo4j graph, by extensively using the Neo4j Browser to execute the Cypher queries.

With our product data successfully assembled into a graph, we can now think about how customers might interact with products, and how to simulate and store this information in the Neo4j database. This will be the purpose of the upcoming section.

Simulating customer interactions

Depending on its size, an online retailer could have thousands of customers browsing products on their web application or app. Each of these customers sends queries to a backend database when they search for a product, are recommended a product, or purchase something, among other actions. This way, a retailer can serve a customer with the information they need, as well as storing data on customer behavior.

We will be focusing on the product recommendation system for our online electronics store, as this is often handled with a graph database. From our graph schema in *Figure 6.2*, we can see that we want to store data on customer purchases, where each customer has a unique ID, a name, and an address.

Of course, we don't have real customers interacting with an application to store data on for this example, but we can mock up some fake customers and simulate the queries they would send to our database. In a real software development team, creating fake customers and customer interactions might be part of a testing framework for a new data pipeline.

These types of query transactions are, in practice, often handled by a publish/subscribe messaging service (pub/sub) or similar, which in turn is often managed with a cloud computing service. These transactions typically take place between multiple machines, which has implications on machine setup, security, and permissions, which is an entire subject in itself, the field of DevOps. For our purposes, in this chapter, our fake customers will be generated in Python, and make purchases by sending queries from Python to Neo4j. This will all take place on a local machine, meaning we can focus on graph data modeling and network analysis.

Let's begin by creating a customer. In our schema, a customer has a productID, name, and address. Python has some nice tools for generating fake data, which we will lean on in this chapter by using the `Faker` library.

`Faker` comes bundled with a variety of methods to simulate different types of data, from simple things such as telephone numbers to entire sets of fake personal information. For our purposes, we need to generate names and addresses to give to our customers.

In the upcoming steps, we will generate fake data to use in our graph use cases going forward:

1. To import Faker, we import the `Faker` class from the `faker` (lowercase) library. We then create an instance of `Faker` by assigning it to a variable, here named *fake*. We can optionally set the random seed of the `Faker` library, so that our randomly generated data is consistent between Python script runs:

    ```
    from faker import Faker
    fake = Faker()
    Faker.seed(0)
    ```

2. We can now use our instantiated *fake* object to generate names and addresses, by simply calling the `name()` and `address()` methods of the class:

    ```
    name = fake.name()
    address = fake.address()
    print(name)
    print(address)
    ```

    Printing our results shows some realistic name and address data. You may notice from the address that this data is US-localized, which is the default setting. It is possible to change the locale of the `Faker` library if needed, for which you should consult the `Faker` documentation.

3. Now that we can create fake data, let's attach this data to a customer. A sensible way to do this is to create a `Customer` class, which holds a `customerID`, `name`, and `address` attribute for each person. We can use the `__init__()` method to assign attributes to each customer

when it is instantiated. We will pass a unique customerID to each customer, and use `Faker` to generate a name and address for the `Customer` object when it is created:

```
class Customer:
  def __init__(self, customerID):
    self.customerID = customerID
    self.name = fake.name()
    self.address = fake.address()
```

4. Let's test our new class by generating a customer. For testing purposes, we can create a customer with an arbitrary ID, `9999`, and print the attributes of our `Customer` object:

```
new_customer = Customer(9999)
print(new_customer.customerID)
print(new_customer.name)
print(new_customer.address)
```

5. Each time the `Customer` class is called, the `__init__()` method will automatically generate our customers' names and addresses. With our new class, we now have the ability to quickly generate customers to populate our graph database.

6. To pass this customer information to our graph database, and for the rest of our pipeline, we will need to access Neo4j from Python, as we did in *Chapter 5, Working with Graph Databases*. When instantiated, this class establishes a connection to Neo4j using the credentials passed to it. It can also establish a session with Neo4j and run a query with the `query()` method, as well as closing the connection with `close()`. This is the same `Neo4jConnect` class we used in the previous chapter, so for more information on connecting Python to Neo4j, please consult *Chapter 5, Working with Graph Databases*. Albeit we have also included a custom package entitled Graphtastic where you can import this class quickly using `from graphtastic.database.neo4j import Neo4jConnect`. For transparency, the full implementation of this connection method is contained again in the following block:

```
from neo4j import GraphDatabase
class Neo4jConnect:
    def __init__(self, uri, user, password):
        self.driver = GraphDatabase.driver(uri,
                auth=(user, password))
    def close(self):
        self.driver.close()
    def query(self, query):
        session = self.driver.session()
        result = session.run(query)
        return result
```

7. We are now ready to generate and add customers to Neo4j. This can be thought of as a customer *signing up* to our online retail app or website. We next need the ability to pass our generated

customer data to the graph database. To do this, we can create a method, `add_customer()`. The method will take a `Customer` object, `c`, and an authenticated Neo4j connection, made with our `Neo4jConnect` class. With these parameters, we can create a Cypher query to add a customer, substituting node attributes for the attributes of our customer, using `c.customerID`, `c.name`, and `c.address`. This is all handled with Python's `f` string functionality, wrapping around a simple `MERGE` function. The additional curly braces used are to escape `f` string behavior in places, as Cypher syntax for specifying node attributes uses the `{ }` characters too. Looking at our graph schema, we also specify that the `customerID` attribute of our new node should be an integer, using Cypher's `toInteger()`. The assembled query can then be called using `connection.query()`:

```python
def add_customer(c, connection):
    query = f'MERGE (:Customer {{customerID: toInteger({c.customerID}), ' \
        f'name: "{c.name}", ' \
        f'address: "{c.address}"}})'
    connection.query(query)
```

8. Let's give this new method a try, by creating another example customer. Using our `Customer` class, we can generate a new `Customer` object with the attributes we need. As with all Cypher queries to Neo4j from Python, we then establish a connection with `Neo4jConnect`, before calling our new `add_customer` method with our generated `Customer` and our Neo4j connection, which handles writing a node to our graph database. Finally, we close the session with `connection.close()`:

```python
test_customer = Customer(9999)
connection = Neo4jConnect('bolt://localhost:7687',
    'admin', 'testpython')
add_customer(test_customer, connection)
connection.close()
```

9. Back in the Neo4j Browser, we can check whether the node was added correctly in a number of ways, but for something more visual, let's open up Neo4j Desktop for the `Store DB` database that we have written to. Using some very simple Cypher to match all nodes of type `Customer`, we can return our customers to the browser:

```
MATCH (c:Customer) RETURN c
```

We should see that one node is returned. Clicking on that `Customer` node should show the node properties on the right of the Neo4j Browser window, confirming that our attributes have been set correctly. Up next, we can now add customers to our graph, but at present they remain disconnected from the rest of the nodes in our database. According to our schema, we need to create relationships to represent product purchases, but we still need a process for simulating these transactions.

10. Let's next create a method for adding a customer purchase, in a similar way to how we defined `add_customer()`. We can name our method `add_purchase`, and this time, we will require more parameters in order to model a purchase correctly. The function will take a customer, c, a product ID, the current time, and a Neo4j connection. We will again handle the assembly of a Cypher query with f strings. When a customer chooses a product and purchases it, to model this in our graph, we need to `MATCH` on the `customerID` attribute of the correct `Customer` node and `MATCH` on the `productID` of the matching `Product` node. These IDs are appropriate to match on as we have defined them as unique in our schema – no two customers or two products should share the same ID. The last step in our query is to `MERGE` an edge between our aliased `Customer` and `Product` nodes, c and p. We use a `PURCHASED` relationship to describe this edge and stamp the `time` parameter on the `datetime` edge attribute. Again, the last step is to send the query to our Neo4j database with `connection.query()`:

```
def add_purchase(c, productID, time, connection):
    query = f'MATCH (c:Customer {{customerID: toInteger({c.
customerID})}}) ' \
        f'MATCH (p:Product {{productID: toInteger({productID})}})
' \
        f'MERGE (c)-[:PURCHASED {{datetime:"{time}"}}]->(p)'

    connection.query(query)
```

11. Now we can test the behavior of `add_purchase()`. Let's use our already created `Customer` object with ID 9999, which is also already present in the database, and simulate a purchase. We can find a product for the customer to purchase in the `products.csv` raw data, or in Neo4j – for this example, we will use the node with `productID` 1010.

12. First, we import `datetime` from `datetime`, in order to access the current time at the point at which the purchase is made. We then establish a connection to the database. We use our `add_purchase()` method, and pass it our existing `test_customer`, along with `productID` 1010, the current time with `datetime.now()`, and the Neo4j connection. The addition of the edge will be handled by our function, so we can finish up by closing the connection:

```
from datetime import datetime
connection = Neo4jConnect('bolt://localhost:7687',
    'admin', 'testpython')
add_purchase(test_customer, 1010, datetime.now(),
    connection)
connection.close()
```

13. As we did before, let's go into the Neo4j Browser for the `Store DB` database and see if we can find our newly created edge. We can again run some Cypher to find edges between `Customer` and `Product` nodes that have the edge type PURCHASED, and RETURN the nodes we matched:

```
MATCH (c:Customer)-[:PURCHASED]->(p:Product) RETURN c, p
```

If the edge was added correctly, in the browser, we should see the two nodes connected by a `PURCHASED` relationship. As we did with the newly added `Customer` node, we can check that the `datetime` attribute was correctly added to our new edge by clicking on it and examining its properties on the right-hand side of the Browser window.

14. In our graph schema, we noted that customers may want to make the same purchase twice and that this behavior should be represented by multiple edges between the same pair of `Customer` and `Product` nodes. We should make sure that this behavior is possible with our Python pipeline methods. To do this, let's run the same code again, where `test_customer` purchases the product with ID `1010` a second time:

```
connection = Neo4jConnect('bolt://localhost:7687',
    'admin', 'testpython')
add_purchase(test_customer, 1010, datetime.now(),
    connection)
connection.close()
```

15. When our code has run, let's check that a new, separate relationship between our `Product` and `Customer` nodes has been added by running another Cypher query in the Neo4j Browser. We can either use the previous query we ran to visually display two edges between our nodes, or run a query to print customer and product details to a table, along with the `datetime` of any relationships between the nodes:

```
MATCH (c:Customer)-[purchase:PURCHASED]->(p:Product)
RETURN c.name, p.name, purchase.datetime
```

We should see that two edges between this pair of nodes have been successfully added. In `add_purchase()`, we use `MERGE` to add the edge, and we learned in *Chapter 5*, *Working with Graph Databases*, that Cypher's `MERGE` function won't create a new node or edge if one matching the pattern specified already exists. In our graph, we can allow multiple edges by specifying `datetime` in our `MERGE` pattern. Because no edge with the exact date and time in milliseconds already exists between our pair of nodes, the pattern is not matched, and a new edge is created.

16. Our tests have shown us that `add_customer()` and `add_purchase()` are working as intended, and successfully writing customer data to our Neo4j database. Let's quickly clean up the test customers and purchases we added to our graph before going any further. To do this, we can `MATCH` customer nodes specifically, preventing any of our product data from being deleted. We can then `DETACH` any relationships from them, and `DELETE` them from the database. This can be run from the Neo4j Browser:

```
MATCH (c:Customer) DETACH DELETE c
```

17. With our custom methods set up, we now have everything in place to simulate the basic behavior of a customer using our application. However, in real scenarios, there are often many customers interacting with online retailers in a short space of time. We can next use the Python functions

we have already written to mock up many users interacting with an application, and store data on these interactions in our graph database.

18. Earlier, we tested our `add_purchase()` method with a hardcoded `product ID, 1010`. However, if we want to simulate purchases for many customers, we can assume they will likely want to buy different products. To begin, although less realistic, let's assume that customers buy products at random. Here, we're aiming to test the capacity of our pipeline to handle more than one query in quick succession, rather than realistic behavior, at present.

19. Let's briefly define a method for retrieving products from Neo4j. Because, at first, our customers will make purchases at random, we only need product IDs from our `Product` nodes in Neo4j. To get the IDs, we can first write a Cypher query inside a method, `get_product_ids()`, using a MATCH statement. In the same query, we can then RETURN the product IDs for each node. Next, we run the query using `connection.query()`. The result is returned as a list of dictionaries, each with one key-value pair, with the key `productID`. So, we can use a list comprehension to extract the product IDs from each dictionary, and add them to a list:

```
def get_product_ids(connection):
        query = 'MATCH (p:Product) RETURN p.productID as
productID'
    result = connection.query(query).data()
    result = [product['productID'] for product in result]
    return result
```

20. We will make sure `get_product_ids()` works, by opening a Neo4j connection and calling the method:

```
connection = Neo4jConnect('bolt://localhost:7687',
    'admin', 'testpython')
product_ids = get_product_ids(connection)
connection.close()
print(product_ids)
print(len(product_ids))
```

Our `print` statements should show a list of IDs, and that that list has 27 elements, equal to the number of data rows in `products.csv`.

21. Now we can generate lots of customers that will sign up to our online retail application and make purchases. We can create instances of the `Customer` class in a list comprehension, which will each have data generated for them by `Faker`. If we do this over the *range* of `10000` to `10100`, we will generate 100 customers with unique customer IDs:

```
customers = [Customer(customerID) for customerID in range(10000,
10100)]
```

22. Now we can add all of our customers to our graph database in quick succession, using a `for` loop. We can create a connection and make a call to `add_customer()` for every customer in our list:

```
for customer in customers:
    connection = Neo4jConnect('bolt://localhost:7687',
        'admin', 'testpython')
    add_customer(customer, connection)
    connection.close()
```

Note that we open and close a Neo4j connection each time to avoid errors, where data will fail to be written to the database. Should you try to open many connections without closing them, the connection pool the Neo4j driver maintains will be exhausted, and the next session that requests a connection will time out, resulting in errors.

With our customers added, we can next add some purchases to the graph. At present, let's add purchases at random to begin populating our graph database with edges between customers and products.

23. To do this, we can use Python's inbuilt `random` library. For each customer in our list, we can randomly sample a product from the `product_ids` list we created earlier by querying Neo4j. We can then open connections and use our `add_purcahse()` method to create edges in our graph that resemble customer purchases:

```
import random
for customer in customers:
    product = random.choice(product_ids)
    connection = Neo4jConnect('bolt://localhost:7687',
        'admin', 'testpython')
    add_purchase(customer, product, datetime.now(),
        connection)
    connection.close()
```

We have now added customer data to our graph, which gives us a good starting point for considering how we might recommend further purchases to our online retailer's users next. At this point, we could take a look at some of the customer data visually in the Neo4j Browser, by querying subsets of the graph, or, for example, counting nodes and paths.

24. Additionally, we could also run the previous loops a few times to generate more customers and purchases. If you want to monitor the population of the graph in real time, consider slowing down the loops Python is running by using the `sleep()` method from Python's `time` library, and adding calls to `sleep()` into the logic. For example, the following would delay Python's execution of code by one second:

```
from time import sleep
sleep(1)
```

By using `sleep()`, as the script runs, you can switch to the Neo4j Browser and see the numbers of nodes and edges increase gradually. Using `f` strings to assemble Cypher queries in Python is a powerful way to generalize graph database processing. Of course, similar behavior is available in other languages frequently used in data pipeline construction, such as Java, though Python is a good place to start when thinking about the design elements required by our processes and schema.

At this point of creating our newly defined classes and methods, we have everything we need to store data on customer interactions with our online retail application. We could stop here, knowing that we're capturing data correctly, but that wouldn't be making the most of the graph data model we have set up. Instead, let's next look at how we can use the data we've collected to drive further customer interactions.

Making product recommendations

Often, when using an online retail application or service, you will find that products are recommended to you. This can be driven by browser cookies, products that you have viewed already, or previous purchases. In our case, we have information on previous product purchases, so we will use that data to make suggestions.

Even with the choice of using prior purchases to inform our recommendations, the decision to recommend a specific product to you can be made in many different ways. If a customer has purchased an item from a specific brand, would they be interested in owning more products from the same brand? Or, should we recommend a product to a customer based on other customers behavior?

In the following sections, we will design and test a few different recommendation methods, and this starts in the next section by looking at product recommendations by brand.

Product recommendations by brand

As we briefly discussed in the *Schema design* section, we can think of our product information as the *backbone* of our graph structure. It contains categorical information on types of products and brands and can be thought of as a kind of product ontology. We can exploit the information in this ontology to create a simple method for recommending products to customers, based on their previous purchases.

To do this, we can make the assumption that a consumer is more likely to be interested in purchasing a product from a brand that they have purchased a product from in the past. We will cover this in the next steps of this section:

1. Let's define a new method, named `rec_by_brand()`. Similar to our existing methods, this will again take c, a `Customer` object, and *connection*, an authenticated Neo4j session. In this function, we can write a Cypher query that makes use of several `MATCH` statements.

2. We first match the customer represented by c, by looking for their customer ID. In the same statement, we find the products our customer in question has already purchased by matching a PURCHASED edge to a Product node. The alias p is assigned to these products, and we use this node to find these products brands through HAS_BRANDS edges. These brands are in turn aliased to b, and our last pattern matching step is to use MATCH to traverse back onto Products associated with these brands, r. At this point, we need to make sure that we don't recommend the same product as the user has already purchased, which will have the same brand. To accomplish this, we add a WHERE clause, specifying that we only want results where the Customer node does not already have a relationship to the recommended Product nodes. To finish the query, we RETURN the product ID node attribute of nodes aliased to r, renaming it to product ID. We also use DISTINCT to produce a set of results, ensuring no duplicate products are recommended. In the same method, we run the query and get the returned data by calling data() and assigning it to *result*, before using a list comprehension to access each product ID in the returned list of dictionaries, assigning them to a list, and returning it:

```
def rec_by_brand(c, connection):
    query = f'MATCH (c:Customer {{customerID: toInteger({c.
customerID})}})' \
            '-[:PURCHASED]->(p:Product)' \
            'MATCH (p)-[:HAS_BRAND]->(b:Brand)' \
            'MATCH (b)<-[:HAS_BRAND]-(r:Product)' \
            'WHERE NOT (c)-[:PURCHASED]->(r)' \
            'RETURN DISTINCT r.productID as productID'

    result = connection.query(query).data()
    result = [product['productID'] for product in result]

    return result
```

3. Now we can test out the method, and get some results for a single customer. Once again, we open a connection with Neo4jConnect, and choose a single customer in our list to pass as a parameter to rec_by_brand():

```
connection = Neo4jConnect('bolt://localhost:7687', 'admin',
'testpython')
brand_recommendations = rec_by_brand(customers[10], connection)
connection.close()
print(brand_recommendations)
```

4. This should print a list of product IDs to recommend to the specific customer. At this point, we could validate this further by opening the Neo4j Browser and running a query to find paths between this customer and products with the same brand as previously purchased products, using similar logic to the query in our rec_by_brand() method:

```
MATCH (c:Customer {customerID:10010})-[:PURCHASED]->(p:Product)
MATCH (p)-[:HAS_BRAND]->(b:Brand)
```

```
MATCH (b)<-[:HAS_BRAND]-(r:Product)
WHERE NOT (c)-[:PURCHASED]->(r)
RETURN c, p, b, r
```

Instead of returning product IDs for recommendation, in this query we return the `Customer`, `Brand`, and `Product` nodes we have matched, and can validate that the paths between them are as expected. We can adjust the `RETURN` statement to filter to just the recommended products or other types of nodes of interest.

5. When we're happy that our recommendations by brand are functioning correctly, we can perform these for all customers, and simulate purchases based on these recommendations. For each `Customer` object in our customer list, we can make recommendations with `rec_by_brand()`, and assign these to a list. We specify a condition that `brand_recommendations` must not be of length 0, as we cannot choose a product to recommend to a new customer with this method that has no purchase history. An empty list would also cause the next step to fail, where we again use the `random.choice()` method to choose a recommended product from our list for a customer to buy. We again use the `add_purchase()` function to create an edge in our graph between our `Customer` and their newly purchased product, based on our recommendation:

```
for customer in customers:
    connection = Neo4jConnect('bolt://localhost:7687', 'admin',
'testpython')
    brand_recommendations = rec_by_brand(customer, connection)
    connection.close()
    if len(brand_recommendations) != 0:
        product = random.choice(brand_recommendations)
        connection = Neo4jConnect('bolt://localhost:7687',
'admin', 'testpython')
        add_purchase(customer, product, datetime.now(),
connection)
        connection.close()
```

6. Of course, we may want to recommend products through other simple methods, for example, based on the type or subtype of previous purchases. This would be a case of changing the path-matching logic in `rec_by_brand()` to traverse different types of relationships, to different types of nodes. We may also want to prevent products being recommended based on whether they are the same product type as one already purchased, assuming that a customer is less likely to make a purchase of something they already have. In the Neo4j Browser, the Cypher to start designing this process might look something like this, making use of pattern matching to find product types, and negating matching these types for recommendations, using an additional clause in the `WHERE` statement:

```
MATCH (c:Customer {customerID:10010})-[:PURCHASED]->(p:Product)
MATCH (p)-[:HAS_TYPE]->(st:Type)
MATCH (p)-[:HAS_BRAND]->(b:Brand)
```

```
MATCH (b)<-[:HAS_BRAND]-(r:Product)
WHERE NOT (c)-[:PURCHASED]->(r) AND (r)-[:HAS_TYPE]->(st)
RETURN DISTINCT r
```

Once satisfied this logic was working correctly, we could update the `rec_by_brand()` method to use this logic. For now, though, let's move on to another type of product recommendation commonly used by real online retailers. This will be covered in the next section.

Drawing on other customers purchases

Recommending a product based on brand is a simple but sensible way to use our graph ontology to drive further customer purchases. However, it is not the only method employed by online retailers to promote sales and only uses part of the data we have available in our graph database.

By this point, we have been collecting lots of data on our simulated customer purchases, and we can use this data in a more holistic way to find products of interest to our customers. Consider a customer that has made a purchase in the past through our web application. This will have been stored as an edge in our graph, alongside edges representing other customers purchasing the same product. By traversing these relationships with other customers, we can find the other products that customers buying the initial product went on to purchase, and recommend them. This type of recommendation relies on the assumption that customers are more likely to buy a similar set of products to one another than they are to purchase items at random.

The following steps show how we can achieve this:

1. Let's write a method to recommend a product to a customer using other customer purchases, named `rec_by_copurchase()`. The structure of this method is similar to that of `rec_by_brand()`, with the Cypher modified to traverse back along the PURCHASED edges from the products our customer in question has purchased to other customers. We use a WHERE clause to prevent traversal back to the original customer we are making a recommendation to. We can then go from customers with the same purchase history, aliased to c2, to other products they have purchased. We also make sure that we don't recommend a product that our customer, c, has already purchased, again using WHERE. The remainder of this method is the same as for `rec_by_brand()`, and returns a list of product IDs:

   ```
   def rec_by_copurchase(c, connection):

       query = f'MATCH (c:Customer {{customerID: toInteger({c.
   customerID})}})' \
                   '-[:PURCHASED]->(p:Product)' \
                   'MATCH (p)<-[:PURCHASED]-(c2:Customer)' \
                   'WHERE c2 <> c ' \
                   'MATCH (c2)-[:PURCHASED]->(r:Product)' \
                   'WHERE p <> r ' \
                   'RETURN DISTINCT r.productID as productID'
   ```

```
result = connection.query(query).data()
result = [product['productID'] for product in result]
return result
```

2. Let's briefly check that this method functions for a single customer, before making recommendations to lots of customers at once:

```
connection = Neo4jConnect('bolt://localhost:7687', 'admin',
'testpython')
copurchase_recommendations = rec_by_copurchase(customers[10],
connection)
connection.close()
print(copurchase_recommendations)
```

This should result in a few product recommendations for the customer with ID 10010, printed to the console.

3. With our method for co-purchase-based recommendations set up, let's do as we did with brand-based recommendations and create purchases for each customer in our database. Again, here, we use a `for` loop to iterate through our list of 100 customers, calling `add_purchase()` for each recommended product:

```
for customer in customers:
    connection = Neo4jConnect('bolt://localhost:7687', 'admin',
'testpython')
    copurchase_recommendations = rec_by_copurchase(customer,
connection)
    connection.close()
    if len(copurchase_recommendations) != 0:
        product = random.choice(copurchase_recommendations)
        connection = Neo4jConnect(
            'bolt://localhost:7687', 'admin',
            'testpython')
        add_purchase(customer, product,
            datetime.now(), connection)
        connection.close()
```

There are many more ways we could use similar path-based methods to recommend our products to users of our online retail application. Choosing an appropriate set of methods, in practice, would probably be done with A/B (a test of two different solutions) software testing, and would depend significantly on customer research in the specific retail sector of interest. For one more example, let's look at a different type of method that could be employed in recommendation systems.

Using similarity scores to recommend products

There is one last method for recommending products that we will consider in this chapter, which leans more heavily on Python and its interface with our Neo4j database. The previous system of recommending products based on joint customer purchases makes use of customer data and might be used after a purchase is made on our retail application, to point the user toward additional products of interest. However, we can extend the idea that customers are likely to purchase similar sets of products by looking at overall purchase history similarity. This type of general recommendation, based on sets of past purchases, would more likely be delivered to a customer on the home page of our application.

To compare customer purchases, we can look at similarity measures. These measures return a score based on the similarity between the elements in two sets. Several methods, each stemming from set theory, can be employed to calculate the similarity between groups of nodes. Examples are overlap similarity, the dice coefficient, and Jaccard similarity due to its ease of implementation and explainability.

Jaccard similarity is defined as the intersection between two sets, divided by the union of the same sets. Essentially, this results in a value from 0 to 1, where 0 represents no similarity, and a score of 1 means two sets are identical. We can use this measure to find similar customers, in terms of their purchases. We will be defining our own simple implementation for the calculation of Jaccard similarity, but more information and examples are available in the *scikit-learn* documentation.

For our purposes, when similar customers are found, with a high but not perfect overlap in product purchases, we can identify the differences remaining between their sets of purchases and recommend these to a customer. By now, our database contains lots of purchases for our 100 customers, so taking full advantage of the data available to us, let's go ahead and implement the final recommendation method for this chapter in Python. These steps will show how we can use Jaccard similarity in our use case:

1. Calculating the Jaccard similarity between customers purchases is a little more involved than the previous methods, and while Cypher excels in path-based calculations, Python is a more suitable language for similarity calculations. Due to this, let's first define a simple method to extract all purchases for a given customer ID, c_id, using similar steps to what we used for rec_by_brand() and rec_by_copurchase():

```
def get_customer_purchases(c_id, connection):
    query = f'MATCH (c:Customer {{customerID: toInteger({c_
id})}})' \
            '-[:PURCHASED]->(p:Product)' \
            'RETURN DISTINCT p.productID as productID'
    result = connection.query(query).data()
    result = [product['productID'] for product in result]
    return result
```

2. Calling this method for one customer should return a list of product IDs they have purchased:

```
connection = Neo4jConnect('bolt://localhost:7687',
    'admin', 'testpython')
purchases = get_customer_purchases(
    customers[10].customerID, connection)
connection.close()
print(purchases)
```

3. To make sure this is correct, we could compare the printed list to that found by a simple, equivalent query in the Neo4j Browser:

```
MATCH (c:Customer {customerID:10010})-[:PURCHASED]-(p:Product)
RETURN DISTINCT p.productID as productID
```

4. Now that `get_customer_purchases()` is working, we can get all customer purchases by using a dictionary comprehension over all customers in our list of `Customer` objects. For every customer, we call our method, and pass our Neo4j connection:

```
connection = Neo4jConnect('bolt://localhost:7687',
    'admin', 'testpython')
all_purchases = {customer.customerID:
        get_customer_purchases(customer.customerID,
        connection)
                 for customer in customers}

print(all_purchases)
```

This results in a dictionary with keys containing customer IDs, and values containing lists of product IDs that a customer has purchased.

5. We next need to define a function to calculate the Jaccard similarity between these sets of purchased products. We can do this according to the standard implementation, which requires two sets, so first, the parameters `list1` and `list2` are converted to Python `sets`. Next, we find the `intersection` between `set1` and `set2`, as well as finding the `union`. Finally, the Jaccard similarity is calculated by dividing the length of the set's intersection by the length of the set's `union`, and we return the value:

```
def jaccard_similarity(list1, list2):
    set1 = set(list1)
    set2 = set(list2)
    intersection = set1.intersection(set2)
    union = set1.union(set2)
    jaccard = len(intersection) / len(union)
    return jaccard
```

6. Jaccard similarity can be calculated by hand easily for simple sets, so we can ensure that our method is functioning as expected by creating some test data and using `assert` to check we get back the correct similarity scores:

```
list1 = [1, 2, 3, 4]
list2 = [5, 6, 7, 8]
list3 = [1, 2]
assert jaccard_similarity(list1, list1) == 1
assert jaccard_similarity(list1, list2) == 0
assert jaccard_similarity(list1, list3) == 0.5
```

7. With our `jaccard_similarity()` method defined and tested, we are ready to calculate the similarities between pairs of our customers purchase histories. For this, we need a list of all pairs of our customers IDs, and a quick way to get this is by using Python's inbuilt `itertools` library. If we first get all keys containing customer IDs from our `all_purchases` dictionary, we can then find all unique pairs with `itertools.combinations()` by passing our customer IDs and the value 2, which specifies to return combinations of two elements only:

```
import itertools
customer_ids = list(all_purchases.keys())
print(customer_ids)
customer_pairs = list(itertools.combinations(
    customer_ids, 2))
print(customer_pairs[:10])
```

Now, with our `customer_pairs` list, let's calculate Jaccard similarity for the customer's purchases using another dictionary comprehension. This comprehension will go through every pair in `customer_pairs`, using the values of each pair as keys to access the purchase list values stored in the `all_purchases` dictionary. These lists are then passed to our `jaccard_similarity()` method. This results in a further dictionary with customer pairs as keys, and similarity scores as values, which we will name `similarity`:

```
similarity = {pair: jaccard_similarity(all_purchases[
    pair[0]], all_purchases[pair[1]]) for pair in
    customer_pairs}
```

8. Let's look at the distribution of scores for our customer pairs in the `similarity` dictionary. We can use the `collections` library and the `Counter` method for this, as we have done in several previous chapters, and print a quick view of the distribution of our dictionary's values:

```
from collections import Counter
grouped_similiarities = Counter(similarity.values())
print(grouped_similiarities)
```

9. At this point, depending on how many purchases and customers your database contains, you will have differing distributions. However, there are likely to be some pairs of customers with a Jaccard similarity of 1, meaning that their purchases are identical. In this scenario, we wouldn't

be able to sensibly recommend a product to either customer, as they both already have every product the other customer has. There are also likely to be customer pairs who have a similarity score of 0. It would also be difficult to make recommendations in this case, as a score of zero indicates no overlap in purchase history, and therefore no sign that one customer would particularly benefit from products that the second customer has purchased, and vice versa.

Instead, we want to focus on customers who have some overlap in their purchase history, which hints that there might be a reason one customer may purchase a particular set of products and that the second may want to do the same for a similar reason. For example, this may apply if a set of products works well together, such as a TV and soundbar. Or, simply if two customers have a similar taste in brands or the style of products. The beauty of using similarity to recommend products here is that we don't need to know the underlying reason for customers having similar purchases; it is still more likely that they will be interested in the products a similar customer has purchased than it is that they will choose to purchase a separate, randomly chosen item.

With this in mind, we want to target similar, but not identical purchase histories, and use these histories to recommend further product purchases. To this end, we will define a Jaccard similarity threshold, based on the results of the similarity analysis we've carried out. Let's bring all of this together and define one last method that could be employed in a pipeline to recommend products to customers based on their similarity.

10. Our new method will be named `rec_by_similarity()`, and take two customer IDs, c1, and c2. Part of our process will be adding new purchases, but our existing `add_purchase()` method takes `Customer` objects as a parameter. So, we should redefine the `add_purchase()` method to accept customer IDs, as follows, and name it `add_purchase_id()`:

```
def add_purchase_id(c_id, productID, time, connection):
    query = f'MATCH (c:Customer {{customerID: toInteger({c_id})}})' \
        f'MATCH (p:Product {{productID: toInteger({productID})}})' \
        f'MERGE (c)-[:PURCHASED {{datetime:"{time}"}}]->(p)'
    connection.query(query)
```

11. Let's return to defining `rec_by_similarity()`, and look at another parameter we'll need, `threshold`. Our threshold will target customers above a certain level of Jaccard similarity. Here, we will set it to 0.7, but this can be changed to target customers with a range of similarities:

```
threshold = 0.7
```

12. Now, with our parameters planned out, we're ready to define the `rec_by_similarity()` method. We start by finding customer purchases from both c1 and c2, by reusing the `get_customer_purchases()` method we defined earlier. Then, using the returned product lists, we calculate the Jaccard similarity between them, with `jaccard_similarity()`. Next, we can check whether the similarity is above a certain threshold, as well as checking that the two sets of products are not identical, with an `if` statement. If the Jaccard similarity value

fits this criteria, we can continue, and find the products for both customers that they have not already purchased, using two list comprehensions, and store these in the variables p1_recs and p2_recs. Now all that is left to do is to simulate purchases of our retailer's products based on these recommendations, by calling our add_purchase_id() method for each new product in both p1_recs and p2_recs:

```python
def rec_by_similarity(c1, c2, threshold, connection):
    p1 = get_customer_purchases(c1, connection)
    p2 = get_customer_purchases(c2, connection)
    similarity = jaccard_similarity(p1, p2)
    if similarity >= threshold and similarity != 1:
        p1_recs = [p for p in p2 if p not in p1]
        p2_recs = [p for p in p1 if p not in p2]
        for p in p1_recs:
            add_purchase_id(c1, p, datetime.now(), connection)
        for p in p2_recs:
            add_purchase_id(c2, p, datetime.now(), connection)
```

13. With everything set up for our new type of recommendations, we just need to call rec_by_similarity() to make similarity-based recommendations for all of our customers, as we did for our previous recommendation methods:

```python
for pair in customer_pairs:
    connection = Neo4jConnect('bolt://localhost:7687', 'admin',
'testpython')
    rec_by_similarity(pair[0], pair[1], 0.7, connection)
    connection.close()
```

To explore the effect of this type of recommendation on our stored customer data, at this point, it may be interesting to open the Neo4j Browser and run some simple queries. With many different recommendation systems in place, an online retailer might pit different systems against each other in A/B testing, and monitor how they drive purchases. These systems represent just a few recommendation methods possible with a graph data model representing customer and product data.

This brings this chapter to a close. We will extend the work we have done here to look at refactoring considerations to make when setting up your schema, and also to look at evolving schema. This chapter has been a blast and we have enjoyed putting it together, as this is how many of our pipelines we have set up function, that is, with the interface between Neo4j and Python – let's call this a happy marriage.

Summary

We started this chapter by looking at design considerations for a graph database pipeline, and we also refamiliarized ourselves with how to set up a Neo4j graph database. Our use case for this chapter was creating a graph database for retail, and we designed a schema and pipeline. With our schema considerations mapped out and considered, we then looked at how you can add static data and introduced fake data to simulate customer interactions. Obviously, this would not be fake in practice but served as a good way to test out if our desired schema functioned the way we would want it to in a production environment.

The ultimate aim of this chapter was to set up a schema that would enable us to make product recommendations based on similar products customers buy. The first step was to get refamiliarized with Cypher (Neo4j's query language – similar to SQL) and Python for working with this data, followed by making recommendations by brand. This then led on to recommendations based on other customers purchases, and finally, using Jaccard similarity to select products that a customer might be interested in, based on their purchase history.

These pipelines are something you will need to get familiar with as a graph data scientist, as these are how production-grade systems are developed and deployed. In our experience, getting the schema right is a crucial step to enforcing good data quality. With the tools and approaches you have learned here, you are now ready to think about how you might set up a schema to solve your business needs.

This chapter reinforced the aim of creating a flexible schema that will function as your data grows. We will draw on this again in the next chapter, when we look at evolving schemas, and refactoring based on changing application requirements.

7
Refactoring and Evolving Schemas

This chapter will spend some time discussing what makes a good schema and approaches to take if you need to refactor or change your schema. We will explore what and how entities can change in a graph database. This will then lead us to why you need to consider evolving schemas. Here, the focus will be on making your schema bulletproof when it comes to its evolution.

Following on from this, we will present a use case of Twitter circles, which will look at setting up your interface between Neo4j and Python (this is something we have extensively covered in other chapters), adding constraints to the Cypher queries we will write to build the graph data model in Neo4j, and some considerations you need to make pre-schema change concerning node and edgelist relationships. Then, we will change the schema with our hypothetical needs, without disrupting a *live* service. Finally, we will reflect on why the design of evolving schemas is pivotal for successful graph data pipelines.

To summarize, the main areas we will cover in this chapter are as follows:

- Refactoring reasoning
- Effectively evolving
- Putting the changes into development

Technical requirements

We will be using Jupyter Notebook to run our coding exercises, which requires `python>=3.8.0`, along with the following package, which will need to be installed with the `pip install` command into your environment:

- `neo4j==5.5.0`

For this chapter, you will also need Neo4j Desktop installed. Please see the *Technical requirements* section of *Chapter 5, Working with Graph Databases*, if Neo4j is not yet installed, as it will be needed to follow along with the tutorials in this chapter.

All notebooks, with the coding exercises, are available at the following GitHub link: `https://github.com/PacktPublishing/Graph-Data-Modeling-in-Python/tree/main/CH07`.

Refactoring reasoning

As an organization grows and develops, its needs can change, including its data storage requirements. Data that is sufficient to operate a service or process can change over time, and it often pays to plan for changing requirements in advance. Managing change in database systems varies in difficulty depending on your current schema and database type, and in this chapter, we will discuss and demonstrate the advantages of using a graph data model when dealing with evolving data structures.

In this section, you will learn about the tools to help you prepare for refactoring effectively. This will include changes in relational schema, the impacts these can have on substantial schema rework, and what you should consider at the point of design, relating to evolving schemas that can effectively handle these changes.

Change in relational and graph databases

In more traditional relational database systems, adding new types of data can sometimes be challenging, depending on the current database schema. We explored this concept briefly in *Chapter 1, Introducing Graphs in the Real World*, comparing the flexibility of relational and graph databases, but we will revisit it in this section.

In the case where a new descriptive feature of a single entity is added, things are simple. For example, we could have a relational database containing a table of data about our customers with names, dates of birth, and so on. If we want to start storing their current shipping addresses, this will simply involve adding a new column to the existing table, as there is a one-to-one relationship between customers and their current shipping address on file.

In a graph database, this change would be equally simple. In a standard customer-based schema, we might have customers represented as nodes, with their information stored as node attributes. The current shipping address could be added as an additional node attribute.

However, things begin to get more complex for relational databases, depending on the relationships between data points. Imagine now that we want to store multiple shipping addresses for each customer in our system so that a customer can choose between them. In our relational database, one column will no longer be sufficient to describe this data. Each customer can have any number of addresses, so creating a column in our customers table for each address is not a viable option either. In this case, we wouldn't know how many columns to create, and even if we did, customers with a large number of addresses on file would likely be uncommon, resulting in columns containing many null values for all other customers.

Instead, adding multiple addresses per customer would involve refactoring the relational database. A typical solution would be to create a new table, containing one row per customer-address pair, and removing the Address column from our main customers table. This maintains the relationship between the unique customer and their address but involves replication of the customer ID (or another uniquely identifying feature) between two tables.

The following figure shows the impact an evolving schema can have on a traditional relational database schema:

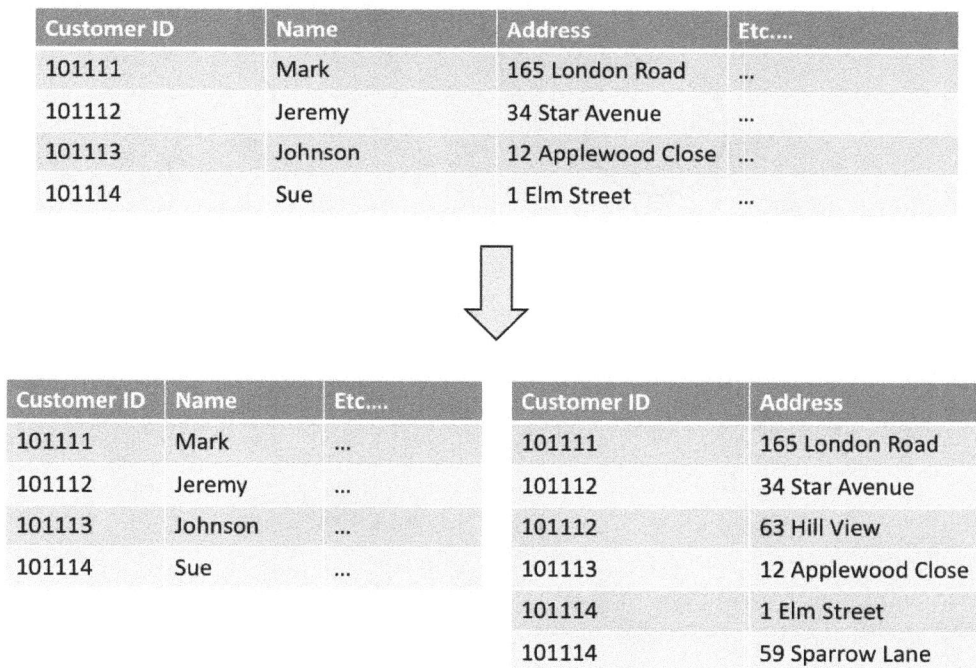

Customer ID	Name	Address	Etc....
101111	Mark	165 London Road	...
101112	Jeremy	34 Star Avenue	...
101113	Johnson	12 Applewood Close	...
101114	Sue	1 Elm Street	...

Customer ID	Name	Etc....
101111	Mark	...
101112	Jeremy	...
101113	Johnson	...
101114	Sue	...

Customer ID	Address
101111	165 London Road
101112	34 Star Avenue
101112	63 Hill View
101113	12 Applewood Close
101114	1 Elm Street
101114	59 Sparrow Lane

Figure 7.1 – Evolving database schema impact

In a graph database, this type of schema change is more simple to implement. Graphs benefit from having no fixed structure, a property conferred by the way relationships between data points are modeled. A graph database, when used correctly, is agnostic to the type of relationship being modeled; whether it be one-to-one, one-to-many, or many-to-many, a relationship is always represented by an edge between two nodes. This is the sort of change that is highlighted in *Figure 7.2*:

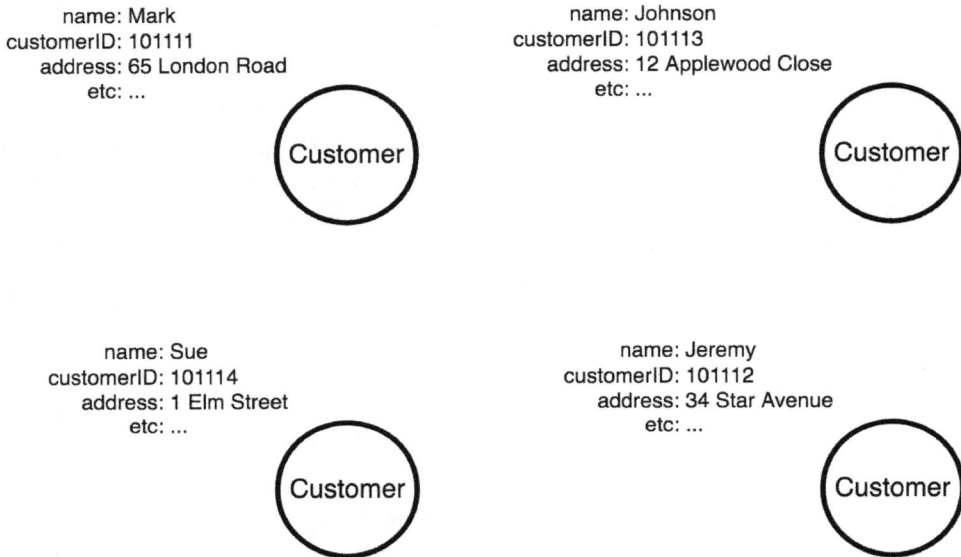

name: Mark
customerID: 101111
address: 65 London Road
etc: ...

Customer

name: Johnson
customerID: 101113
address: 12 Applewood Close
etc: ...

Customer

name: Sue
customerID: 101114
address: 1 Elm Street
etc: ...

Customer

name: Jeremy
customerID: 101112
address: 34 Star Avenue
etc: ...

Customer

Figure 7.2 – Graph database pre-schema change

With multiple addresses per customer possible, we can move the **address** attribute to a separate node of the **Address** type, connected by an edge. Now, when additional addresses are added for a customer, we just add another node and edge to the graph. Here, there is no need to have a pre-existing number of addresses allowed per customer, nor is there any need to duplicate data in separate parts of the database.

This is illustrated in the following diagram to show the flexibility of a graph schema over a relational schema:

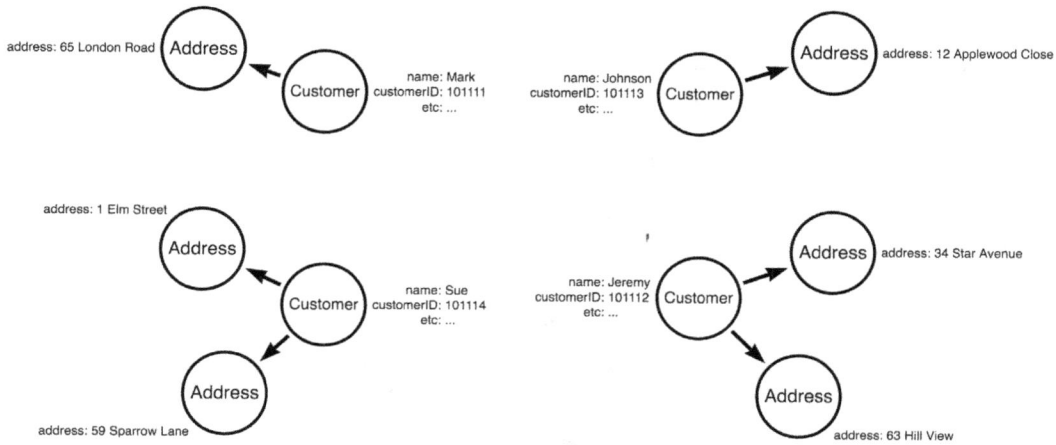

Figure 7.3 – Evolving graph schema

With a graph data model, the way in which data is represented is highly flexible, making graphs suitable for modeling data with high complexity.

However, with this flexibility to model data in many different ways, we must consider the impact of particular schemas on the performance of our database too, which we will learn about next.

Effectively evolving with graph schema design

When planning a schema in the previous chapters, we assumed that our graph data model would not change. In practice, this is rarely the case. Data requirements can change regularly with the needs of a solution or business, and it is important to consider this in advance. We saw in the last section that it is often more simple to change the schema of a graph than the structure of a relational database.

On the other hand, when a graph database becomes a key part of the tech stack that underpins a valuable system, we would not want to allow drastic shifts in structure and schema, especially those that may disrupt a live service. We have to strike a balance between taking advantage of the mutable structure and schema of a graph database and setting sensible constraints that ensure data is as expected.

For the rest of the chapter, let's consider a new example, using data from Twitter. Twitter, like many other social media platforms, has changed over time in terms of the services it provides to customers and its core product. Any visible changes to Twitter on the frontend application are likely to rely on backend database changes too.

Let's consider Twitter at its first stages of launch, and how it might represent data concerning a user's *follows*. Each Twitter user would likely be represented by a User node, with a unique ID of some sort. Following another user on Twitter, unlike Facebook, which we explored in *Chapter 2, Working with*

Graph Data Models, is a directional relationship. If one user follows another, there is no requirement for the reverse to be true.

Now, imagine that later in its ongoing development, Twitter is releasing a new feature, *Circles*. In an early release, each user could be part of a single *circle*, with other users. Here, we might make the decision to add the ID of a user's circle as an attribute to the User node. Using an attribute to represent this makes sense because, currently, the relationship between a user and their circle is one-to-one.

The following diagram shows how you would set up a **User** with a **FOLLOWS** relationship if the user belongs to just one circle:

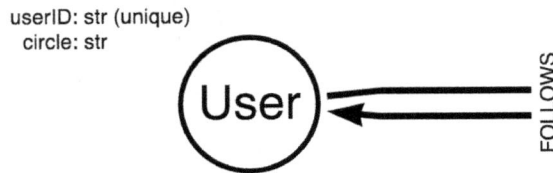

Figure 7.4 – Schema with one circle per user

This schema would work perfectly well if each user can only belong to one circle. However, what would happen if a new Twitter update allowed users to be a member of more than one circle? The relationship between a user and a circle after this update would be one-to-many. If we listed them in a property, this may become unwieldy, where we would potentially have very large strings representing user circle memberships. As time goes on, this would become very difficult to query should we want to use the information held in the graph database to drive any behavior in the frontend application concerning circles. Query performance would be impacted by having to search for a specific circle inside a long list.

Instead, we could plan ahead and move the `circle` property to its own node type, `Circle`. Each node could have a unique ID, and relationships could be made from User to Circle nodes. We will call this relationship MEMBER_OF.

As well as preventing long lists of properties from building for each User, the addition of Circle nodes removes duplication of the circle IDs being held in this property. Each *circle* is now represented by a single node that has several User nodes connected to it. This will further increase performance, allowing graph queries to traverse through the User/Circle network that has now been connected.

This diagram shows User as a member of a particular circle, with a relationship to show who also follows the user:

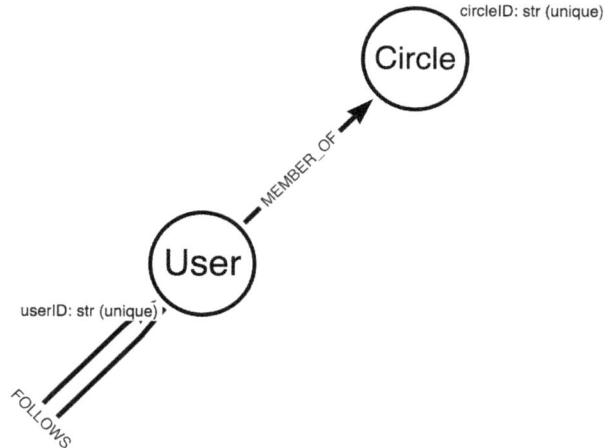

Figure 7.5 – Updated schema with a one-to-many relationship between User and Circle

In the next section, we will look at putting these conceptual considerations into development and allow the pipeline to factor in our proposed changes.

Putting the changes into development

In this section, let's model the changes to Twitter over time by creating our initial schema and refactoring it to meet the new needs of the application, following a planned update. This will include how to set up your database and adding constraints to the database and why and how you should use them. Then, we will look at the steps to implement the pre-schema change and the final step, implementing the changes to our schema. The following sections will cover our main use case of how to put our schema changes into production.

Initializing a new database

As in *Chapter 5, Working with Graph Databases*, and *Chapter 6, Pipeline Development*, we will start by creating a new Neo4j graph database. The steps to do this are detailed here:

1. Open Neo4j and choose **Add** and then **Local DBMS**. This will create a new local graph database, which we are going to work with in this section.

2. For this chapter, we will call the new database `Refactor DB`, and again use the password `testpython`. Make sure to create a database with these settings, for repeatability. However, you could call this whatever you wish.

3. Once the database is created, click on it and choose **Start** to spin it up for the first time, which may take a minute or so. Once it has started, click **Open** to open up the new database in the Neo4j Browser.

4. Again, as before, we need to add a new user with administrator privileges, in order to run Cypher on the Neo4j database from Python. In the Neo4j Browser console, run the following:

```
:server user add
```

5. This will open a window where you can enter a username and password for the new user. Here, we will use the username admin and the password testpython. In the drop-down **Roles** list, choose both **admin** and **PUBLIC**. Finally, click **Add User**.

With our database set up, we're ready to add the first iteration of the Twitter schema.

Adding constraints

In a graph database, where data accuracy is absolutely critical, we may want to consider additional ways of making sure data conforms strictly to our schema. We have previously explored using MERGE statements, instead of CREATE, to ensure that duplicate nodes are not added to our database when sending write queries. However, using constraints adds a separate layer of control over our graph data.

Constraints can be set up in a Neo4j database to ensure that nodes, edges, and their properties conform to stringent rules. We previously explored using MERGE statements, instead of CREATE, to ensure that duplicate nodes are not added to our database when sending write queries. However, using constraints adds an additional layer of control over our graph data when preventing duplicates. There are many types of constraints that are possible in Neo4j; see https://neo4j.com/docs/cypher-manual/current/constraints/ for more implementations.

In our Twitter schema, we have identified some node properties that should be unique across all nodes of a particular type. Let's add a uniqueness constraint to our User nodes, which should each have a unique userID property. To do this, we need to write some Cypher. The steps to create our constraint are as follows:

1. We can add a constraint using the CREATE CONSTRAINT function and give it a name, unique_user. We then set the type of node that the constraint applies to using FOR, followed by a node and a chosen alias – here, u. We then specify what type of constraint applies to this node, using REQUIRE, and assert u.userID IS UNIQUE:

```
CREATE CONSTRAINT unique_user
FOR (u:User)
REQUIRE u.userID IS UNIQUE
```

These lines can be run in the Neo4j Browser of our database to set up the constraint. When run, the browser should confirm that one constraint has been added. This is shown in *Figure 7.6*:

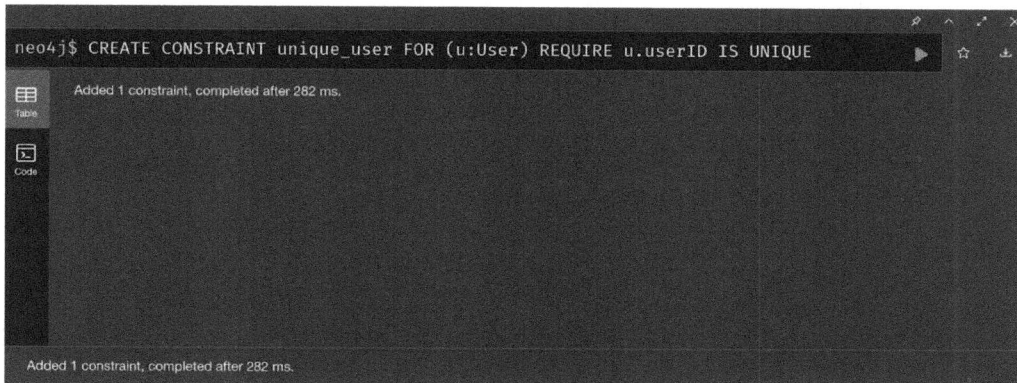

Figure 7.6 – Neo4j Browser constraint

2. Let's test to see what happens now when we attempt to violate the constraint's rule, in the Neo4j Browser window. First, we can create a node with `userID` set to `100`:

    ```
    CREATE (u:User {userID:'100'})
    ```

    Then, try to run this same query again. If the constraint is set up properly, the browser window should return something such as "Node(2) already exists with label `User` and property `userID = '100''`". This constraint prevents writing a new node with an existing user ID by throwing an error.

3. In contrast, let's try to use `MERGE` to add the same node:

    ```
    MERGE (u:User {userID:'100'})
    ```

    When run in the Neo4j Browser, we should see that there are no changes to the database. The `MERGE` statement has matched the existing node with ID `'100'` and has subsequently written no new data to the database.

4. Before continuing, we should clear out the test data we added to the database in this section by running the following in the Neo4j Browser, as we have done in previous chapters:

    ```
    MATCH (n) DETACH DELETE n
    ```

Constraints are a great way to absolutely ensure data conforms to schema requirements such as the uniqueness of properties. With our uniqueness constraint set up on users, and more tight control over our graph data model, let's next look at adding some Twitter data to Neo4j.

Pre-change schema

As we saw in the previous section, the original data we will be working with contains information on Twitter users, who follows who, and what *circle* they belong to.

To begin, let's look at the structure of the data we have to import into our graph database. Looking at the first few lines of edges1.csv, we see the following:

```
166712218,106118793
27617013,192318065
116798290,19294743
106118793,197401382
192318065,111310036
```

This is a fairly standard edgelist, containing the node IDs of accounts that follow each other. The accounts in the first column follow the accounts in the second column.

We have one more file to consider at the moment, circles1.csv. Let's also open this in a text editor or similar and take a look:

```
2,5402612
5,106118793,166712218,14157134
10,47069130,43996908,19281401,116798290,19294743,115430599,27617013,74
265849,111310036,192318065,264224758,197401382,108352527,130104942
```

Here, we have a small amount of data showing what circle each Twitter user is a member of, in our imaginary case where users are only allowed to be in one circle. The first column contains the circle ID, while the remaining columns list each user ID belonging to the circle ID on the same row. Pre-schema change, these circles will be node attributes.

In the following steps, we will be connecting to our graph database and then we will be performing operations on the data that we have already done throughout this book. Let's look at the process step by step:

1. We will be adding nodes and edges to our Neo4j database using Python, so we'll need to run `import GraphDatabase` to import `GraphDatabase` from the Neo4j library, and add our custom `Neo4jConnect` class used in previous chapters (this can be imported from the graphtastic package and is found under the graphtastic.database.neo4j directory where we import the `Neo4jConnect` method). For more information on how this class and its functions work, see *Chapter 5, Working with Graph Databases*:

   ```
   from graphtastic.database.neo4j import Neo4jConnect
   from neo4j import GraphDatabase
   ```

2. With functions ready to connect to our Neo4j database, we can think about populating our graph with data, first from our edgelist. We will need to open edges1.csv using the inbuilt Python csv library, and convert each row into a list, resulting in a list of lists:

```
import csv
with open('./data/edges1.csv', 'r') as c:
    reader = csv.reader(c)
    edgelist = [edge for edge in reader]
print(edgelist[:5])
```

3. Our print statement shows that edges have been read into Python correctly. We now need a way to transfer these user IDs and their FOLLOWS relationships into Neo4j, so we will write a separate function for this. The functions will take n, the ID of a user who follows another user, with ID m. It will also take a Neo4j connection established using Neo4jConnect. We can then use these parameters to assemble a simple Cypher query, using MERGE so that existing nodes and edges are not replicated. Each User node is first merged into the graph, followed by the FOLLOWS edge between them. Quotes are used around the user ID properties to ensure they are added as a string, as per the schema we designed in the last section. The last step is to use our connection to send the write query to the database:

```
def add_edge_neo4j(n, m, connection):
    cypher = f'MERGE (u1:User {{userID: "{n}"}}) ' \
             f'MERGE (u2:User {{userID: "{m}"}}) ' \
              'MERGE (u1)-[:FOLLOWS]->(u2) '
    connection.query(cypher)
```

4. Let's test that this function is working by adding a single edge to the database from Python. We can use list slices to get the source and target of the first edge in our imported CSV:

```
connection = Neo4jConnect('bolt://localhost:7687', 'admin',
'testpython')
add_edge_neo4j(edgelist[0][0], edgelist[0][1], connection)
connection.close()
```

5. If this worked successfully, you should see that two User nodes and a FOLLOWS edge have been added to Neo4j, when using the Neo4j Browser. To confirm, we could run the following in the Neo4j Browser Terminal:

```
MATCH (u:User) RETURN u
```

After running this, you will see a result where you have a node-follower relationship:

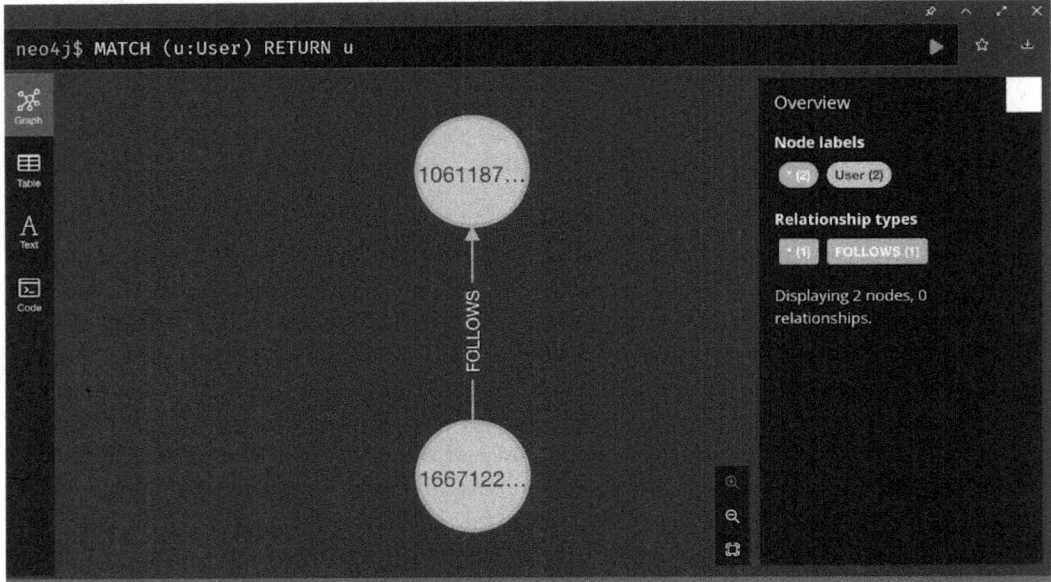

Figure 7.7 – Neo4j: two user nodes with a FOLLOWS edge

6. With our function working, we are now ready to add every node and edge in our edgelist. We can write some Python code to loop through this edgelist and add MERGE each edge into Neo4j:

```
for n, m in edgelist:
    connection = Neo4jConnect('bolt://localhost:7687', 'admin',
'testpython')
    add_edge_neo4j(n, m, connection)
    connection.close()
```

After running this Python code and navigating back to Neo4j, we can check that our edges have been added correctly and that our database has started to become more populated.

> **Important note**
>
> This time, we didn't need to remove our test data before adding edges. Because we are using MERGE, and because we tested our function with an edge that is present in our edgelist, for the test edge, MERGE will match the nodes and edges. Since the MERGE statement matched, no updates were made to the graph.

7. Now, considering that we are conforming to the schema in *Figure 7.3*, we can add the one-circle-per-user data to the graph too. We need to define a new function to add a circle to a User

node attribute, using data read in from a CSV. We will first import the `circles1.csv` data, similarly to how we imported our edgelist, using the `csv` library:

```
with open('./data/circle1.csv', 'r') as c:
    reader = csv.reader(c)
    circles_raw = [row for row in reader]
print(circles_raw)
```

Our `print` statement shows that we have a list of lists, with each list containing the circle ID in the first element and the users that belong to it following that. We will need to parse this format into something more easily handled in a Cypher query.

8. Let's define a quick function to convert this data format into pairs of circle ID and user ID. We will call this `get_user_circle_pairs()`, which will take just the data we read in from `circle1.csv`. We define an empty list and for each circle and its list of users, take the circle ID from index 0, as well as a user ID, using a list comprehension. Because the first element in the list resulting from this comprehension will contain the circle ID twice, we take forward a slice from the second element onward. We then append each pair to the `pairs` list and return it:

```
def get_user_circle_pairs(circles):
    pairs = []
    for circle in circles:
        circle_pairs = [[user, circle[0]] for user in circle]
    [1:]
        [pairs.append(pair) for pair in circle_pairs]
    return pairs
```

9. Once this function is defined, we can pass our `circle` data to this function, and then we can print the relevant output to the console:

```
pairs = get_user_circle_pairs(circles_raw)
print(pairs)
```

The result of `print()` will show circle ID/user ID pairs. With this more consumable data format, we can move on to adding the circle ID property to the `Users` in our graph.

10. Once this function is defined, we can pass our circle data to this function, and then we can print the relevant output to the console.

11. We will need to define another function for adding data to Neo4j. Let's call it `add_circles_neo4j()`. This will receive a user ID, a circle ID, and an authenticated Neo4j connection. As we did with `add_edge_neo4j()`, we will create a Cypher query using f strings to replace parts of a string. Our query will use MATCH to find a `User` node with a specific user ID, then use SET to add the `circle` property to that node. Then, all that remains is to execute the `write` query against the Neo4j database, using `connection.query()`:

```
def add_circles_neo4j(user_id, circle_id, connection):
    cypher = f'MATCH (u:User {{userID: "{user_id}"}})' \
```

```
                    f'SET u.circle = "{circle_id}"'
        connection.query(cypher)
```

12. With our function to add the `circle` property defined, let's run `add_circles_neo4j()` for each user ID/circle ID pair:

```
for user_id, circle_id in pairs:
    connection = Neo4jConnect('bolt://localhost:7687', 'admin',
'testpython')
    add_circles_neo4j(user_id, circle_id, connection)
    connection.close()
```

13. Head over to the Neo4j Browser and confirm that the desired properties have been added for `User`, by implementing a Cypher query similar to the following:

```
MATCH (u:User) RETURN u.circle
```

Our graph database, as it's currently set up, now contains our schema for Twitter data, before the hypothetical change to the `Circles` feature. Now, imagine a new feature is requested, to allow users to be members of more than one Circle. Changes will need to be made to our schema and database to reflect the data resulting from this new feature.

In the next section, we will cover how to make changes to the schema to allow the pre-schema changes to be updated effectively.

Updating the schema

To best illustrate why we might favor one schema design over another, when it comes to allowing multiple Twitter Circles per user, we will imagine what queries we would need to run in order to retrieve this data. These will be outlined in these steps:

1. Currently, finding users in a specific circle, when a user can only have one, can be done with a simple `MATCH`, specifying the `circle` property:

```
MATCH (u:User {circle: '5'}) RETURN u
```

2. However, if we started to add to the `circle` property in order to store additional information on additional circles a user is part of, for example, as a list, we would need to change this query to include a `WHERE` statement and locate a specific circle:

```
MATCH (u:User)
WHERE '5' in u.circle RETURN u
```

Upon running the Cypher, the query in the Neo4j Browser window will look as follows:

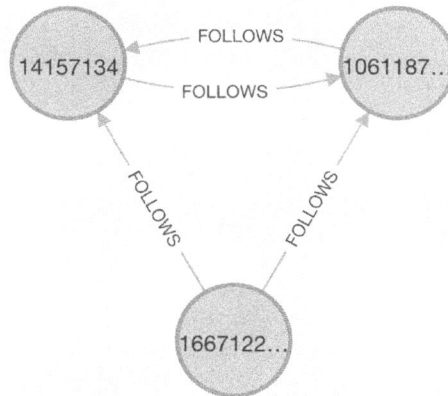

Figure 7.8 – Follower connections with the updated schema

3. Now, while this kind of query is acceptable when the number of circles per user is small, as it might be when this feature update is released, this could scale very poorly. As users become members of more and more circles, the database engine will need to search lists of increasing length in order to find members of a particular circle. Queries could also become very complicated if we were looking for users who share several circles, or perhaps if we were to try to find users that don't follow each other but share a circle, in order to recommend following a new Twitter user. By planning ahead, we can avoid these performance pitfalls later on, as the database becomes increasingly populated over time.

4. Instead, we can refactor our database and change the schema to that in *Figure 7.5*, where circles are added as a node rather than a property. With this schema, we can take better advantage of our data, as path-based queries to find relationships between distant users and circles are more easily computed.

5. Importantly, considering in this example that our database is serving an active platform, we can't do what we have done in previous chapters and run something like MATCH (n) DETACH DELETE n. We want to preserve the data currently in our database in order to continue supporting our application's current state.

6. So, we will begin by adding data according to our new schema, and finish up when our hypothetical feature has been deployed, by removing data conforming to the old one-user-per-circle data model.

7. As well as our schema change, we still have new users, follows, and circles to incorporate into our database. Two files contain the data already added to the Neo4j database, as well as additional information: `edges2.csv` and `circle2.csv`. Let's begin by importing them into Python as lists of lists, in the same way that we did previously for the edgelist and circles:

```python
with open('./data/edges2.csv', 'r') as c:
    reader = csv.reader(c)
    edgelist2 = [edge for edge in reader]

with open('./data/circle2.csv', 'r') as c:
    reader = csv.reader(c)
    circles2 = [row for row in reader]
```

8. Nothing has changed concerning `User` nodes and their `FOLLOWS` relationships, so let's add the newly imported nodes and edges to Neo4j with our previously defined `add_edge_neo4j()` function:

```python
for n, m in edgelist2:
    connection = Neo4jConnect('bolt://localhost:7687', 'admin',
'testpython')
    add_edge_neo4j(n, m, connection)
    connection.close()
```

9. Additionally, we need to parse the circle data in `circles2` as we did earlier, using `get_user_circle_pairs()`:

```python
pairs2 = get_user_circle_pairs(circles2)
```

10. Now, in both our new and old data models, when a new user joins, we can add a node for them, and when they follow someone, we add a relationship. This is already handled by the `add_edge_neo4j()` method. However, with our new schema, when a user joins a circle, we add a relationship, `MEMBER_OF`. When a circle is created, we add a new `Circle` node with a unique ID.

11. In order to satisfy the new schema requirements, let's prepare a new method for adding circles to our database, `add_circles_neo4j_new_schema()`. As with `add_circles_neo4j()`, the input to our new function will be the same, taking user ID, circle ID, and a Neo4j connection. However, the logic in our Cypher query will differ. We first find a `User` node by matching on `userID`, before using `MERGE` to either match or create a new `Circle` node with a unique `circleID`. These two nodes are aliased to u and c, with these aliases being used in the last bit of Cypher to create the `MEMBER_OF` relationship between `User` and `Circle`. The query is then executed, as for all of our Neo4j-interfacing methods, with `connection.query()`:

```python
def add_circles_neo4j_new_schema(user_id, circle_id,
connection):
    cypher = f'MATCH (u:User {{userID: "{user_id}"}})' \
            f'MERGE (c:Circle {{circleID: "{circle_id}"}})' \
```

```
            'MERGE (u)-[:MEMBER_OF]->(c)'
   connection.query(cypher)
```

12. In this step, we can use `add_circles_neo4j_new_schema()` to add `circle` nodes to the graph, by looping over the `user`/`circle` pairs in `pairs2`:

```
for user_id, circle_id in pairs2:
    connection = Neo4jConnect('bolt://localhost:7687', 'admin',
'testpython')
    add_circles_neo4j_new_schema(user_id, circle_id, connection)
    connection.close()
```

13. With our new `Circle` nodes added, let's move over to the Neo4j Browser and create a Cypher query to extract the user and circle information. Our new schema allows us to use MATCH to find paths, rather than searching through large property lists with WHERE, which is a more suitable type of query for a graph. Now, we can use MATCH to find users that have the MEMBER_OF relationship to a specific circle:

```
MATCH (u:User)-[:MEMBER_OF]->(c:Circle {circleID: '5'})
RETURN u, c
```

This returns the MEMBER_OF relationship to the specific circle, as visualized in the results of the Neo4j Browser:

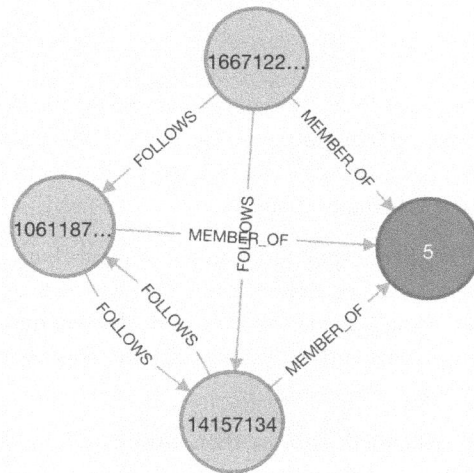

Figure 7.9 – MEMBER_OF relationship

14. The last step we need to do, now that we have rolled out our new graph data model to reflect our simulated changes to Twitter Circles, is to remove the old data. Imagine now that with our feature fully online, we are no longer using the `circle` property on `User` nodes, but rather the `Circle` nodes instead, to present information to an application's frontend. Because of

this, we can safely remove the `circle` property and clean up our database. We can do this by matching all `User` nodes and using the `REMOVE` function:

```
MATCH (u:User)
REMOVE u.circle
```

Our database structure is now such that we can extend queries to match larger paths, such as users that belong to several circles or users that could potentially know each other because of shared circle membership. Feel free to try out some more queries in the Neo4j Browser using what we've learned about Cypher in the last few chapters, to get a feel for the new schema. To help with this, you can check out the Neo4j website for a comprehensive breakdown of how to construct Cypher queries: `https://neo4j.com/developer/cypher/`. More specific to this chapter, check out tips from Neo4j on how to refactor graph databases: `https://neo4j.com/developer/graph-model-refactoring/`.

Refactoring our data model has allowed us to avoid poor graph database standards even while requirements change, and also enabled potential future functionality based on relationships between parts of the Twitter platform. In an industry situation, staying abreast of changes that impact a graph database and planning ahead can save a lot of headache in the future. Take it from us, you learn from your mistakes, and these tips have been built from years of industry experience. Essentially, you need to learn from what has gone wrong in past graph projects to know what does and doesn't work in terms of schema design.

Summary

This was a pivotal chapter if you want to really expand and extend the skill sets you have learned throughout this book and start putting them into practice. Prior to this chapter, we focused on graph pipelines. This extends the knowledge and insights you have gained further by looking at the importance of having a flexible and responsive schema to change.

Stemming from the tools you have been equipped with for schema change, we looked at what this means for your existing schema and what you need to know to build an adaptive schema. Furthermore, we looked at the reason for refactoring schemas, focusing on why you may need to refactor such as because of graph database relationships and the various changes that need to be considered when building your initial schema design.

Following the initial concepts of schema design, we then moved on to looking at how to effectively evolve your schema in production.

This focused on a use case of adding additional Twitter Circles (networks of people who converse with each other on Twitter) to a known schema. Here, we built a Neo4j database to store our graph database and applied constraints to our schema design – in Cypher – as a way of enforcing and controlling evolving schemas.

From this point, we looked at building our initial schema (labeled a pre-change schema), which involved the combination of Python and Neo4j scripts (written in the Cypher query language).

Finally, the last stage was to take into account all that we have learned and apply the changes to our updated schema design.

This chapter focused on building everything you would need to handle evolving and updating schemas, which is something that you should bear in mind at design time as much as possible.

In the next chapter, we will further build on all the knowledge we have acquired so far when we look at graph projections and how they can be useful for downstream analytical tasks. These projections can contain analytically relevant, potentially aggregated, topological and property information of a main graph. This stored view will contain analytically relevant, potentially aggregated, and topological property information of the graph.

Part 4: Graphing Like a Pro

In this part, we explore what graph projections are and how they can be used. This will give you the rudimentary knowledge you need to extract projections to perform analysis. These projections can then be extracted for further statistical and analytical uses. You will learn all about how to do this in this chapter. In addition, you will also get an understanding of how to export your projects in igraph and Neo4j. Buckle up and let the analysis flow with the use case looking at analyzing movies with relationships such as *acted in* and *starred with*.

Finally, the section on common errors and debugging jumps into the types of errors we have encountered in our careers, and how you can easily get around and resolve these errors and bugs effectively. Let's think of this as your reference whenever anything untoward occurs in your code.

This part has the following chapters:

8

Perfect Projections

In this chapter, we are going to focus on creating graph projections, which you will be able to perform sophisticated analysis on, and even use other algorithms, such as machine learning and statistical methods, to form insights. We will start by explaining what projections are, leading on to how to use projections in practice. We'll draw upon how you can create projections in igraph and Neo4j, using a combination of the Cypher query language and Python.

For our use case, we will focus on popular movies, with a focus on using graph data science to find what films actors have appeared in, co-starred in, and multiple other relationships we can define with flexible graph structures. By the end of this chapter, you will be able to create a projection and put it to work for your use case.

We will be covering the following main topics:

- What are projections?
- How to use a projection
- Putting the projection to work

Technical requirements

We will be using Jupyter Notebook to run our coding exercises, which requires `python>=3.8.0`, along with the following packages, which will need to be installed with the `pip install` command into your environment:

- `neo4j==5.5.0`
- `igraph==0.9.8`
- `matplotlib==3.6.3`

For this chapter, you will also need Neo4j Desktop installed. Please see the *Technical requirements* section of *Chapter 5*, *Working with Graph Databases*, if Neo4j is not yet installed, as it will be needed to follow along with the tutorials in this chapter.

All notebooks, with the coding exercises, are available at the following GitHub link: `https://github.com/PacktPublishing/Graph-Data-Modeling-in-Python/tree/main/CH08`.

What are projections?

Data in graph data models usually comprises relationships between *things*, whether they be people, languages, transport hubs, or any of the other examples we've seen throughout the previous chapters. Plenty of data models have several types of nodes and relationships, making one node or edge not equal in meaning or value to another.

These types of graphs are known as heterogeneous graphs, and we have seen them throughout this book. One type of heterogeneous graph is a bipartite graph, where there are two types of nodes. In bipartite graphs, only different types of nodes can share edges. For example, a citation network might be represented as a bipartite graph, with authors connected to articles they have written.

Analysis of heterogeneous graphs with multiple node and edge types can be tricky. To illustrate this, first consider the authorship graph in *Figure 8.1*. We can answer some simple questions easily, using this graph's native structure, such as finding the number of articles an author has written using node degree, or contrastingly, the number of authors for an article, with the same method.

However, to measure the tendency for groups of authors to work together, for example, using an algorithm such as community detection (as we used in *Chapter 4, Building a Knowledge Graph*), we would need to traverse paths through both articles and authors in order to find sensible communities. The results from running an algorithm such as community detection across a bipartite graph may not necessarily make sense when trying to examine the connectedness of groups of solely authors or solely articles:

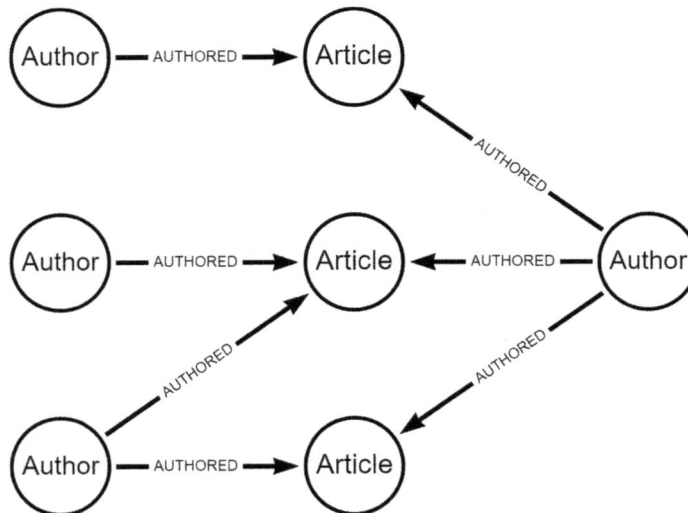

Figure 8.1 – A sample from a bipartite authorship graph

To answer these types of questions that primarily concern the authors, rather than the articles themselves, we can use a projection. A projection is a representation of a graph – often a simplified version of a complex network. Projections often *collapse* graph data into more simplified interactions between specific entities, meaning that information is lost during the conversion. Although information is lost, analysis becomes easier and more intuitive and allows more direct questions to be asked of the graph.

Figure 8.2 contains a unipartite projection of the bipartite graph shown in *Figure 8.1*. The graph now contains only **Author** nodes, which share an edge if the original bipartite graph nodes shared relationships to the same co-authored **Article**. Through this projection, we have lost certain information, for example, the individual articles that each pair of authors collaborated on. However, we have gained the ability to run graph algorithms over a homogenous graph, for example, what was mentioned previously, community detection. We can sensibly split our graph into communities of authors algorithmically when our graph exclusively contains Author nodes:

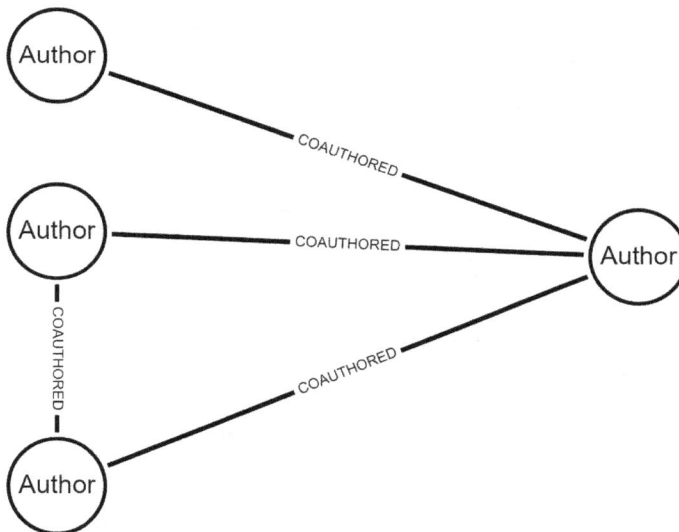

Figure 8.2 – Corresponding unipartite projection of the authorship graph

Other types of heterogeneous networks can be more complicated, with numerous node and edge types, such as in a knowledge graph.

A knowledge graph can represent a wealth of information in a highly complex schema – for example, a graph containing detailed customer information, which could contain many different ways in which information relates to each other.

Figure 8.3 shows a sample of an example customer graph database, with many types of nodes and relationships. In this case, unlike the bipartite graph, a simple graph measure, such as the degree of certain types of nodes, would give you little useful information. If we find the degree of **Customer** nodes in this graph, this is an amalgamation of both products a customer has purchased and their address information.

In addition to this, with a high number of node and relationship types in a graph data model, asking certain types of questions in an efficient way can be difficult. Consider how we would relate address information to brands of purchased products; we would have to traverse three relationships to go from **Address** nodes to **Brand** nodes:

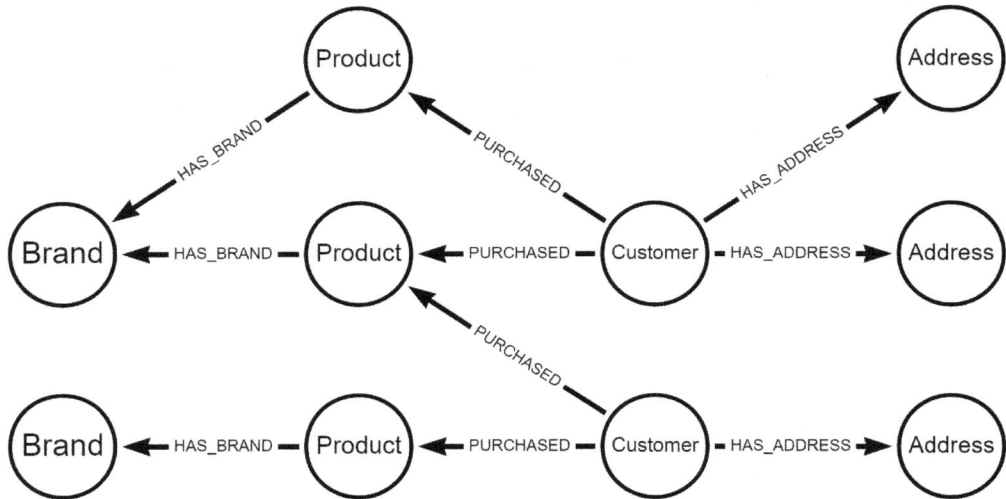

Figure 8.3 – Heterogeneous customer data graph

Instead, here we might consider using a graph projection of the customer data in order to answer a particular question, especially if this is a question we might ask of a graph database regularly, for example, as part of a recommendation system.

To answer questions on how brands relate to addresses of customers, we could collapse paths between these two node types into a single edge. In doing this, we lose information about the way addresses relate to brands through customers and products, but we hugely increase the efficiency of answering questions about how these node types relate by drastically reducing the number of hops required to traverse between these nodes. We can now easily compute the number of brands associated with an address, or perhaps locations of the world associated with purchasing particular brands of products.

These brands that are associated to distinct addresses can be seen in the following diagram, with an established **HAS_PURCHASE_FROM** edge-to-node relationship:

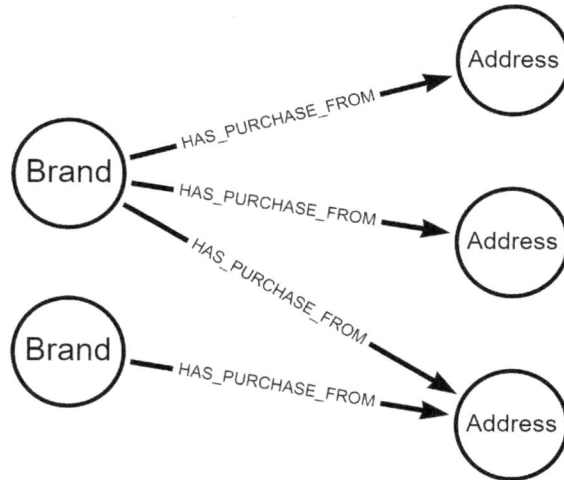

Figure 8.4 – Bipartite projection of complex heterogeneous customer data

Now that you have an idea of why we might use a projection, we're going to put this idea into practice in the next section. We will be exploring a large dataset of film information, creating projections to answer some questions that would be tricky to answer in a heterogeneous knowledge graph, and using some tricks in Neo4j to process data in efficient ways.

How to use a projection

The steps that follow will refer to setting up a Neo4j instance, creating a data store, and using Cypher to work with our projection. This will combine the skills we have learned in subsequent chapters and distill them all in one place:

1. Let's first create a new Neo4j database again, as we did in the last few chapters, to store our film knowledge graph. We will call it `Projection DB` and use the password `testpython` again, before starting up the database.

2. As we have detailed previously in *Chapters 5*, *6*, and *7*, we will create a new admin user using `:server user add` (in the Neo4j Browser), with the name `admin`, the password `testpython`, and the `PUBLIC` and `admin` roles added. For more detailed information on how to do this, please refer back to any of the previous three chapters.

3. In this chapter, because our dataset is large, we are going to use `LOAD CSV` to import data into Neo4j. To do this, we must first move `movie.csv` into a folder Neo4j can access.

    In the main Neo4j Desktop window, click the **...** icon next to **Projection DB**, then select **Open folder | Import**. This will open the data `import` folder for this database in the file explorer, in which we should then copy `movie.csv` (this can be found in the supporting GitHub repository's `data` folder).

4. We will also be using the **Awesome Procedures on Cypher (APOC)** plugin (`https://neo4j.com/labs/apoc/4.1/installation/`) for Neo4j in our data import step. To install this, go to the main Neo4j Desktop window, select the **Projection DB** database, and look on the right of the window for the **Plugins** tab. Click on this tab, and under **APOC**, click **Install and Restart**.

5. Once installed, restart the **Projection DB** database.

6. With all this set up, it's time to think about adding data to our database. As always, so we know what we're working with, let's take a look at the first few rows of the `movie.csv` file we added to our database's `import` folder:

```
002 Operazione Luna,COUNTRY,Italy
002 Operazione Luna,DIRECTOR,Lucio Fulci
002 Operazione Luna,STARRING,Ciccio Ingrassia
002 Operazione Luna,STARRING,Franco Franchi
002 Operazione Luna,STARRING,Linda Sini
```

Here, we see that `movie.csv` contains edge data, with the first and third columns containing the names of related entities. These entities, on inspection, can be different types of film-associated data. Each of these entities is related by the concept in the second row – COUNTRY, DIRECTOR, and so on. This type of data structure is often seen when creating graph databases, and each row is known as a *triple*.

7. This time, our dataset seems a lot larger than those we worked with previously. We should check some of the properties of our `import` data before diving into loading it to Neo4j. In Python, we can read in the dataset and check the number of rows first:

```
import csv
with open('./data/movie.csv', 'r') as c:
    reader = csv.reader(c)
    data = [line for line in reader]

print(len(data))
```

8. From our `print` statement, we see that `movie.csv` contains over 410,000 triples. We can also check how many types of edges we will be importing into the Neo4j database, by taking a `set()` of the second column:

```
edge_types = set([triple[1] for triple in data])
print(edge_types)
```

This shows that we have four different edge types in `movie.csv`: AWARD, DIRECTOR, COUNTRY, and STARRING. This means our node entities must correspond to awards, directors, countries, and actors, as well as the films they relate to. Now that we have a better understanding of what data we have access to, we can design an approach to Neo4j data ingestion.

9. With a much larger dataset, we need to ensure that performance is maintained in Neo4j. With graphs containing hundreds of thousands of nodes, it's important to configure our database so that reading and writing aren't too slow, which risks query timeouts. To mitigate the effect of having a huge number of nodes and edges on our queries, we can add an index. Our graph will initially contain just one node type, `Entity`, which will have a `name` property. We will need to access this property repeatedly when we merge each row containing an edge into our graph, to check whether a node already exists. We will also be accessing these node properties many times to create projections later.

10. Based on *step 9*, we will use `CREATE INDEX` in the Neo4j Browser to create an index-named entity. A benefit of an index is that it speeds up the query performance, as it knows exactly what it is trying to locate, in terms of specific nodes. Other benefits associated with indexes are faster query execution, reduced traversal times, efficient sorting and ordering, enhanced scalability (meaning that as the graph grows, indexes are crucial for keeping the query times down to an acceptable limit), and optimal resource utilization (creating more efficient query execution plans and therefore using less compute). This index will be `FOR` nodes of the `Entity` type and with `ON` in the `name` property:

```
CREATE INDEX entity
FOR (e:Entity)
ON (e.name)
```

11. With our index in place, we can start to think about loading our film data into Neo4j. We will be loading this directly from the CSV file into the graph database, as we have done in previous chapters. However, if we simply use `LOAD CSV` as we have before, we may run into issues with running out of memory. When loading a large amount of data, we can give Neo4j hints on how to handle this in batches, to avoid memory problems.

12. We will surround our logic for adding nodes and edges to the graph with a subquery, using the `CALL` function. With `CALL`, and `IN TRANSACTIONS OF 1000 ROWS` at the end of our subquery, we can tell Neo4j to load information contained in a certain number of CSV rows at a time (the data needs to be in the `import` folder at this stage; otherwise, you will get an error), and add them to the graph according to the Cypher inside the curly braces. Our logic for adding nodes is simply to use `MERGE` to add or match `Entity` nodes with the `name` property, which is taken from each CSV row. Creating edges, however, is slightly more complicated, as Cypher does not natively allow relationship type assignment using variables stored in a row. Instead, we can use the APOC library's `create.relationship` function. To do this, we use `CALL`, which is used here to run a non-native function, followed by a call to `apoc.create.relationship()`.

13. We then specify the parameters of the nodes we have merged, *n* and *m*, and the relationship type in the second column of the CSV file, assigned to the variable type using `WITH` in the previous line. This creates a relationship in the database with the type equivalent to the value in column 2 of our CSV. The third parameter of this function takes a dictionary of relationship attributes – in this case, we have none and so pass an empty dictionary. Many APOC functions need to be

followed by YIELD, which carries over an output of apoc.create.relationship. We can carry over the rel output, but we will not use it, as we are writing to the graph and don't need to use any returned value. Similarly, our subquery requires that something is returned, but because we don't need this, we can return a dummy variable, x:

```
:auto LOAD CSV FROM 'file:///movie.csv' AS row
CALL {
    WITH row
    MERGE (n:Entity {name:row[0]})
    MERGE (m:Entity {name:row[2]})
    WITH n, m, row[1] as type
    CALL apoc.create.relationship(n, type, {}, m)
    YIELD rel
    RETURN 1 as x
} IN TRANSACTIONS OF 1000 ROWS
RETURN x
```

This query will run in batches and may take up to a few minutes, depending on the machine the Neo4j database is running on. Once the data is loaded in, we can check that the data is structured as intended by running queries in the Neo4j Browser.

14. Let's look for an edge we know should be present in the database, for example, the edge corresponding to the first row in movie.csv. This has two entities, a film, 002 Operazione Luna, and Italy, connected by a COUNTRY edge. We can match this edge using Cypher and return it to confirm it exists in Neo4j. Running this query, we should see the nodes and COUNTRY edge returned in the Neo4j Browser:

```
MATCH (n:Entity {name:'002 Operazione Luna'})-[:COUNTRY]-
(m:Entity {name:'Italy'})
RETURN n, m
```

The country matching to the movie will be shown in the graph relationship diagram:

Figure 8.5 – Entity matching on an edge

With our film dataset loaded into a persistent database, we can create various projections in order to answer different questions using our graph data. If we want to see what actors work together on various films, we could create a projection of co-starring actors. We could also create a projection to dive deeper into what films share common actors, and how much this is influenced by the country used in filming. We are next going to tackle how to generate both of these predictions, before moving on to using projections to sensibly and efficiently analyze our data.

Creating a projection in igraph

Let's create our first projection in Python, by reading from the Neo4j database and importing it into igraph. To do this, we will use a package we have created to import the functions we will use again and again in these graph projects. The function we will use is the Neo4jConnect function and this can be imported from the graphtastic package that is found in the associated GitHub repository (link in the *Technical requirements* section of this chapter). The following steps will cover the importing of this module to connect to Neo4j and then how you create a projection, step by step, with igraph and Python. Let's get projecting:

1. Import the Neo4jConnect class from the graphtastic package:

    ```
    from graphtastic.database.neo4j import Neo4jConnect
    ```

2. With our class and methods in place to connect to the Neo4j database, we can now figure out how to get some data from Neo4j, in the form of a graph projection. The projection we're aiming for is a graph containing information on what actors co-star alongside each other in films. In our Neo4j database, we have the STARRING relationship, which connects film Entity nodes to actor Entity nodes.

3. Let's quickly take a look at these relationships by looking up a pair of actors that starred in the same film, with some Cypher in the Neo4j Browser. Here, we can identify the correct types of Entity nodes by using MATCH with the specific STARRING relationship type:

    ```
    MATCH (act1:Entity)<-[:STARRING]-(film:Entity)-[:STARRING]-
    >(act2:Entity)
    RETURN act1, film, act2 LIMIT 1
    ```

    We can see from the browser results that actors are connected through films. However, in our projection, we want to connect co-starring actors. So, any Cypher query we run in Python to get edge data for our projection needs to find nodes and edges that have this pattern and return just the nodes containing actor information.

4. Knowing this, we can write a method in Python to access this actor data, get_co_stars_ neo4j(). This method will take only a Neo4j connection object and use the pattern we found in a MATCH statement using the Neo4j Browser to find co-starring actors. We only need to return the node on the edge of our pattern, here aliased to act1 and act2. We execute the query using the connection.query() method, and access a list of dictionaries containing our query result with result.data(). As a last step, we clean up the data structure by accessing

the name properties of our resulting nodes, contained in dictionaries, and turn these into a pairwise list of co-starring actors:

```
def get_co_stars_neo4j(connection):
    query = 'MATCH (act1:Entity)<-[:STARRING]-(film:Entity)' \
            '-[:STARRING]->(act2:Entity)  '  \
            'RETURN act1, act2'

    result = connection.query(query).data()
    result = [[act['act1']['name'], act['act2']['name']] for act
in result]

    return result
```

5. We can now create a Neo4j connection using the Neo4jConnect class with our credentials, and call get_co_stars_neo4j() to get pairs of co-stars, before remembering to close the database connection. Let's make sure things look as expected by printing the first few pairs:

```
connection = Neo4jConnect('bolt://localhost:7687', 'admin',
'testpython')
co_stars = get_co_stars_neo4j(connection)
connection.close()
print(co_stars[:5])
```

6. With a list of lists containing actor pairs, we essentially now have an edgelist in Python, with which we can create a graph. As we have covered in earlier chapters, we will also need a list of nodes and lists of attributes to assemble it in *igraph*.

7. We can get a list of unique nodes by using a double list comprehension to get a list of all nodes in the edgelist and taking a set of that list:

```
nodes = list(set([node for edge in co_stars for node in edge]))
```

8. Also, we can assign ascending integer *igraph* IDs to these nodes by creating a dictionary. Using a dictionary comprehension, we can use enumerate() on our unique node list, creating mapped ascending IDs for each node:

```
igraph_ids = {film:node_id for node_id, film in
enumerate(nodes)}
```

9. In *igraph*, we will need to use these new IDs to add edges to the graph, so we must substitute each node name for the unique *igraph* ID from igraph_ids. We can again use a comprehension for this task, resulting in an edgelist of paired integers corresponding to our films:

```
edgelist = [[igraph_ids[n], igraph_ids[m]] for n, m in co_stars]
```

10. We now have everything we need to assemble our graph:

    I.   Let's first import *igraph* and create an empty graph using `igraph.Graph()`.

    II.   Next, we can add nodes to the graph with `add_verticies()`, equivalent to the length of our unique *igraph* node IDs.

    III. Then, we can link these nodes by using the `add_edges()` method of our graph object, g, and passing the ID's edgelist as a parameter.

    IV.   Finally, by accessing `g.vs`, we can add the `actor` attribute listwise to each node, which is the name of each actor from our unique `nodes` list:

    ```
    import igraph
    g = igraph.Graph()
    g.add_vertices(len(igraph_ids))
    g.add_edges(edgelist)
    g.vs['actor'] = nodes
    ```

11. As a last step, we should make sure that the elements of the graph are as expected. We can use `assert` statements in Python to make sure that node attributes are named correctly, comparing them to the `nodes` actor name list. We can also make sure that the number of nodes is as expected too:

    ```
    assert g.vs[2]['actor'] == nodes[2]
    assert len(g.vs) == len(nodes)
    ```

12. For one final test to confirm that our projection has been applied as intended, let's find an edge in our *igraph* graph, and find the equivalent path in the original graph database stored in Neo4j. To first find the nodes on an edge in *igraph*, we can access the `g.es` attribute of our graph and find the ID of the nodes connected by the edge with index 0 by accessing the `source` and `target` attributes, in turn. Using these *igraph* node IDs, we can then feed this index into `g.vs` and locate the `actor` properties we will use to find the corresponding path in Neo4j, assigning them to the `actor1` and `actor2` variables:

    ```
    actor1 = g.vs[g.es[0].source]['actor']
    actor2 = g.vs[g.es[0].target]['actor']
    ```

13. Now, we can open a connection to Neo4j with `Neo4jConnect` and plug these actor names into a Cypher query. We can use f-strings to form a valid Cypher query, looking for the `Entity | Film | Entity` pattern we originally queried Neo4j for to create our projection. Returning the actors and film, we can then create a result dictionary with `.data()`, before closing the connection with `.close()` and printing it to the console:

    ```
    connection = Neo4jConnect('bolt://localhost:7687', 'admin',
    'testpython')
    query = f'MATCH (act1:Entity {{name:"{actor1}"}})' \
            '<-[:STARRING]-(film:Entity)' \
    ```

```
            f'-[:STARRING]->(act2:Entity {{name:"{actor2}"}}) ' \
            'RETURN act1, film, act2'
result = connection.query(query).data()
connection.close()
print(result)
```

Our `print` statement here should show a valid path in the original graph, corresponding to our projected edge in *igraph*, confirming that the projection has been taken correctly:

```
[{'act1': {'name': 'Roger Pryor (actor)'}, 'film': {'name':
'The Man with Nine Lives (film)'}, 'act2': {'name': 'Boris
Karloff'}}]
```

With this, we have taken a projection of co-starring actors from our original, complex knowledge graph in Neo4j, and set it up in *igraph* ready for further analysis. We will return to this projection in the last section to explore the data some more. For now, we will move back to the Neo4j Browser to go through another method of generating a projection, should you want to store a projection more permanently.

Creating a projection in Neo4j

While a projection in Python allows for some highly advanced data analytics, it is stored in memory and therefore not persistent. Should we want a projection that we access repeatedly or need to store long term, we might want to use a graph database such as Neo4j for this too. To develop our Neo4j projection we are going to need to take the following steps:

1. In `Projection DB`, we're next going to create a projection of films sharing the actors and the countries they are filmed in, in order to enable some more analysis. For the purposes of the chapter, we can store this projection alongside the original graph data, as long as we make sure to keep this graph separate by using new labels and edge types. This will prevent any mixing of information when querying the graph for insights later.

2. Our new graph will contain `Film` nodes that have a stored name. As we did with our main movie information graph, we will first create an index for `Film` nodes, on the `name` attribute. This will drastically speed up operations where we match using film names. We will use the same syntax as we did earlier on in this chapter, in the *How to use a projection* section, in *step 9*:

    ```
    CREATE INDEX film
    FOR (f:Film)
    ON f.name
    ```

3. Next, we can move on to querying our existing `Entity` nodes for specific information and add this to a new, separate graph projection. We are going to be using some fairly advanced Cypher again here, drawing once again on the APOC plugin. This time, we are using the `apoc.periodic.iterate()` function to split the execution of a query into batches. This prevents Neo4j from loading too much into memory at once and hitting a memory limit that causes it to raise an error. We'll kick off this query by using `CALL` to call `periodic.iterate()`, with

an open parenthesis, with the first parameter containing the Cypher logic to match Entity nodes. We want to connect films that have actors in common in our projection, so we need to match paths that contain two films, each with a STARRING relationship to another entity, containing an actor. Once this path is matched, we finish off the first Cypher string by returning film1 and film2, the nodes we want to add to our projection.

In periodic.iterate(), the second parameter contains another Cypher string, which contains the logic for what to do with the returned results of the previous query. For each path we find, we want to merge two new Film nodes and give them the name property. We can then connect f1 and f2, our newly created node aliases, with a HAS_COMMON_ACTORS edge. The last parameter for our function is a dictionary containing information on how to execute our batched query. A batchSize value of 1000 tells the function to find 1,000 results from the first Cypher query parameter before executing the second parameter's Cypher using the results of the first. The other option we pass is parallel, which, when set to True, enables parallel processing in batches of 1,000. In this specific case, parallelizing these batches would lead to errors due to the locking of nodes during updates, which we will go into more detail about in *Chapter 9, Common Errors and Debugging*. For now, let's close our complex APOC function with a parenthesis and run our query in the Neo4j Browser:

```
CALL apoc.periodic.iterate(
    "MATCH (film1:Entity)-[:STARRING]->(actor:Entity)
    <-[:STARRING]-(film2:Entity)
    RETURN film1, film2",
    "MERGE (f1:Film {name:film1.name})
    MERGE (f2:Film {name:film2.name})
    MERGE (f1)-[:HAS_COMMON_ACTORS]->(f2)",
    {batchSize:1000, parallel:false}
)
```

This batched query may take up to a few minutes to run, depending on the specifications of the machine running it. Once it has finished, the Neo4j Browser will display information on how many batches were needed to complete the apoc.periodic.iterate() task, as well as whether any batches failed. Had we used parallel:True for this, we would have likely noticed some batch failures, and several write operations will not have been completed, due to the potential for multiple writes to the same nodes at once.

4. With our graph's structure set up, we can now add additional properties to our nodes. For our graph projection, we are interested in the countries the films are shot in, and in our main graph, these relationships are represented with COUNTRY edges. It is possible to move this relationship to a property as a list of countries that a film was filmed in.

> **Important note**
>
> Note that this operation of moving a one-to-many relationship from edges and nodes to a node property is not always a sensible idea, as we learned in *Chapter 7, Refactoring and Evolving Schemas*, when keeping track of multiple addresses per customer. However, with a finite number of countries and a low likelihood of a huge number of countries for any given film, when using this list property later for further analysis, searching through these lists is unlikely to be a large memory overhead for any query.

5. To move relationship and node information to a property node, we will again make use of `apoc.periodic.iterate()` to batch our processes over the graph database. In the first parameter, we will again use a Cypher string to match the relationship information of interest, where `Entity` nodes have a `COUNTRY` relationship to another `Entity`. We can then return the country and the related film from the connected nodes, by returning the `name` properties. To move this data over to our graph projection of films that share actors, we can use `MATCH` in the second `periodic.iterate()` parameter to locate the corresponding node of the `Film` type. Then, with that node aliased to `f`, we can use `SET` to modify the `country` property. Here, we are using the `coalesce()` function to either create or add to a list of countries. If the `country` property is `null`, then an empty list is created, and the new country name is appended to the list. On the other hand, if the `country` property already contains data, an additional `country` is added to the list. The use of `coalesce()` here prevents errors when trying to append properties to a `null` object, while appending in `SET` prevents countries from being overwritten if there is already a `country` property written. Finally, we specify extra parameters for the `periodic.iterate()` function, as we did for adding nodes and edges to the graph. However, this time, because the `SET` operation and paths we are looking for in the original data result in far less memory usage, we can increase `batchSize`, this time to 10,000 operations. Because we are not adding relationships to nodes, and because it is unlikely we will add two properties to a node at the same time, here we are safe to use the `parallel:True` option, to speed up our batched query and allow parallel processes to take place. We can now run this query in the Neo4j Browser:

```
CALL apoc.periodic.iterate(
    "MATCH (film:Entity)-[:COUNTRY]->(country:Entity)
     RETURN film, country",
    "MATCH (f:Film {name:film.name})
     SET f.country = coalesce(f.country, []) + country.name",
    {batchSize:10000, parallel:true}
)
```

Again, pay attention to the output of `periodic.iterate()` in the Neo4j Browser window. Check how many batches were required and whether any failed. If at any point any of the batched processes failed during the previous steps, or if any mistakes were made, we will likely need to use batched processes to remove nodes and relationships too, before trying again. Using a similar pattern to `MATCH (n) DETACH DELETE n` with this large dataset can result in running out of memory too, so batching the delete process is recommended.

6. To remove all `Film` nodes and edges, in the event of an issue or mistake with graph projection, we can use the following query, with another `CALL` to `apoc.periodic.iterate()`. Here, we match `Film` nodes and return them in the first Cypher parameter, and use `DETACH DELETE` on the returned nodes in the second. Here, we won't be able to parallelize the operations, since processes could conflict if the same edge is removed from two connected nodes at the same time:

```
CALL apoc.periodic.iterate("
    MATCH (f:Film) RETURN f",
    "DETACH DELETE f",
    {batchSize:1000, parallel:false}
)
```

In these last steps, we have added thousands of `Film` nodes to Neo4j to create our projection, which is also densely populated with millions of edges. With our common actors and countries graph set up and stored in a database, we have permanent access to this projection, which is ideal for performing repeat queries and analysis.

In the next section, we will move on to harnessing the projections we have made in both *igraph* and Neo4j to perform some analysis that would otherwise either be impractical or generate misleading results.

Putting the projection to work

We have two projections to put to use now, one read from Neo4j and converted to a Python *igraph* and one stored more permanently in Neo4j, alongside the original graph data. It's time to generate some insights about the films and actors in our knowledge graph, drawing on our projections. Now that our projections have a nice, simple, and clean schema to work with, our analysis can be more powerful than if we approached the original knowledge graph data directly. Let's begin by returning to Python and our co-star graph.

Analyzing the igraph actor projection

As a reminder, we used Python and the Neo4j API to query our knowledge graph using Cypher and return actors who starred alongside each other in the same film. We then converted our results to an edgelist and imported this into *igraph*, ready for graph analytics. The analysis steps are as follows:

1. Let's start with the basics and learn about some of the properties of our co-star graph. It's good practice to check the size of our graph, in terms of nodes and edges, which we can retrieve by accessing the `vs` and `es` attributes of our *igraph* graph, stored as `g`:

```
print(len(g.vs))
print(len(g.es))
```

From this, we can see that our graph has around 82,000 nodes and over 1.4 million edges, making it fairly strongly connected. This makes sense, as actors rarely appear in films without a large number of other stars.

2. The number of nodes in our projection is useful to know, but we could have found the number of `Actor` nodes in our data by searching for unique nodes with an incoming `STARRING` relationship in our original knowledge graph. The number of edges, equivalent to the number of co-starring actors, would have been slightly more complex to find but would have involved searching for unique paths of the same pattern as we searched for when constructing the projection.

3. Let's move on to something that would be trickier to calculate using the knowledge graph and trivial with a projection – the degree distribution. Searching for paths by starting at films and going back to co-stars for every node representing an actor in order to find the number of co-stars would be time consuming in our original graph data. However, with our co-star projection, we can simply count the number of edges incident to every node.

4. We can find the number of edges for each `Actor` node, and therefore the number of co-stars each actor has, using the `degree()` method on our *igraph* `g` object:

```
degree = g.degree(igraph_ids.values())
```

5. Let's plot the degree distribution of our graph, to learn more about its structure. We can do this by importing `matplotlib.pyplot` and using its `hist()` method to plot a histogram of our node degrees. Here, we use a log scale for the *y* axis, as real-world graphs typically have long-tailed degree distributions. These graphs have many nodes with a small number of edges and few with a very large number of edges. Using `yscale('log')` will ensure that we can see the frequency of high-degree nodes on the right-hand side of the degree distribution:

```
import matplotlib.pyplot as plt
plt.hist(g.degree(), bins=20, edgecolor='#1260CC',
color='#3A9BDC')
plt.xlabel('Node degree')
plt.ylabel('Frequency')
plt.yscale('log')
plt.show()
```

The chart shows our histogram of frequencies by node degree (indicating the number of edges connected to the respective nodes):

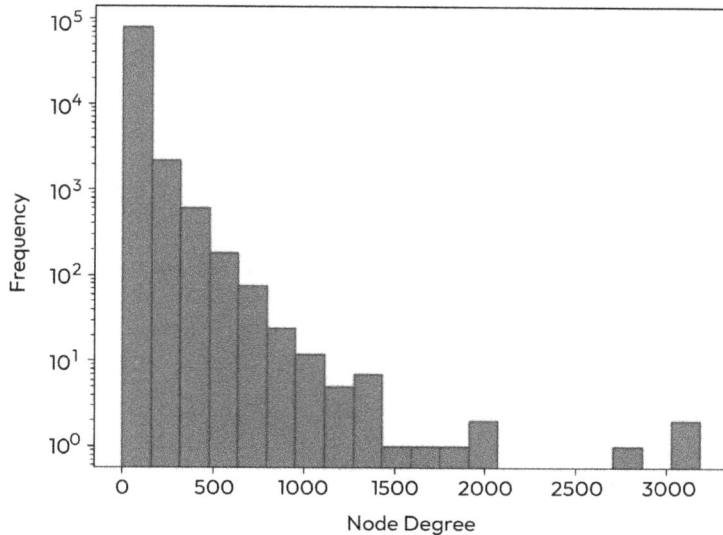

Figure 8.6 – Degree distribution of the co-star projection

Sure enough, our co-star graph does feature a long-tailed degree distribution. This tells us that the vast majority of actors have co-starred with few other actors, while a very small number have worked with thousands in their careers.

We can also see that on the far right of the distribution's long tail, we have three Actor nodes that have a disproportionate number of co-starring actors in their films. Let's check who these actors are.

6. We can use zip() to create a list of degree and actor name pairs, by accessing our list of node degrees and the actor attributes of all nodes with g.vs['actor']. The order of degree results for each node in g.vs is preserved, so we can safely use zip to get them side by side. We can then use the sorted() method to sort by the first element in each pair in our actor_degree list using an anonymous function, and use reverse=True to sort in reverse order:

```
actor_degree = list(zip(degree, g.vs['actor']))
actor_degree = sorted(actor_degree, key=lambda x: x[0],
reverse=True)
print(actor_degree[:3])
```

Printing the first three actors in our sorted list shows us that in our dataset, Moe Howard, Larry Fine, and Mithun Chakraborty are the most well-connected actors in terms of working alongside other actors, each with around 3,000 connections through co-starring roles.

Exploring connected components

Another feature of our graph worth exploring is the number of connected components. As discussed before in previous chapters, running the weakly connected components algorithm reveals whether our graph is wholly connected or it is split into disconnected parts, as is often the case in real-world graph data. In our original knowledge graph, before taking a projection, finding connected components of co-starring actors would have been challenging. Using the weakly connected components algorithm in the knowledge graph doesn't give us any information on actor relationships, but rather a very rough measure of whether there are components of information in our graph that don't overlap with other film knowledge we store. This would be a very coarse-grained measure – the existence of the country nodes and relationships would likely make our knowledge graph appear much more strongly connected than you might expect.

The following steps take you through how to explore the connected components in your constructed graph:

1. With a projection, we can much more reliably ask a specific question about connectivity among co-starring actors in particular – in our data, are there groups of actors in films that are entirely disconnected from other groups of co-stars? To answer this question, let's run the weakly connected components algorithm across our graph in Python, using *igraph's* components() method. Specifying the mode='weak' parameter here ensures that we still consider an edge as a connection, regardless of direction. This is important as although edges can be stored in *igraph* with a source and target, for the purposes of a co-star actor graph, the edge direction is irrelevant:

   ```
   cc = g.components(mode='weak')
   print(len(cc))
   ```

   Printing the length of our connected components object, we can see that our graph contains over 3,000 components and is therefore far from fully joined. There are isolated silos of actors in our data that have no connections to other actors through co-starring in films in our graph.

2. We can explore this further by looking at the size of the largest connected components. Using a list comprehension, we can take the length of each component, which corresponds to its number of nodes, and sort the list of lengths in descending order. Printing a list slice will show us the sizes of the top components:

   ```
   cc_size = [len(component) for component in cc]
   cc_size.sort(reverse=True)
   print(cc_size[:10])
   ```

Our largest component has 71,115 nodes, nearly comprising the entire graph. Our second and third-place components, by size, have only 45 and 34 nodes, respectively, so it seems that we have a long-tailed distribution of weakly connected component sizes in our co-actor graph too.

3. Because we have such a drastic reduction in size from the largest to the near-largest components, and yet have over 3,000 connected components in total, we may want to examine the sizes of components at the smaller end of the scale too. We can do this using `Counter()` from the inbuilt `collections` module in Python, which will convert our list of connected component sizes, `cc_size`, into a dictionary of sizes and frequencies. We can then sort this dictionary by its keys (which contain the component size), using another anonymous function, to find the frequency of component sizes, from large to small:

```
from collections import Counter
cc_freq = dict(Counter(cc_size))
cc_freq = sorted(cc_freq.items(), key=lambda x: x[0],
reverse=True)
print(cc_freq)
```

From our output in the Python console, we can see that we have a huge number of tiny components completely separate from the graph. Each tuple in our printed list contains the component size in the first element and the number of components of this size in the second element:

```
[(71115, 1), (45, 1), (34, 1), (30, 2), (25, 1), (24, 1), (23,
3), (22, 2), (20, 1), (19, 2), (18, 2), (17, 3), (16, 5), (15,
7), (14, 5), (13, 5), (12, 8), (11, 17), (10, 23), (9, 37), (8,
69), (7, 86), (6, 125), (5, 242), (4, 416), (3, 675), (2, 1157),
(1, 522)]
```

The most common component size is 2, likely from actors who have starred in the same film and, in our dataset, are yet to star in any others.

Exploring cliques in our graph

Up to this point, we have used our co-star projection to take a look at some graph features that would have been difficult to either compute or interpret using our main source of data, the knowledge graph. Let's take a look at answering a different type of question.

There are groups of actors who regularly appear in the same films. For a more advanced type of analysis using our projection, we may want to identify groups of actors that have all starred alongside each other at some stage in their careers. We can do this by finding *cliques* in our graph.

In graph theory, a clique is a subgraph in any given network where a set of nodes are all interconnected with each other. If this subgraph were an entire graph in itself, we would call this *fully connected*.

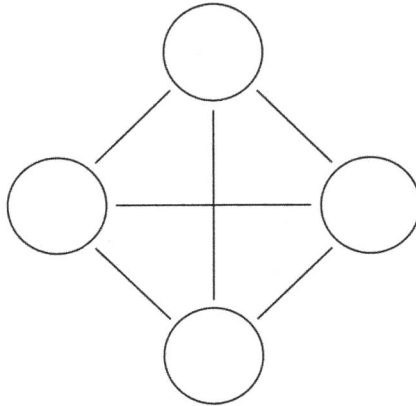

Figure 8.7 – A clique containing four nodes

In our original knowledge graph schema, before taking a projection, we wouldn't be able to use any regular clique-finding algorithm for co-stars, as the nodes would have been related through two edges and a Film node. We could have written a custom, more complex method for finding co-star cliques using the original data structure, but this would likely have poorer performance too due to the additional edges it would have to traverse.

Instead, with our projection, we can use *igraph* and its largest_cliques() method to find the biggest fully connected subgraph inside our graph. This returns a list of nodes inside a set. So, let's take the first element of that with a list slice to simplify the output.

In the following steps, we will explore the largest clique among actors:

1. We can take a look at the size of our biggest clique of co-stars and what nodes belong to it:

```
largest_clique = g.largest_cliques()[0]
print(len(largest_clique))
print(largest_clique)
```

2. Our print statements show that the largest clique in our projection is formed of 65 nodes. We can also see the node IDs belonging to that clique, but since it would be more meaningful to check what actors these nodes represent, let's next use the vs attribute of our graph, g, and our largest_clique list to find the actor attribute for each of our clique nodes.

   This last step will reveal the actors who have all worked with each other in some capacity, in our dataset, during their careers:

```
clique_actors = g.vs[largest_clique]['actor']
print(clique_actors)
```

We have carried out a lot of analysis on our *igraph* projection of co-starring actors and learned a lot about how actors work together in films by examining the structure of the graph.

In the next section, we have a second projection to analyze, which is complementary in some ways to our co-starring network.

The projection we previously set up in Neo4j represents films that share a common actor, so let's dive into using our projection to gain insight into any interesting patterns present.

Analyzing the Neo4j film projection

The projection we have in Neo4j contains `Film` nodes only, which share an edge if they have actors in common. Let's begin, as we did in *igraph* for the co-stars projection, by characterizing some basic information about our graph.

The following steps will inform you of the Cypher queries you need to execute in the Neo4j Browser to get similar results to the Python analysis we have done in previous sections:

1. First, let's count the number of nodes in the graph with a simple Cypher query in Neo4j Desktop, by using `MATCH` to find nodes of the `Film` type only, and returning the number of these nodes with the `count()` function:

   ```
   MATCH (f:Film) RETURN count(f)
   ```

   The console output shows us that we have 79,478 `Film` nodes in our projection. When creating the projection, we had to write a batched query to read and write our data, and around 80,000 nodes wouldn't usually cause us any issues.

2. Let's also check how many `HAS_COMMON_ACTORS` relationships we created when building our projection, by matching this relationship between our `Film` nodes with a pattern. This time, we alias the relationship to `r`, and again return the number of nodes with `count()`:

   ```
   MATCH (:Film)-[r:HAS_COMMON_ACTORS]->(:Film) RETURN count(r)
   ```

   Now, we have found the source of our time-consuming projection storage, with our graph containing 5,774,715 edges. This makes our graph projection very highly connected in general. Thinking back to what our projection represents, this makes sense – for each actor in our dataset, there are a number of `HAS_COMMON_ACTORS` relationships between films, based on every film they have appeared in. When an actor has appeared in, for example, five films, in our projection, this would generate a clique of five `Film` nodes. Considering that there are many actors that have appeared in far more films, the high connectedness of our shared actors projection is unsurprising.

3. We have a node attribute on our `Film` nodes in our Neo4j projection where a country is added to a list for each country of filming found in our knowledge graph data. We can use the `country` attribute to perform some analysis around common actors between films, and their filming locations.

4. Let's write a Cypher query to find films with common actors that are filmed in separate countries, and find the most common pairs of locations. We can start with a `MATCH` statement, specifying

only `Film` nodes and `HAS_COMMON_ACTORS` relationships that are part of our projection, and ensuring we are not querying the rest of the knowledge graph stored in the same database. Then, we can use `WITH` to access the `country` attributes of our Film nodes and alias them to `c1` and `c2`. We are interested in films that share actors that have different filming locations, so we will use the `<>` operator to compare the countries. Then, using `WITH` to pair up the country lists, we can return `country_pair` alongside the `count()` of each unique pair, which implicitly aggregates our results. The very last step is to order the results by `count(country_pair)` in descending order so that we can focus on the most common pairings:

```
MATCH (f1:Film)-[:HAS_COMMON_ACTORS]->(f2:Film)
WITH f1.country as c1, f2.country as c2
WHERE c1 <> c2
WITH [c1, c2] as country_pair
RETURN country_pair, count(country_pair)
ORDER BY count(country_pair) DESC
```

In our results, we can see that films sharing actors often have very closely located countries of filming, with some top results being the United States and Canada. Language also seems to have an impact, with another frequent location pairing for our shared-actor films being the United States and the United Kingdom. Our most common result shows us a pair of `Cinema of Hong Kong` and `Hong Kong`, which hints to us that our data could have benefitted from additional cleaning – this is fairly common in scraped semantic data, and could help to direct data quality improvements in the original knowledge graph.

Summary

In this chapter, we have used both Python and Neo4j to create, store, and analyze graph projections, demonstrating their power in both the efficiency and interpretability of results. Each technology has its own separate strengths. In Neo4j, we have less readily available access to complex graph data science algorithms to analyze our projection, compared to what we can easily carry out in Python with *igraph*.

However, using Neo4j is a more permanent storage option and suitable for a projection we might want to repeatedly read and write to. For any given use case, it is important to consider what the most appropriate projection creation and storage tool is for the task at hand.

These skills you have acquired will allow you to navigate between Neo4j, Python, and igraph with ease and will have set a strong foundation to build pipelines between the two technologies – a happy marriage indeed.

In the next, and final, chapter, you will learn about some of the common headaches of a graph data scientist. These lessons will focus on debugging (really, the only way to learn in data science is by creating imperfect code, and then going on a mission to debug this code, very much like Sherlock Holmes). Then, we will assist you by giving you insights into some of the common errors you will find when working in graph data science.

Common Errors and Debugging

In this chapter, we will be working through common errors that you will be presented with as a newly qualified graph data scientist or engineer (which you will be when you have finished reading this book). The focus will be on how to debug graph issues. This will lead on to common issues and how to get around them when working in *igraph*. Following on from this, we will look at common Neo4j issues, as we have been working igraph, Python, and Neo4j for a large proportion of this book; therefore, it is useful to know how to get around graph database issues as well. We will also touch on how to modify your *igraph* and Neo4j scripts to achieve the best performance.

There are many examples under each of these sections, with use cases of how and why these issues may present themselves. Therefore, you will be perfectly prepared, after reading this chapter, to debug and solve these common issues in your projects. In the upcoming sections, you will delve into common errors and issues you may face when working with igraph, Neo4j, and Python libraries for graph data modeling.

To summarize, in this chapter, we will be covering the following topics:

- Debugging graph issues
- Common igraph issues
- Common Neo4j issues

Technical requirements

We will be using Jupyter notebooks to run our coding exercises, which require `python>=3.8.0`, along with the following packages, which will need to be installed in your environment with the `pip install` command:

- `neo4j==5.5.0`
- `igraph==0.9.8`

For this chapter, you will also need Neo4j Desktop installed. Please see the technical requirements section of *Chapter 5, Working with Graph Databases*, if Neo4j is not yet installed, as it will be needed to follow along with the tutorials in this chapter.

All notebooks, with the coding exercises, are available at the following GitHub link: `https://github.com/PacktPublishing/Graph-Data-Modeling-in-Python/tree/main/CH09`.

Debugging graph issues

With graph data models and analysis being more readily employed in industry, and graph database solutions and software gaining popularity, it is likely that you will be exposed to data problems that can be solved in a graphical way. At the same time, graph solutions are still fairly new to many businesses, and you will almost certainly run into errors and issues as a graph data practitioner.

Here, we will cover some of the most common problems you are likely to encounter when using the *igraph* Python library, as well as some standard errors and issues you may see when using Neo4j. Each issue will be demonstrated with a short example, as an aid in debugging your own issues.

Each error or problem will be shown alongside a real example you can follow along with and resolve. We will need some data with which to demonstrate some issues you may encounter when using Neo4j and Cypher.

For this chapter, our examples will use social network data collected from GitHub. This will include data relationships between GitHub developers. Each edge in our edgelist, `musae_git_target.csv`, represents two developers that mutually follow each other.

We also have the names of our developers, which will be our nodes, in `musae_git_target.csv`. Our data represents a reasonably large graph, with around 38,000 nodes, and nearly 290,000 edges. Of course, there are many types of graphs you could run into problems with, as in all the example data we have worked with so far, but here, for the purposes of demonstrating some issues around bugs and scaling issues in both *igraph* and *Neo4j*, the GitHub social network will be used.

The following section will look at the common issues you will face when working with the igraph library.

Common igraph issues

While *igraph* is a powerful library for graph data and its analysis, much of its power comes from the fact that Python acts as an interface to *igraph's* implementation behind the scenes, which is in C. Because of this, *igraph* comes with some quirks, which you need to bear in mind when using its features. In the following subsections we will take you through some common problems users come across when working with *igraph* in Python.

No nodes in the graph

Some graph and network science libraries in Python can be created directly from a list of tuples, an edgelist. In *igraph*, because of how node indexing is implemented in C, nodes have to be added to a `Graph` object before edges can connect them together. In the next steps, we will demonstrate this problem and the subsequent errors that arise:

1. We can first read in edge data from `musae_git_edges.csv` as our example graph to load into *igraph*, using the inbuilt `csv` module. This file has headers, so we are using a list slice at the end of the list comprehension, building a list from the `reader` object, to remove them:

    ```
    import csv
    with open('./data/musae_git_edges.csv', 'r') as c:
        reader = csv.reader(c)
        edges = [row for row in reader][1:]
    ```

2. At this point, in many libraries, you might create a graph directly from the `edges` list. But, if we try to do this, we will encounter an error:

    ```
    import igraph
    g = igraph.Graph()
    g.add_edges(edges)
    ```

    This produces the following error:

    ```
    ValueError: no such vertex: '0'
    ```

3. There are actually two things going on here. No vertex exists in the graph with the name `0` because we haven't yet added any nodes. In addition, we are trying to pass strings into `add_edges()`, with which *igraph* is incompatible. We can fix this issue first by converting the values in our edgelist to integers with `int()`, and a list comprehension. Then, we can try to add the edges again:

    ```
    edges = [[int(edge[0]), int(edge[1])] for edge in edges]
    g.add_edges(edges)
    ```

    We will see that this still doesn't work, and get a new error:

    ```
    igraph._igraph.InternalError: Error at src/graph/type_
    indexededgelist.c:261: Out-of-range vertex IDs when adding
    edges. -- Invalid vertex ID
    ```

    This is now the error we encounter when we have a node ID in our list of edges that doesn't yet exist in the graph. In *igraph*, we must always add nodes to the graph before edges are added.

4. As we have shown in previous chapters, we can find the number of unique nodes by using a double list comprehension to get all node IDs in both columns of our edgelist, contained in the edges variable, and taking a set of these. Then, we just calculate the length of this set:

```
nodes = set([node for edge in edges for node in edge])
print(len(nodes))
```

We can confirm we are getting the correct number of nodes by comparing it against the README. txt file provided with the dataset. The number of nodes shown in the length of this set, and the README file, should be 37,700.

Note that this edgelist is 0-indexed already and that there would be additional steps to take here to avoid errors if it was not. We would need to generate IDs for each node if this were the case, which we will cover in the next subsection.

5. Now that we know how many nodes we should add, let's add nodes to our Graph object before adding edges:

```
g.add_vertices(len(nodes))
g.add_edges(edges)
```

6. We get no error this time, and edges are successfully added to the graph. Let's check that the number of edges is as it should be, by again comparing it to the README file. We can print the length of the es attribute of our graph to find the number of edges:

```
print(len(g.es))
```

Our count of edges is as it should be, 289,003.

Node IDs in igraph

Many, many times throughout this book, in our worked examples, we have loaded graphs into Python with *igraph*. Each time, we have had to make sure to create *igraph IDs*.

In the *igraph* library, a graph must have 0-indexed nodes – no exceptions. This is one of the features that allows *igraph* to load in data and run graph algorithms so quickly, using its C implementation behind the scenes. When we have data that is not 0-indexed, we need to first transform it to ensure that it is, and keep a record of this transformation, for example, in a dictionary.

Here's a worked example of the steps to show the conversion of these 0-indexed identifiers, as mentioned in the aforementioned sentences:

1. Firstly, we initialize a graph, as usual (we've already done this multiple times in the previous chapters):

```
g = igraph.Graph()
```

Thankfully, for the previous section, the GitHub developer social network is already 0-indexed. However, many datasets and edgelists are not and could need adjustment before *igraph* can be used. In this case, we can imagine that additional developers have been added to the network – there is no reason that they would all have sequential ID numbers, so we would have to deal with this if we wanted to load the social network into a graph for analysis in Python.

2. Let's see what happens in *igraph* when we add edges to our imported edgelist. We know our graph has exactly 37,700 nodes, making the highest valid node ID 37,699 (since 0 is also a valid node). To break this pattern, we can add several edges to our `edges` list of lists, where the nodes have IDs that are out of range. We will add these to create `new_edges`:

```
new_edges = edges + [[40000, 0], [99999, 1], [40000, 99999]]
```

3. Because we have new nodes in `new_edges`, we will need to again use a double list comprehension and `set()` to find the new total number of unique nodes:

```
new_nodes = set([node for edge in new_edges for node in edge])
print(len(new_nodes))
```

We have added nodes 40,000 and 99,999, so the length of our new unique node set should be 37,704.

4. As always, let's now add nodes to our `igraph.Graph` object, g, equivalent to the length of `new_nodes`, and add our edges from `new_edges`:

```
g.add_vertices(len(new_nodes))
g.add_edges(new_edges)
igraph._igraph.InternalError: Error at src/graph/type_
indexededgelist.c:261: Out-of-range vertex IDs when adding
edges. -- Invalid vertex ID
```

When we try to add edges to the graph, we see the preceding error. This is because when `add_vertices()` is called, *igraph* has added nodes with IDs 37,000 and 37,001, and doesn't know that nodes in our edgelist are named differently. *igraph* doesn't know what to do with the IDs 40,000 and 99,999 in our edgelist, as there is no equivalent node added, and no way for *igraph* to map these node names to node IDs. An *igraph* graph is always constrained to 0-indexing on nodes.

5. To solve this issue, we can consider mapping these new nodes to igraph IDs that are sequential and 0-indexed. Let's take the `new_nodes` list we previously assembled by finding all unique nodes in the edgelist and create a dictionary that maps their IDs to sequential, 0-indexed *igraph* IDs. We use `enumerate()` to do this, which counts through the unique IDs and creates a sequential ID for each, which we use as the value for each original ID key in our dictionary, `igraph_ids`:

```
new_nodes = sorted(list(new_nodes))
igraph_ids = {node: igraph_id for igraph_id, node in
enumerate(new_nodes)}
```

6.   We can check what has been assigned to our new nodes by accessing the *igraph* ID values of our new dictionary, specifying the keys:

```
print(igraph_ids[40000])
print(igraph_ids[99999])
print(igraph_ids[0])
```

Our `print` statements show that node 40,000 in our edgelist has correctly been assigned the *igraph* ID of 37,000, and node 99,999 has been assigned 37,701. Just to make sure, we can also check that our node with name 0 has still been assigned an *igraph* ID of 0, confirming that our dictionary of ID mappings has been created successfully.

7.   With our new dictionary mapping, we can recreate our edgelist using a list comprehension. Here, we create a new edgelist, `ig_edges`, where each node in each edge is replaced with its equivalent *igraph* ID, according to our mapping. We can then use the `add_edges()` method to add these new edges to our graph:

```
ig_edges = [[igraph_ids[edge[0]], igraph_ids[edge[1]]] for edge
in new_edges]
g.add_edges(ig_edges)
print(len(g.es))
```

Printing the number of edges by accessing the length of the `es` attribute of our graph, g, shows that we now have 289,006, three more than with our original edgelist, which is correct.

In the following section, we will look at best practices, or tips, for adding node properties.

Adding properties

Properties can be added to nodes and edges by accessing the `vs` and `es` attributes of an *igraph* graph object. This can be used to keep track of node properties and measures, or simply to add additional information such as IDs to our graph elements.

We have shown in previous chapters that node and edge attributes can be added to a graph listwise, which is far more efficient than adding one attribute at a time. Let's demonstrate this by adding GitHub developer names to the nodes in our graph. This will be covered in the following steps:

1.   First, let's import the data in `musae_git_target.csv` into Python, using the `csv` module, as we did for the edgelist:

```
with open('./data/musae_git_target.csv', 'r') as c:
    reader = csv.reader©
    node_attributes = [row for row in reader][1:]
```

2. With our data loaded, we could simply iterate through the imported `node_attributes` list with a `for` loop, and add the developer name as a node attribute to each node in turn, by accessing different nodes in `g.vs`:

```
for node_id, name in node_attributes:
    g.vs[int(node_id')]['developer_n'me'] = name
print(g.vs['']['developer_n'me'])
```

3. This works as intended, but is not an efficient method, as our graph, g, is repeatedly accessed for every node. Instead, it is much more efficient to add node properties listwise, extracting the `developer_name` attribute from the second elements of our list using a list comprehension, before adding them to `g.vs`:

```
developer_names = [row[1] for row in node_attributes]
g.vs['developer_name'] = developer_names
print(g.vs[0]['developer_name'])
```

The result here is identical but requires less processing. However, it is important to bear in mind that when properties are added to nodes or edges in a listwise fashion, that ordering is extremely important. Attributes are added to nodes so that the *igraph* node with ID 0 is assigned the attribute value at index 0 of the list. The order of the attribute list added to our graph must be in line with the order of our node IDs in *igraph*.

4. This can be particularly dangerous if there is duplicate node attribute information. We can demonstrate what might go wrong by adding a duplicate of the first element to our `developer_names` list, before adding these names to our graph:

```
developer_names_dup = [developer_names[0]] + developer_names
g.vs['developer_name'] = developer_names_dup
```

5. This will complete successfully and throw no errors, despite the length of our list being one element longer than the number of nodes in the network. Essentially, this line errors silently because it results in incorrect developer names not just for the first node, but for all nodes, where intended names are offset by one. Accessing the names of nodes with ID 0 and 1, we can see what has gone wrong:

```
print(g.vs[0]['developer_name'])
print(g.vs[1]['developer_name'])
```

6. Because of this silent error, it is good practice to use `assert` statements to ensure the intended behavior of node attribute addition. We know that the length of our node attributes list should be identical to the number of nodes in our graph, so this is an easy test to carry out:

```
assert len(g.vs) == len(developer_names_dup)
```

This will fail and throw an `AssertionError`, warning us that something has gone wrong with data preprocessing.

That concludes how we can effectively add properties to nodes and edges. In the next section, we will direct our focus toward the `select` method.

Using the select method

In *igraph*, as we have explored in previous chapters, it is possible to sample a series of nodes or edges from the graph using the `select()` method, on either the `vs` or `es` attribute of a `Graph` object, respectively. The `select()` method can sample nodes by their attributes, or, with special method parameters, calculations on nodes and edges that are performed on the fly, like different types of centrality.

While this is useful functionality in analysis, using the `select()` method in this manner can result in significant efficiency issues when used in a data pipeline. This is particularly noticeable when calculating a more computationally complex node or edge measure. The next steps demonstrate how to use this on the GitHub developer social network:

1. Firstly, if it is not already created, use the steps at the start of this section to load the GitHub edgelist `csv` into Python, as an *igraph* graph, g. Now, let's find nodes with a high degree in the graph, by using `vs.select()`, with the `_degree_gt=2000` parameter, specifying nodes with `degree` above `2000`:

    ```
    high_degree = g.vs.select(_degree_gt=2000)
    ```

2. Here, the calculation of `degree` is performed on the fly, and discarded once the high-degree nodes are selected. For a one-off analysis, this would be an acceptable use of the `select()` method. However, should this be used as part of an analysis pipeline, or even calculated again in the same Python script, it may make more sense to calculate degree centrality across the graph, and write this to nodes as a property. This prevents duplicate calculations of the same measure. To do this, we can simply calculate the degree, or whatever other measure is desired, with *igraph*, and the results will be returned as a list. This can then be added listwise to the nodes in the graph by accessing the `vs` attribute of g, and adding a new property name:

    ```
    degree = g.degree()
    g.vs['degree'] = degree
    ```

3. Now that the degree of each node is added as a node property, we can just retrieve the `degree` property of each node each time we want to use the degree of a node in our code. This means we don't have to repeatedly calculate the degree of our nodes if we use it more than once. Note that this time, our `select()` method uses the `degree_gt` parameter, with no `_` prefix, specifying that we want to access the property, rather than the `igraph degree()` method:

    ```
    high_degree = g.vs.select(degree_gt=2000)
    print(list(high_degree))
    ```

Note that any calculation on our graph takes some time to process – measuring `degree` for each node is fairly simple, but calculating something like betweenness centrality for each node involves finding the shortest possible path between all pairs of nodes in the graph, which while informative for certain analysis purposes, is far more inefficient. This requires a large amount of computing power, related to the size of the network. When calculating particularly computationally complex measures on a graph, this use of `select()` is far more optimal.

In the next section, we will put under the microscope chained statements and their usage with `select`. This will show some of the ways to avoid issues with these methods.

Chained statements and select

The `select()` method can be used in conjunction with `vs` and `es` to access nodes and edges in all manner of different ways, by their indices, their properties, and measures calculated on the fly. However, caution is advised if using `select()` to sample nodes or edges with chained statements. Using `select()` in a chained manner can have unintended consequences.

When `select()` is used, it generates either a `VertexSeq` or `EdgeSeq` object depending on whether it was used to find nodes or edges. The `vs` and `es` attributes of a graph have `VertexSeq` and `EdgeSeq` classes too. It is therefore possible to also use `select()` on the results of a `select()` call.

We will now take you through a worked example of this:

1. Let's demonstrate how this can cause some issues using the GitHub developer social network. We can sample nodes with specific indices by using an iterable as the first parameter in a `select()` call. Here, we are selecting nodes with IDs 0, 1, and 2:

    ```
    sample = g.vs.select([0, 1, 2])
    print(list(sample))
    ```

2. `Select()` can, as we have previously seen, also be used to sample nodes with a specific property, or measure. Here, we are using the method to find all nodes with `degree` equal to exactly 100, by using `_degree_eq` as a special parameter:

    ```
    degree_100 = g.vs.select(_degree_eq=100)
    print(list(degree_100))
    ```

    Our `degree_100` variable now contains a `VertexSeq` object, containing nodes sampled from our original graph, g. We can use `select` on this too to refine our node sample further. However, we should be wary when using IDs to sample or check the existence of specific nodes.

3. Imagine a scenario where we want to test our sampling method with `select` is working correctly, by checking for the existence of a node. We know that the node with ID 1075 should be present in this `VertexSeq`, as it has a degree of exactly 100. So, we could use an `assert` statement to ensure this:

    ```
    assert degree_100.select([1075])
    ```

Perhaps surprisingly, this `assert` statement will cause an error, which tells us that this node is out of range of the object. This will produce a similar error message as hereunder:

```
ValueError: vertex index out of range
```

4. Though we know that node `1075` is contained in the `select()` results, using `select()` reindexes nodes in the returned `VertexSeq`. Node `1075` has instead been reindexed into the 0th element, and can actually be accessed as such:

```
sample = degree_100.select([0])
print(list(sample))
```

We won't necessarily know what reindexing has taken place when running `select()`, so rather than searching for or further sampling the resulting `VertexSeq` objects using node IDs, it is best practice to sample by a node property, such as a unique identifier added to each node in the original graph. Reindexing will have no effect on accessing a node by its attribute, and so chaining `select()` would be safer.

In the next section, we will look at issues arising from path lengths and work through a case where this may occur.

Efficiency and path lengths

Not all graph algorithms are equal, with each allowing the calculation or estimation of different features of nodes, edges, or an entire network. Nor are they equal in complexity, where some can run in milliseconds, and some take hours to compute.

When choosing a measure to learn something about the nodes in a graph, we need to take into account the computational complexity of the method used to measure a feature. This is often highly correlated with the size and connectivity of the graph.

To illustrate this point, we can compare the degree centrality and betweenness centrality algorithms, which both seek to calculate the importance of nodes in a graph, but in different ways. Degree centrality is a simple measure, counting each node's connected neighbors, and scales proportionally to the number of nodes in a graph.

On the other hand, betweenness centrality traverses paths between all pairs of nodes in the graph, and so scales not only with the number of nodes, but the number of edges. In addition, due to its routine of finding short paths between nodes to estimate node importance, it is far more computationally demanding than calculating degree centrality.

While degree centrality is good for finding important hub nodes with many incident edges, betweenness centrality can show us nodes that act as important thoroughfares for paths through a graph. These concepts are linked and often correlate, but are not identical. However, betweenness centrality will always take longer to compute on a graph than degree centrality, by several orders of magnitude. It is important to choose a suitable algorithm not only to ensure you are measuring what is intended in your analysis but also to ensure that it is suitable for the size and structure of your graph.

To demonstrate this, we can use one specific algorithm to examine our graph, harmonic centrality. Harmonic centrality seeks to measure the ease of reaching other nodes in the graph from a given node. Formally, it is equal to the mean inverse distance from a node to every other node in a network:

1. Let's run it across our GitHub developer graph to estimate how easily each vertex can be reached from any point in the graph:

```
harmonic = g.harmonic_centrality()
print(harmonic)
```

2. You will notice that harmonic centrality takes a very long time to run across our graph, and may even need to be stopped midway. This is due to the algorithm's need to traverse paths from each node to every other node in the network in order to calculate a node's score and therefore has fairly high computational complexity. It is easy to see that, even if this feature was useful, it would be difficult to add to any data pipeline where processing speed was important.

3. However, we have options in order to still obtain a measure of a node's centrality in a similar way. If speed is important, perhaps an estimate of the same measure will suffice – *igraph* allows us to choose the maximum length of paths traversed to calculate a node's harmonic centrality, using the `cutoff` parameter. Here, we set this to 3, and rerun the algorithm:

```
harmonic = g.harmonic_centrality(cutoff=3)
print(harmonic)
```

This time, the harmonic centrality algorithm will reach completion much faster, and we have a result we could use in further analysis or decisions. If an estimate of how easily each vertex can be reached is enough for a specific use case, then we can use this. Different algorithms have vastly different complexity, and some are more suitable for large graphs than others – it is important to consider both the aim of a measurement algorithm and its scalability when adding it to your analysis. This is particularly important when working with graph data that is likely to increase in size over *time*.

In the next section, we will delve into some common Neo4j issues you may encounter when working with the Neo4j graph database and the explorer.

Common Neo4j issues

To demonstrate some examples of common Neo4j errors, we will need to follow the steps hereunder to build the Neo4j database and set admin credentials and login information. This will then aid us in the following subsections:

1. First, we will have to create a new empty graph database in Neo4j. You can call this whatever you like, but we will be using the database name Common Issues DB.

2. Head to the Neo4j browser and use the `:server user add` command in the browser, as we have done multiple times in previous chapters.

3. We will then add a new user and call this user `admin`. We will also need to set up a password for this user. Here, we will use `testpython`. You will have to type this password twice under **Password** and **Confirm Password.**

4. Once we have done this, we will need to apply the **admin** and **public** roles in the Neo4j browser.

5. For full details of all the steps, we have covered this multiple times in *Chapters 5 to 8.*

6. We will also need data with which to demonstrate some issues you may encounter when using Neo4j and Cypher, so let's move `musae_git_edges.csv` and `musae_git_target.csv` to our database's Import folder.

7. We can access this folder from the main Neo4j browser window, by clicking on the three dots next to `Common Issues DB`, then choosing **Open folder** and **Import**. So that Neo4j can access our data, drag the data files into this folder.

Now we have all the data in our Neo4j database, ready for the next step in the process. The subsequent sections will include, with demonstrations, the common issues you may experience with Neo4j. The first of which is the problem with slow writing from a file in Neo4j. Here, we will focus on how to *amp up* the writing speed to the graph database.

Slow writing from file to Neo4j

When working with Neo4j and tabular data, it is quite common that you will be using huge files, for example in `.csv` or `.json` format. We often use the LOAD CSV function to access a file in the database's `import` folder and use the data in each row to add nodes and edges to Neo4j. However, there are a number of different ways to use LOAD CSV, and not all are equal.

First, let's try to import nodes and edges from `musae_git_edges.csv` into `Common Issues DB`, with the following Cypher script.

Here, we are simply calling LOAD CSV, adding WITH HEADERS because our data contains the headers `id_1` and `id_2`, and assigning each row to the `row` variable. We can then MERGE each GitHub developer node into the graph with a `githubId` attribute taken from `row`, as well as creating a relationship between the aliased nodes `d1` and `d2`. Run this code in the Neo4j Browser and see how it performs:

```
LOAD CSV WITH HEADERS FROM 'file:///musae_git_edges.csv' AS row
MERGE (d1:Developer {githubId:row.id_1})
MERGE (d2:Developer {githubId:row.id_2})
CREATE (d1)-[:FOLLOWS]->(d2)
```

You will probably have noticed that this query runs extremely slowly, depending on your machine's specifications. But whatever the power of your process or availability of memory, this Cypher is very poorly optimized for the data import it is trying to perform.

When writing this query in Neo4j, you may have noticed that the query becomes underlined, and mousing over it displays a warning message. The message warns us that the query uses the EAGER operator, which can consume a lot of memory while the query runs. We will look in more detail at the EAGER operator, and why it should be avoided, in a later subsection.

One option for getting this query to run more effectively is to use a subquery to effectively split up the query into several transactions of a smaller size. This reduces the memory load on Neo4j, as it loads in only a set number of rows from the csv at a time as it writes nodes and edges.

This type of transaction behavior query needs to begin with the :auto statement, followed by our LOAD CSV WITH HEADERS function. Next, we enclose our logic for adding the GitHub nodes and edges to the graph with CALL and curly braces to specify our subquery. The only change is that we need to bring the row variable inside the subquery using WITH. After the subquery is defined, we can tell Neo4j how many csv rows to process at a time using IN TRANSACTIONS OF 1000 ROWS. Run this Cypher script in the Neo4j Browser, and compare the runtime to that of the previous query with no transaction control:

```
:auto LOAD CSV WITH HEADERS FROM 'file:///musae_git_edges.csv' AS row
CALL {
  WITH row
  MERGE (d1:Developer {githubId:row.id_1})
  MERGE (d2:Developer {githubId:row.id_2})
  CREATE (d1)-[:FOLLOWS]->(d2)
} IN TRANSACTIONS OF 1000 ROWS
```

You should see that this query runs much faster than the previous one because Neo4j no longer needs to hold on to the entire CSV data in memory as the query runs. This frees up memory to actually handle the writing of nodes and edges, therefore speeding the whole process up.

This is certainly an improvement, but there are other things we can do to speed up the loading of large datasets, for example, using indexing.

Indexing for query performance

While splitting our large write query into transactions certainly improved the efficiency of our query, we can do more to speed it up, by creating an index.

In Neo4j, like in other databases, we can create an index to improve search performance. Indexes are created for specific node or edge attributes and essentially result in a stored, ordered list of information on node or relationship properties. The index is used when queries involve searching the attribute in question, and the ordered nature of these property lists drastically improves query performance at the cost of some storage space, and some initial time required to create the index. This will be done in a series of steps:

1. Let's demonstrate this by comparing the speed of our write query in the previous section with and without an index. First, if our graph still contains data, we can remove it using MATCH and DETACH DELETE:

```
MATCH (n) DETACH DELETE n
```

2. Now, with our empty graph, let's create an index for Developer nodes, on the githubId property. We do this using CREATE INDEX, specifying a name, githubId_index, before identifying a node type it applies to with FOR, and the node property to build an index for with ON:

```
CREATE INDEX githubId_index
FOR (d:Developer)
ON (d.githubId)
```

3. Now, try running the write query from the previous section again, used to add Developer nodes to the Neo4j database. You will notice that the speed of this query has increased dramatically. As nodes are created using data from the CSV, an index is built up for the githubId attributes. Then, when the MERGE statements are used to add new Developer nodes, using our index, Neo4j can either find existing nodes or establish that they don't exist, far more quickly.

   It is worth bearing in mind that indexes are used for every type of query that involves matching on a particular property, not just write queries. A read query matching many paths involving Developer nodes and returning information about them would run far faster with an index in place than without.

   The one potential downside of indexes is that indexes can take up a large amount of storage space and so it is not always optimal to store an index of a property that is rarely queried, especially in the case of very large graphs.

   Should you need to remove an index on a rarely queried property, you can use DROP INDEX, followed by the name of the index set up when CREATE INDEX was called previously:

```
DROP INDEX githubId
```

Now, let us examine the issues you may experience with cached queries in Neo4j and how to get around them with a little bit of Cypher.

Caching results

One less obvious source of query performance increases is caused by repeated similar or identical queries. Neo4j maintains a cache of information related to the outputs of previously run queries. When a query is run on a new or recently restarted database, nothing has yet been cached, but once queries start to traverse through nodes and relationships held in the database, subsequent query performance is affected by cached data.

Let's run a query to demonstrate this. The following query will search for developers in our GitHub social network that follow the repositories of at least 10 other developers. We do this by matching all relationships from each developer, d, to other developers, d2. Then, we use collect() to form a list of all the followed developers for each node and take its size. This is equal to the out degree for each node, so we name it as such. We limit the results to where out degree is at least 10, and return results ordered by this property:

```
MATCH (d:Developer)-[:FOLLOWS]-(d2:Developer)
WITH size(collect(d2)) as degree, d
WHERE degree >= 10
RETURN d.githubId, degree ORDER BY degree DESC
```

This represents a fairly exhaustive list of graph traversals across our nodes so that each node and relationship is considered in the initial MATCH statement. Try running this query once, make a note of its speed, and run it a few more times. Depending on the specifications of your machine, you should notice an increase in query speed in runs past the first execution.

This method of running a query on startup is known as *warming the cache*. Provided there is enough memory available, Neo4j will store as much information about the nodes and relationships it encounters during queries as it can fit into memory. When memory becomes limited, the oldest cached data will start to be replaced. We will examine this more closely in the next section.

Memory limitations

When asking Neo4j to perform certain highly complex queries, it is likely that you will run into issues with available memory. If a particularly large or complex pattern is being matched, or a large amount of reads/writes are taking place in a single query, Neo4j may run out of memory in which to store intermediate information between query steps, resulting in dramatically slower query processing.

In extreme cases, it may run out of available memory altogether, resulting in canceled queries and Java error messages, such as the following:

```
java.lang.OutOfMemoryError: Java heap space
```

Running more simple queries to get around this issue isn't always an option, so instead we can control the way Neo4j processes intermediate results by using the APOC library (https://neo4j.com/developer/neo4j-apoc/), and specifically, functions that are part of APOC.periodic. We first encountered this in *Chapter 8, Perfect Projections*, when working with a very large graph. To add the APOC plugin to our database, open the main Neo4j Desktop window, and select the database we have set up for this chapter, **Common Issues DB**. To the right side of the window, a menu will appear, from which you should select the **Plugins** tab. From this tab, choose APOC, and click **Install**.

A common example of a slow query is the Cypher used to clear a Neo4j graph database, removing all nodes and edges:

```
MATCH (d) DETACH DELETE d
```

On relatively small graphs, this will perform relatively well with no issues. However, due to the query's structure, on large graphs with many thousands or millions of nodes, this query is unlikely to complete successfully without erroring, depending on the specifications of the machine running Neo4j.

This is because before any DETACH or DELETE operation is carried out for any node in the graph, all nodes in the database must first be matched. Holding all of this node information at once can result in Neo4j having either no memory left and erroring, or having little memory remaining to perform the latter part of the query.

Using APOC, we can control the flow of how Neo4j executes this query. Instead of simply matching every node first, we can use CALL and APOC.periodic.iterate, wrapping the function inside some execution logic. Our first parameter contains a MATCH statement for finding nodes, while the second contains Cypher telling Neo4j what to do once those nodes are matched. The trick here is in the third parameter, which tells Neo4j to execute the MATCH and then the DETACH DELETE functions in batches of 1,000. This means that Neo4j only has to hold information about 1,000 nodes in memory at any given time, meaning more memory is available for node and edge removal:

```
CALL apoc.periodic.iterate("
    MATCH (d:Developer) RETURN d",
    "DETACH DELETE d",
    {batchSize:1000, parallel:false}
)
```

The result is a drastically faster query, which scales to far larger graphs. Even on the relatively small GitHub developer social network, the difference in execution speed will be noticeable. APOC has many useful functions for advanced Neo4j and Cypher users, a few more of which we covered in *Chapter 8, Perfect Projections*.

The number of functions is too large to cover them all in this book, but when encountering issues with scaling, it is worth navigating to the APOC documentation to check what options are available to you. APOC also contains tons of handy solutions for managing very complex Cypher operations in fewer, more simple, lines of code.

In the next section, we will examine how to handle duplicates in your code using the MERGE statement, which we have encountered many times in the preceding chapters.

Handling duplicates with MERGE

Often, when working with real data, it is less ordered and clean than we would like. Working with graph data is no different, particularly when undergoing tasks such as converting tabular data to graph format. Poor initial data quality can dramatically impact the quality of a resulting graph, so Neo4j comes with some tricks to prevent bad-quality data from impacting graph construction and analysis. We can handle duplicates in Neo4j in a few ways, using MERGE and using CONSTRAINTS. In the following steps, we will be focusing on handling duplicate data with the MERGE function:

1. For this subsection, we assume that the Neo4j database is already populated with the GitHub social network. If not, follow the steps toward the start of this section to add data to Neo4j first.

2. In *Chapters 5* to *8*, we used the MERGE function in Neo4j, as opposed to the CREATE function, to prevent additional nodes from being created when reading in tabular data, or when executing write queries from Python. As discussed previously, the MERGE function first runs a match query to find a specified node or pattern, and if it already exists, does not write an additional node to the graph.

3. Let's run a basic query with MERGE to attempt to write a node that already exists to the graph:

    ```
    MERGE (d:Developer {githubId: '1'})
    ```

4. When running this in the Neo4j Browser, the resulting output will show that no changes were made to the database. The node was matched so no write operation took place. To illustrate, let's look at the difference when we run the CREATE function with the same node specification:

    ```
    CREATE (d:Developer {githubId: '1'})
    ```

5. The output will show that one node has been added. If you wish, run a MATCH query with the same command to visually display the two identical nodes that are now present in our database:

    ```
    MATCH (d:Developer {githubId: '1'}) RETURN d
    ```

6. While the behavior of CREATE compared to that of MERGE is fairly obvious, what is less immediately clear is that the matching part of MERGE occurs for the entire pattern specified. So, should you attempt to merge two nodes and a relationship into Neo4j, and all nodes, relationships, and their attributes in the pattern don't already match an entire pattern in the graph, the whole pattern will be created.

7. Let's demonstrate this by merging data we might find in an edgelist. Here, we try to merge in Developer nodes that already exist in the graph, alongside a FOLLOWS relationship between them that does not yet exist:

    ```
    MERGE (d:Developer {githubId: '1'})-[:FOLLOWS]->(d2:Developer
    {githubId: '2'})
    ```

    The Neo4j output shows that some changes have been made to the graph. While the intention may have been to find nodes with githubId of 1 and 2 and add a relationship, because this relationship did not yet exist, two duplicate nodes with an edge between them have now been created.

8. A simple way to resolve this type of behavior is to change our MERGE query to include additional statements, separating the pattern into individual MERGE calls. This type of query structure will be familiar from the previous chapters where we used Neo4j:

```
MERGE (d:Developer {githubId: '1'})
MERGE (d2:Developer {githubId: '2'})
MERGE (d1)-[:FOLLOWS]->(d2)
```

With MERGE statements for individual parts of the pattern, each node will match on execution, and no writes to the database will take place. Then, if the relationship doesn't exist, it will be merged separately, using the d and d2 aliases assigned to nodes when they matched. If the relationship already exists, it too will be matched and no updates will be made.

In the next section, we will build on methods for handling duplicates by introducing constraints into our Cypher mixing bowl.

Handling duplicates with constraints

While we can control the write behavior of Neo4j by being careful with the CREATE and MERGE functions, this is sometimes not sufficient to ensure that a graph contains no duplicate data. For example, imagine a case where multiple users with different levels of Neo4j experience could access the graph, perhaps across a team of data specialists – this could potentially result in unwanted changes to a graph database if somebody wrote an imperfect query.

When we need more control over the duplicate-handling behavior of Neo4j, we can use constraints. Constraints prevent specific write operations on the database by throwing errors when illegal database updates take place.

We will look at steps to set up constraints in your Cypher in the next steps:

1. To set up a constraint, we can use the CREATE CONSTRAINT function. The syntax for adding a constraint in Neo4j is similar to that for creating an index. After CREATE CONSTRAINT, we choose a name for the constraint, followed by FOR and the node type it applies to. The last section of this query starts with REQUIRE (or ASSERT in older Neo4j versions), and then the logic for the requirements of the constraint. Here, we want to make sure that the githubId attribute of Developer nodes is unique, which we simply state as d.githubID IS UNIQUE:

```
CREATE CONSTRAINT githubId_constraint
FOR (d:Developer)
REQUIRE d.githubId IS UNIQUE
```

2. If you have already created an index for this database on Developer nodes, that will also need to be removed before a constraint can be added. Running CREATE CONSTRAINT also creates an index for the node property specified in the constraint, and two identical indexes cannot exist at once. To remove a previous index, use DROP INDEX followed by the index name, for example:

```
DROP INDEX githubId_index
```

3. In addition, if we try to run this `CREATE CONSTRAINT` query while there are duplicate nodes in the graph, we will run into an error, as follows:

```
Unable to create Constraint( name='githubId_constraint',
type='UNIQUENESS', schema=(:Developer {githubId}) ):
Both Node(2) and Node(37701) have the label `Developer` and
property `githubId` = '1'
```

4. This error shows that a constraint cannot be created if it is already invalidated by current data in the Neo4j database. If this is the case, because you have been following the previous worked examples, run `MATCH (n) DETACH DELETE n` to clear all data, as we have done before. Now, with either a blank database or clean non-duplicate data in Neo4j, we can safely create the constraint with our `CREATE CONSTRAINT` query. Running `SHOW INDEXES` in the Neo4j Browser console will show that an index has been created. If the database is blank, add data back into the database using the steps at the start of the *Common Neo4j issues* section.

5. Now, let's attempt to use `MERGE` to add a relationship, with the node and relationship pattern that caused issues in the *Handling duplicates with MERGE* subsection:

```
MERGE (d:Developer {githubId: '1'})-[:FOLLOWS]->(d2:Developer
{githubId: '2'})
```

6. This time, as intended, we will encounter an error, thrown by our database constraint:

```
Node(2027) already exists with label `Developer` and property
`githubId` = '1'
```

The whole `MERGE` pattern does not exist, which means Neo4j tries to add both nodes and the relationship to the database. But because `Developer` nodes with these `githubId`s already exist, the write operation is not carried out. Our constraint is functioning as intended to prevent duplicate nodes from being added to Neo4j.

Following this section, we will look at the `EXPLAIN` and `PROFILE` functions and the eager operator.

EXPLAIN, PROFILE, and the eager operator

Aside from the pointers in each of the previous Neo4j issue subsections, occasionally the complexity of what you need to achieve using Cypher and Neo4j can mean assembling lengthy and complicated queries.

When encountering issues with tricky queries and slow or incorrect execution, Neo4j has two tools you can use to get to the bottom of your problems.

The `EXPLAIN` and `PROFILE` Cypher functions are handy tools to shine a light on exactly how Neo4j will execute a query. Using these, we can show the flow of a Cypher execution plan, and locate inefficiencies.

`EXPLAIN` displays the execution plan for a query without actually executing it, and displays the estimated number of rows operated on at each execution plan step, while `PROFILE` shows the same plan but runs the query across the database, and displays the actual number of rows processed.

Let's display the query plan for matching connected GitHub developers using EXPLAIN:

```
EXPLAIN
MATCH (d:Developer)-[:FOLLOWS]->(d2:Developer)
RETURN d, d2
```

This will result in the Neo4j Browser generating the following flowchart:

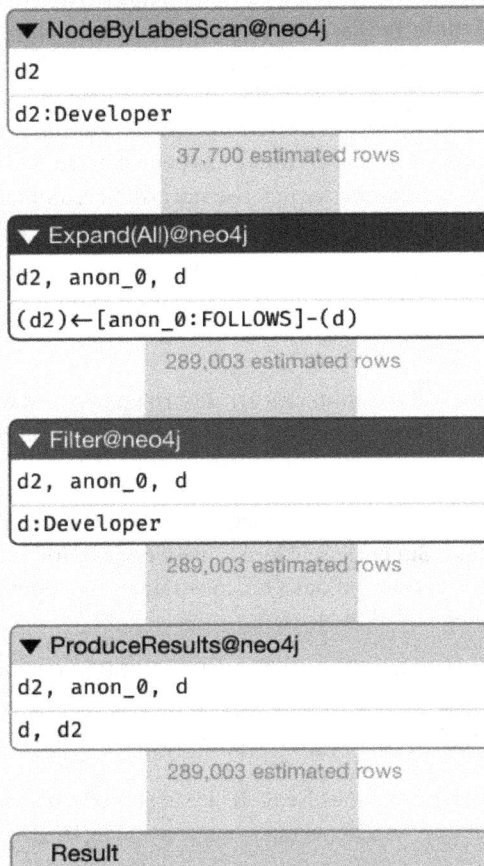

```
▼ NodeByLabelScan@neo4j
d2
d2:Developer
```
                    37,700 estimated rows

```
▼ Expand(All)@neo4j
d2, anon_0, d
(d2)←[anon_0:FOLLOWS]-(d)
```
                    289,003 estimated rows

```
▼ Filter@neo4j
d2, anon_0, d
d:Developer
```
                    289,003 estimated rows

```
▼ ProduceResults@neo4j
d2, anon_0, d
d, d2
```
                    289,003 estimated rows

```
Result
```

Figure 9.1 – Neo4j EXPLAIN results

Each step in the flowchart generated by EXPLAIN or PROFILE represents a process the database is carrying out and is classified by types of operator, such as Expand and Filter. A query plan can often highlight unexpected execution behavior – here, we can see that Developer nodes aliased to d2, on the right-hand side of the path we are querying for, are actually located first, before expanding to nodes with the alias d. This has no impact on the speed of our query execution, but other query plan patterns and operators can be more impactful.

One key thing to look for in an execution plan is the type of operators being used. A major source of slow Cypher query execution is the presence of the eager operator. The eager operator makes sure that a previous operation has been fully completed before moving on to another operation, to avoid issues with read and write conflicts. While the eager operator is clearly important in this regard, to maintain the integrity of our data, this type of execution has significant impacts on query performance. It is often possible to rewrite or split Cypher queries to avoid the need for the eager operator and speed up execution.

The eager operator is particularly common when using LOAD CSV to import data. With EXPLAIN, we can show what is happening when loading data from our csv edgelist. Try using EXPLAIN followed by the LOAD CSV query from the start of the *Common Neo4j issues* section:

```
EXPLAIN
LOAD CSV WITH HEADERS FROM 'file:///musae_git_edges.csv' AS row
MERGE (d1:Developer {githubId:row.id_1})
MERGE (d2:Developer {githubId:row.id_2})
CREATE (d1)-[:FOLLOWS]->(d2)
RETURN d1, d2
```

This returns an execution plan for loading our data.

On examination of the operators, we can see that the eager operator is present. During query execution, Neo4j is having to wait for one MERGE function to fully execute before moving on to other MERGE or CREATE operations, to prevent write conflicts.

Though unintuitive, it can often be more efficient to split LOAD CSV queries into multiple parts, where only one MERGE or CREATE takes place per csv row. Using EXPLAIN, we can take a look at the impact of splitting our data-loading Cypher script into three parts. We have one query for adding nodes in the first column to our database:

```
EXPLAIN
LOAD CSV WITH HEADERS FROM 'file:///musae_git_edges.csv' AS row
MERGE (d1:Developer {githubId:row.id_1})
```

We use a separate query to add nodes from the second csv column:

```
EXPLAIN
LOAD CSV WITH HEADERS FROM 'file:///musae_git_edges.csv' AS row
MERGE (d1:Developer {githubId:row.id_2})
```

And, we have a final query for connecting nodes together, where we match nodes in our graph based on the contents of our CSV:

```
EXPLAIN
LOAD CSV WITH HEADERS FROM 'file:///musae_git_edges.csv' AS row
MATCH (d1:Developer {githubId:row.id_1})
```

```
MATCH (d2:Developer {githubId:row.id_2})
CREATE (d1)-[:FOLLOWS]->(d2)
```

Take a look at the execution plan generated by EXPLAIN for each of these queries, and you will notice that the eager operator is no longer used. This means Neo4j is free to process each query without accounting for the loss of data integrity in write conflicts, resulting in faster execution.

When loading very large datasets into Neo4j, this is often more efficient and less time-consuming overall than adding nodes and edges in a single Cypher query. Combined with the subquery and TRANSACTIONS tricks we discussed at the beginning of this section, this method of loading data can be even more effective for quickly getting data into Neo4j.

This concludes this chapter and now we will summarize what you have learned in this chapter, and draw this book to a close.

Summary

We have learned a lot about common issues that may be presented to us as aspiring graph practitioners. These are based on many years of experience working with these issues, and they do spring up in production code and systems more than we would like. However, over time, these issues tend to be covered by effective error handling in Python code and defense mechanisms we can put in place in Cypher script.

The main things we looked at were issues such as how to debug errors in *igraph* and Neo4j (graph databases). In *igraph*, we have looked at issues such as how to correctly create edges in the graph, where we looked at the problems associated with node indexing; we extended this node indexing problem to analyzing node IDs in *igraph* and how we can fix node ID indexing issues. We then looked at adding properties effectively utilizing the vs and es attributes of *igraph*, getting under the hood of the select() method to understand how to use it, and sometimes, the shortfalls with using the method, such as working with chained statements in tandem with select() and how this can lead to unexpected consequences. Finally, we looked at how we can make algorithms more efficient by looking at path lengths and various ways to amp up the performance of our centrality algorithms.

Relating to Neo4j, we looked at issues relating to slow writing from files and how to overcome this or speed this up with large datasets. Query performance was the next topic, where we looked at indexing and the effect this has on query performance; this was followed by how Neo4j caches results and how you may want to avoid this for large datasets and path traversals. In the query performance section, we looked at handling duplicates in our Cypher queries with the use of the MERGE statement and how we can use constraints to deal with duplicates. Debugging was the last port of call. Here, we looked at how you can use the Cypher EXPLAIN and PROFILE commands to produce an execution plan for your queries and to debug suspicious results. Additionally, in the debugging section, we looked at the eager operator and how to avoid this, allowing Neo4j to effectively execute queries without waiting to execute in places, while still avoiding issues with read and write conflicts.

This brings this chapter to a close, and indeed the whole book. You have all the knowledge you need to replicate what you have learned in this book to go out there and start building graph solutions for your data problems.

Throughout this book, we have focused on getting you to grips with understanding the fundamentals of how graphs are used in the real world; we then explored how to build and work with graph data models – the main focus of this section was to get you familiar with Python libraries for graph data science and to build a basic recommender system for predicting a user's favorite television program, based on their viewing profile; this was followed by moving from a relational database mindset to a graph database mindset – this exposed us to working with MySQL and building a similar recommendation engine, but this time to predict video games that the user might be interested in. Knowledge graphs were the next subject of discussion, where we focused on methods of ingesting and cleaning data, before we built a knowledge graph and applied community detection over the top of the knowledge graph; we then started to introduce the concepts of graph databases and focused on Neo4j as our solution of choice for storing the graph connections and interfacing Neo4j with Python and *igraph* – the use case we used, once we had all our data in the graph database, was to work on a travel optimization solution. We then looked at building production pipelines. This focused on a combination of Neo4j and the interaction between various elements of the Python pipeline. Next, we looked at how to equip ourselves for rapidly changing schemas and the strategies to build these into the design upon inception. Moving on, we looked at how to store and utilize projections from a graph to do analysis and other downstream tasks. Finally, we covered the last piece of the puzzle – looking at some of the common issues and unexpected errors that appear when working with *igraph* and Neo4j.

This really has been a rollercoaster of a ride, and we hope you have enjoyed every twist and turn along the way. It has been a pleasure to take you through years of acquired knowledge, distilling it down into this book.

Index

www.packtpub.com

Subscribe to our online digital library for full access to over 7,000 books and videos, as well as industry leading tools to help you plan your personal development and advance your career. For more information, please visit our website.

Why subscribe?

- Spend less time learning and more time coding with practical eBooks and Videos from over 4,000 industry professionals

- Improve your learning with Skill Plans built especially for you

- Get a free eBook or video every month

- Fully searchable for easy access to vital information

- Copy and paste, print, and bookmark content

Did you know that Packt offers eBook versions of every book published, with PDF and ePub files available? You can upgrade to the eBook version at www.packtpub.com and as a print book customer, you are entitled to a discount on the eBook copy. Get in touch with us at customercare@packtpub.com for more details.

At www.packtpub.com, you can also read a collection of free technical articles, sign up for a range of free newsletters, and receive exclusive discounts and offers on Packt books and eBooks.

Other Books You May Enjoy

If you enjoyed this book, you may be interested in these other books by Packt:

Serge Gershkovich

‹packt›

Foreword by Kent Graziano, Owner and Chief
Strategic Advisor, Data Warrior LLC

Data
Modeling
with
Snowflake

A practical guide
to accelerating
Snowflake
development
using universal
data modeling
techniques

1st edition

Data Modeling with Snowflake

Serge Gershkovich

ISBN: 9781837634453

- Discover the time-saving features and applications of data modeling

- Explore Snowflake's cloud-native architecture and features

- Understand and apply modeling concepts, techniques, and language using Snowflake objects

- Master modeling concepts such as normalization and slowly changing dimensions

- Get comfortable reading and transforming semi-structured data

- Work directly with pre-built recipes and examples

- Apply modeling frameworks from Star to Data Vault

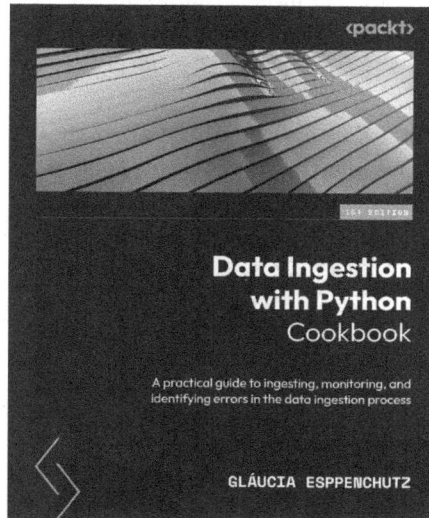

Data Ingestion with Python Cookbook

Gláucia Esppenchutz

ISBN: 9781837632602

- Implement data observability using monitoring tools
- Automate your data ingestion pipeline
- Read analytical and partitioned data, whether schema or non-schema based
- Debug and prevent data loss through efficient data monitoring and logging
- Establish data access policies using a data governance framework
- Construct a data orchestration framework to improve data quality

Packt is searching for authors like you

If you're interested in becoming an author for Packt, please visit `authors.packtpub.com` and apply today. We have worked with thousands of developers and tech professionals, just like you, to help them share their insight with the global tech community. You can make a general application, apply for a specific hot topic that we are recruiting an author for, or submit your own idea.

Share Your Thoughts

Now you've finished *Graph Data Modeling in Python*, we'd love to hear your thoughts! Scan the QR code below to go straight to the Amazon review page for this book and share your feedback or leave a review on the site that you purchased it from.

https://packt.link/r/1-804-61803-9

Your review is important to us and the tech community and will help us make sure we're delivering excellent quality content.

Download a free PDF copy of this book

Thanks for purchasing this book!

Do you like to read on the go but are unable to carry your print books everywhere?

Is your eBook purchase not compatible with the device of your choice?

Don't worry, now with every Packt book you get a DRM-free PDF version of that book at no cost.

Read anywhere, any place, on any device. Search, copy, and paste code from your favorite technical books directly into your application.

The perks don't stop there, you can get exclusive access to discounts, newsletters, and great free content in your inbox daily

Follow these simple steps to get the benefits:

1. Scan the QR code or visit the link below

https://packt.link/free-ebook/9781804618035

2. Submit your proof of purchase
3. That's it! We'll send your free PDF and other benefits to your email directly

www.ingramcontent.com/pod-product-compliance
Lightning Source LLC
Chambersburg PA
CBHW061411210326
41598CB00035B/6170